Section of CALIFORNIA
showing the route of
PORTOLÁ ——— in red,
and the modern
U.S. 101 ‑‑‑‑ in broken
black lines.

NEVADA

MOJAVE
DESERT

Colorado River

ARIZONA

LOS ANGELES

SANTA ANA

SAN JUAN CAPISTRANO

WARNER'S RANCH

SAN PASCUAL

COLORADO
DESERT

SAN DIEGO

YUMA

BAJA CALIFORNIA

THE ROYAL HIGHWAY

● BOOKS BY EDWIN CORLE

Stories: Mojave

Novels: Fig Tree John
               People on the Earth
               Burro Alley
               Solitaire
               Coarse Gold
               Three Ways to Mecca
               In Winter Light
               Billy the Kid

Biography: John Studebaker: An American Dream

Americana: Desert Country
               The Story of the Grand Canyon
               The Royal Highway
               The Gila: River of the Southwest

EDWIN CORLE was born in Wildwood, New Jersey, on May 7, 1906. He attended public schools in Wildwood, Philadelphia, and Hollywood, California. He received his B.A. from the University of California at Los Angeles in 1928, majoring in English, and spent two years in graduate work at Yale University.

His literary career began in 1930 with motion-picture and radio writing. With the acceptance of his first short story by the *Atlantic Monthly* in 1932 he devoted his work entirely to stories and novels, eventually expanding to nonfiction. Most of his writing has been about California and the American Southwest.

In 1942 his work was interrupted by his service in the Air Force in World War II; it was resumed in 1945. He has been published in England, Australia, and New Zealand; and his work has been translated into French, Dutch, Danish, Swedish, German, and Japanese.

BILLY THE KID, a subject that has interested him for many years, is his fourteenth book. At present Mr. Corle is living in Santa Barbara, California.

The
ROYAL HIGHWAY
(EL CAMINO REAL)

by EDWIN CORLE

DUELL, SLOAN & PEARCE • NEW YORK
LITTLE, BROWN & COMPANY • BOSTON

For

JEAN CORLE

Who will doubtless see the highway in the year 2000

TABLE OF CONTENTS

Part I

BEFORE THE HIGHWAY . . . TO 1769

Part II

SPANISH ARCADY, 1769 TO 1821

Part III

MEXICAN MAZE, 1821 TO 1846

LIST OF ILLUSTRATIONS

MAPS

PART { **1**

BEFORE THE
HIGHWAY

...to 1769

The Unknown   { 1

IN THE YEAR 1510, the Spanish author Garcí Ordóñez de Montalvo had published what was unquestionably a best seller of its day. It was a prolix and second-rate imitation of the Portuguese romance *Amadís de Gaula* written more than a century earlier by Vasco de Lobeira. Montalvo had translated the work of the Portuguese author into Spanish. The popular reception accorded it (by those who could read in those days in Spain, and they were a minority) caused Montalvo to try his hand at an original prose composition. It was pretty dreadful and was called *Las Sergas de Esplandián,* or *The Exploits of Esplandián.* Yet the novel, if it may be so designated, has one incontestable claim to fame. In it, for the first time in print, occurred the attractive word *California.*

Where did Montalvo get it? The area we know today as California had not yet been seen by white men. Whether Montalvo simply made it up, or constructed it from the Latin words *calida* and *fornax* ("hot" and "oven") or the Greek root word καλὸς "beautiful") or whether he adapted it from the mythical kingdom of Califerne in the *Chanson de Roland* written about the end of the eleventh century—all matters little. Montalvo called it California and, moreover, he described it. If you will read him, you will understand that there was no doubt in his mind that he knew whereof he wrote. No subsequent Chamber of Commerce pamphlet has ever been more specific than Señor Montalvo when he told his readers:

Know ye that at the right hand of the Indies there is an island named California, very close to that part of the Terrestrial Para-

13

dise, which was inhabited by black women, without a single man among them, and that they lived in the manner of Amazons. They were robust of body, with strong and passionate hearts and great virtues. The island itself is one of the wildest in the world on account of the bold and craggy rocks. Their weapons were all made of gold. The island everywhere abounds with gold and precious stones, and upon it no other metal was found. They lived in caves, well excavated. They had many ships with which they sailed to other coasts to make forays, and the men whom they took as prisoners they killed. In this island, named California, there are many griffins. In no other part of the world can they be found. And there ruled over that island of California a queen of majestic proportions, more beautiful than all others, and in the very great vigor of her womanhood. She was desirous of accomplishing great deeds. She was valiant and courageous, and ardent, with a brave heart, and had ambitions to execute nobler actions than had been performed by any other ruler. . . .

Her name was Calafía.

And her name was Disappointment to those who sought her and her fabulously rich land of California. Yet somehow this euphonious and mellifluous name jumped the Atlantic, crossed Mexico, and was finally given to what was first thought to be an island off the Mexican west coast. Just who bestowed the name on the land is not known. There are theories, of course. Some believe it was Fortún Jiménez, who reached the tip of the peninsula now called Baja California in 1533. Jiménez saw nothing of the black women and their golden arms. Instead, the first California greeters committee consisted of bellicose Indians who killed the exploring Jiménez and twenty of his men.

In 1535 the great Cortés reached the "island." There is no record of his calling it California, although he may have done so in ironic jest as he found it unprofitable and abandoned it as a more or less unwanted child in the growing Spanish colonial family.

But be it California or not, the land in 1535 was a vast unknown area. Lower California had been touched only in the general vicinity of what is today the Mexican city of La Paz. Of the area between what are now the cities of San Diego and San Francisco nothing was known. It has been estimated by anthropologists and ethnologists that there were about 70,000 Indians living along the California coastal strip and in the adjacent valleys between San Diego Bay and San Francisco Bay in 1540. These were the first Californians. Or perhaps it would be better to say that these people, who never heard of California or ever considered themselves as Indians, were the descendants of the first unknown inhabitants.

Just when human beings first came to live along the California coast must remain archaeological theory. But it is reasonably certain that a race known as the Proto-Australoid migrated from central Asia, possibly driven out by force by the Mongoloid stock, and crossed the land bridge, then existent, between Asia and North America by way of Alaska and the Bering Straits, about eighty thousand years ago. One of these long-headed, short-statured, brown-skinned men may have been the first Californian.

Or, about forty thousand years ago, there were later waves of Asiatics who were of the Mongoloid, Caspian and Palae-Alpine races. These people moved on south to the valleys of Mexico and became the Mayans, the Toltecs and the Aztecs. It is not impossible that some of their number lingered in California to form a culture comparable to that of the so-called Basket Makers of Arizona and New Mexico.

At any rate, it can safely be said, without archaeological question, that some form of human beings lived along the California coast as much as twenty-five thousand years ago. They may be classified by modern scientists as existing in a culture somewhere between savagery and barbarism and must have had contact with animals of the Pleistocene period such as the mastodon, the mammoth, the ground sloth and the camel. Skeleton remains of both mastodon and mammoth have been found adjacent to the Bay of San Francisco. It was a California difficult to visualize today; but it was these people of the Pleistocene period, nevertheless, who were the first to pass over the terrain later transversed by what is today U.S. Highway 101.

For practical purposes, anthropologists usually classify the prehistoric races of the California coast under two headings: first were the so-called Oak Grove People about whom little is known except that they survived on acorns and left a few crude tools and weapons; second were the Hunting People who succeeded the Oak Grove race and had a slightly more advanced culture. The first of the races of modern times, are, of course, the people collectively misnamed "Indians," and this word is usually accepted by the public to identify any and all cultures pre-Columbian.

The first white man to look at the present California was Juan Rodríguez Cabrillo in 1542. As the "discoverer," however, his claim is sometimes contested. There are historians who believe the Chinese were in North America before the Spaniards, perhaps as much as one thousand years before the arrival of Columbus. It is argued that these Oriental people were not attempting to reach a new world, but came only because they could not help themselves when their ships were caught in prevailing winds and the Japan Current.

A Buddhist priest named Hwui Shan, reputedly, returned to China from what he called the Kingdom of Fusang in 499 A.D. Fusang, seemingly, was the coast of California or the west coast of Mexico. The evidence, however, leaves a great deal to speculation. And the whole Chinese-got-here-first theory goes from the speculative to the ridiculous with the claims of a white missionary named Shaw who declared he found evidence (in China) of a manuscript stating that a Chinese sea captain reached the California coast as early as the first century A.D. This story was printed in the *New York Tribune* for September 10, 1890, in all seriousness, before someone pointed out that the name of the supposed captain was Hee-Lie.

So it is most unlikely that any race except those people we call Indians ever passed over any part of what was destined to be called by the Spaniards El Camino Real. And all through the unknown years there was nothing even resembling a road. Indian trails no doubt connected the settlement of some tribes with others, and these trails followed in general the route of the road today. But the California Indians were not nomadic, belonged to various linguistic stocks and had little or no commercial intercourse or trade with one another. The average American's idea of an Indian comes from the aborigines of the plains; and the Sioux, perhaps, with their hunting of buffalo, living in tepees, drinking firewater, wearing war bonnets and taking of enemies' scalps, are the most representative type in the common mind. The California Indians were of a different stripe entirely. They didn't wear war bonnets or live in tepees or take scalps and, unless goaded beyond reason, were generally peaceful. They were rather small and stocky brown-skinned people, with a definite culture and philosophy, although it takes a patient search to find these latter attributes. On the whole they were regarded by the white race as somewhat inferior Indians, even though this conclusion is not entirely accurate.

These people lived on the coastal slope or in valleys well hemmed in by mountains. They were not too numerous and therefore did not suffer from lack of sustenance, even in what was in the sixteenth century a somewhat sparse land. They are often referred to as the "Mission Indians," a misnomer which will be obvious later in this book. From San Diego to San Francisco they may be divided into six arbitrary linguistic groups: the Yuman, the Shoshonean, the Chumashan, the Salinan, the Esselenian and the Costanoan. If you were to stop a hundred cars on El Camino Real today—or U.S. 101—it is doubtful if you'd find one person in a hundred who had even heard of any of them. That same person driving from San Diego to San Francisco would pass through the stamping ground of each linguistic stock. But no Palatingwa buck, from what is the present-day Pala Indian Reservation in San Diego County, ever engaged in trade with, let us say, a Costanoan from the San Francisco peninsula. There was no need for a road, or even a trace or a trail. Arteries of communication awaited the arrival of the white man. And he first put his foot down on the soil of this country in 1542. So slow was the development of California that it was another two hundred and fifty years before there was need for a road. When at last it became a reality, though at first only a trail, it was given a name that will ever ring through history—El Camino Real or the Royal Highway.

Rodríguez Cabrillo { **2**

ALTA CALIFORNIA—as contrasted to Baja California—or what is the state of California as we know it today, was discovered in 1542 by Juan Rodríguez Cabrillo, a Portuguese navigator, in the service of Spain. This seemingly harmless statement will immediately bring forth protestations from the champions of Hernando de Alarcón, who sailed up the Gulf of California (or the Sea of Cortés) in 1540, reached the mouth of the Colorado River, and managed to work his way upstream with the sweating assistance of Cocopah Indians who thought he was a sun god and who towed the ship from the banks, canal-fashion. It is generally accepted that Alarcón managed to inveigle the Indians into pulling the ship beyond what is now Yuma, Arizona, and even some distance north of the confluence of the Colorado and the Gila. Without doubt, Alarcón and his crew went ashore numerous times. If they went ashore on the California side, as seems probable—for why not take a look at both banks of a river if you are exploring it for the first time?—then surely Hernando de Alarcón was the first white man to set foot on what is now the state of California. So with this bow to the first man to ascend part of the Colorado River, we can return to Cabrillo. We can safely say of him that he was the discoverer and explorer of the California coast, that his route, in an offshore way, paralleled the land route that was later to be called the Royal Highway and, furthermore, that Cabrillo came ashore and was the first white man to see many points that are landmarks along the Royal Highway today.

Of Cabrillo himself (the word can be translated as "Little Goat")

19

not a great deal is known. It is said that he was a Portuguese and
that his name was Juan Rodríguez and that his mother's name was
Cabrillo and that the use of the latter name was a result of matri-
linear preference. He arrived in New Spain, or what was euphe-
mistically called the "New World," in 1520. He served under
Cortés and apparently made a good name for himself by his
prowess and dependability as a soldier. The original plan for the
exploration of California was hatched by one Pedro de Alvarado,
who was much closer to Cortés than was Cabrillo and who had
almost singlehandedly financed an expedition of thirteen ships.
Alvarado was killed in an Indian foray in Mexico before the expedition could get under way. The viceroy of New Spain, Antonio de Mendoza, who was no friend of Cortés in any circumstances, had a stake in the plan, and it was Mendoza who took over
the executive management in Mexico City and sent the Little Goat
on his maritime way.

The Little Goat never got back. His remains, if any exist, lie
somewhere on San Miguel Island, which is thirty miles off the
California coast from Santa Barbara and is visible from the Royal
Highway on a clear day.

Instead of being an admiral of a fleet of thirteen ships, Cabrillo
was sent out to sea with only two caravels under his command.
Viceroy Mendoza was not a man to squander money, particularly
if some of it was Viceroy Mendoza's.

The two little ships were called the *San Salvador* and the *Victoria,* and they sailed from Navidad on the west coast of Mexico
on June 27, 1542. Cabrillo's orders were to explore the coast, take
possession of the land in the name of the King of Spain, make
friends with the natives and chart any good harbors or navigable
rivers. A further goal was to locate the mythical Strait of Anián
which, for some reason, cartographers believed existed, and which
served to round the northwest corner of North America and con-
nect the Pacific Ocean with the Atlantic. The expedition had an

eight months' supply of food, one priest and a few Indians to serve as interpreters. The fact that the Mexican Indians did not speak the same language as the California Indians was apparently not considered.

The details of this journey have been carefully retraced and outlined by several historians, and, as usual, there is no complete agreement. But such differences that exist amount to hairsplitting, and for the most part a reasonably clear account of what Cabrillo did, where he went and what happened to him is available today.

After working northward along the coast of Baja California, the two ships arrived at a "very large" bay, on September 28, 1542. Cabrillo called it more than a bay; it was a port. He named it San Miguel, and it was later changed to San Diego and San Diego it is today. It became a vital Spanish base of supplies in later years, and was, of course, a key point on the Royal Highway after 1769. But it was Cabrillo and his sailors who met the Indians at this point and were thus the first white men to set foot on the present coast of California.

The two small ships sailed north from San Diego Bay, following the coast line, and at first not finding anything of any great interest. The party touched at what is now Catalina Island, had a friendly reception from the Indians, and unquestionably anchored their craft at what is now Avalon. Over on the mainland there were the smokes of many Indian fires and this was the next stop. Cabrillo called the place La Bahía de Los Fumos, or the Bay of Smokes. It was very likely what is San Pedro and Los Angeles harbor today, although there is one standout authority among historians, George Davidson, who believes it was Santa Monica.

By October 12, 1542, the expedition had passed a mountainous point and discovered a broad valley and a large Indian village. These people were of the Chumashan stock and were the most advanced of the natives so far encountered. U.S. Highway's alternate 101 passes within a few yards of the site of the village today. It is just north of Point Mugu where the Santa Monica Mountains end, and not so very far north from the motion picture colony of Malibu Beach. Cabrillo called the settlement Pueblo de las Canoas, or Canoe Town, to translate freely. The Indians were especially adept at navigating crude canoes capable of holding a dozen men. Presents were exchanged and the explorers and the natives were able to converse to some extent by sign language. This, surprisingly enough, was just fifty years to the day after Columbus had discovered America. Henry VIII was king of England, the girl who was to be Queen Elizabeth was only nine years old and the English had not yet considered the New World worth claiming, much less colonizing.

Continuing along the coast, Cabrillo discovered numerous other Indian towns and villages. While these people had no written language they seemed to display a high degree of aboriginal intelligence. They had even heard of bearded white men far to the east across a great river. These must have been Melchior Diaz and his men who were an offshoot of Coronado's main party exploring Arizona and New Mexico in 1540 two years earlier. News got around in North America, even in those days.

The numerous Chumashan villages were self-supporting inasmuch as the natives lived in crude huts, grew maize, killed animals for food and clothing (scanty though the clothing may have been) and were skillful fishermen. Cabrillo would have done well to settle down at Pueblo de las Canoas or any other of the settlements along the present Santa Barbara Channel. But he was a man of mettle, and, moreover, he could not know what lay ahead, and that he was in for one of the stormiest winters ever known to occur along the California coast.

In spite of storms, hell and high water and a broken right arm suffered off San Miguel Island, Cabrillo continued his attempt to carry out his orders from Viceroy Mendoza. He left Pueblo de las Canoas on Friday the thirteenth. Any superstition as to the inadvisability of attempting anything on this date may not have been extant in 1542. If it was not, Cabrillo might well have begun such a fantasy, for he ran into plenty of trouble from that day on.

The little ships were buffeted and battered, but somehow they managed to sail northward, and Cabrillo discovered such landmarks as are now well-known: Carpinteria, Santa Barbara, the Channel Islands, Dos Pueblos, Gaviota Pass, Point Concepcion, Point Sur, Monterey Bay, Cape San Martin and a number of other salient features such as the Santa Lucia Mountains between San Luis Obispo and Carmel. The peaks of these coastal mountains were snow-covered that winter, and Cabrillo named them the Sierra Nevada. Later the name was changed, and Sierra Nevada was given to an even greater range which is more deserving of the name. But the words "Sierra Nevada," or "snowy mountain," were certainly brought to California by Cabrillo.

Beaten back by bad weather, and for some reason missing San Francisco Bay altogether (probably due to the fact that from a ship standing out at sea the Golden Gate looks more like a headland than an entrance to a navigable harbor), Cabrillo returned down the coast and sought refuge for a second time at San Miguel Island. The spot is known as Cuyler's Harbor today. This is the northernmost and westernmost island of the Santa Barbara Channel group. It would have seemed wiser to return the extra thirty-odd leagues (a Spanish league is 2.6 miles) to the reasonable security of Pueblo de las Canoas and its friendly and hospitable inhabitants. At any rate, Cabrillo decided to remain at San Miguel Island, possibly reasoning that the anchorage there was safer than that at Canoe Town. And on January 3, 1543, the intrepid Little Goat died of complications caused by his broken right arm. His remains were buried in the sand, and the waves of more than four hundred years have washed them to eternity.

Bartolomé Ferrelo, second in command, took over the leadership of the expedition and determinedly attempted to carry out Cabrillo's orders. To some extent he succeeded in spite of the stormy weather, and it is believed the two little ships battled their way as far north as the mouth of the Rogue River in Oregon. If so, they certainly scouted the entire California coast before reaching their northernmost point of advance, latitude 42°, on March 1, 1543.

Eventually the two ships became separated in a storm, and while they had occasionally lost sight of each other before, this time those on the *San Salvador* believed that the smaller *Victoria* must have been lost. When all hope was gone, and the *Victoria* did not appear at the anchorage at San Miguel Island or at Pueblo de las Canoas, Ferrelo decided it was time to return to Mexico and report. He took a few Chumashan Indians with him and sailed south, down the long coast line. At Cedros Island, about halfway down the Baja California coast, the little *Victoria* turned up, having been blown far out to sea and at last getting back to landfall more than four hundred miles from where the ships had become separated.

Each crew was overjoyed to find the other alive. The men on the *Victoria* had all but given up hope, but they were saved, they said, by prayers to the Virgin, and by making a vow that they would all go to church stark-naked if only she would save them. It seems an odd propitiation, but saved they were and there were no Doubting Thomases among them.

From Cedros Island the two ships continued south to their home port, Navidad, on the west coast of Mexico, and there the expedition came to an end on April 14, 1543.

While considerably more was known about California than the mere speculation that had preceded the explorations, the whole attempt was generally considered a failure. No especial wealth had been found, no Strait of Anián had been located, and no reason for a further expedition seemed to be pressing. Viceroy Mendoza was not ecstatic over the results. The bravery and loyalty of both Cabrillo and Ferrelo were shrugged off by Mexico City. And it is not recorded whether the sailors from the *Victoria* ever went to church in the nude.

Nevertheless the courageous exploits of Cabrillo and Ferrelo opened the door to California even if the Spanish authorities did not choose to follow through at once. Today Ferrelo is forgotten; but the brave Little Goat's name will stay with posterity. The broad and beautiful avenue along the coast at Santa Barbara, a part of the Royal Highway, is called Cabrillo Boulevard today. And as you drive along north from Santa Barbara, far on the horizon is San Miguel Island and the unmarked grave of the exploring pioneer.

Sir Francis Drake ⎰ 3

It is more than probable that Sir Francis Drake never set foot on any part of what was to become the Royal Highway, and it is equally likely that none of his men did either, although this cannot be said as a certainty. For surely they were very close to it a number of times as the *Golden Hind* sailed up the California coast in 1579, and they were within a day's marching distance of what was destined to be the northern limit of the highway, at the future site of the Mission San Francisco Solano, when they anchored their ship in what the voyage's chaplain called "a convenient and fit harborough."

As usual, professional historians cannot agree on the location of this harbor. But the consensus brings it down to what is today called Drake's Bay, just north of the Golden Gate. Drake, like Cabrillo and others who were to follow, missed the Golden Gate entirely and probably never knew of the existence of the more perfect and landlocked harbor—San Francisco Bay. Or if he did, the news came too late, and he had no need of it when he sailed from California for England by way of China.

At any rate, it was thirty-six years after Cabrillo before the white race set foot on California soil again. These new arrivals were Englishmen and their 100-ton ship was said to be loaded to the gunwales with loot stolen from the Spanish Pacific Coast ports. The Spaniards knew Drake had sailed north and they were waiting, grimly, for him to come back. If the men of New Spain could help it, the *Golden Hind* was never going to see England with its cargo of pilfered Spanish wealth, reputedly worth 800,000 English pounds. Drake thought otherwise. He simply sailed his ship around the world, leaving the Spaniards to their watchful waiting. Queen Elizabeth was so pleased with this example of derring-do that she made the pirate a knight.

But even if his contribution is slight, Drake cannot be ignored among the early forces that finally brought the highway into reality. And he did a number of things during his stay of thirty-six days that made history. For one thing, he said that the land wasn't Spanish at all, but English, and he christened it New Albion. It should never have been called California in the first place, and now that name could be forgotten and the land was a province of England. Neither the Spaniards nor the English seemed to think that the land belonged to the people who already lived on it—the Indians.

Besides taking formal possession of the land and renaming it, Drake engaged in ceremonies with the Indians identified as the Coast Miwok, and held the first Protestant religious service on the Pacific Coast of America. Drake seemed to believe that the white ceremonies were immensely impressive to the Indians and that their friendly response indicated their willingness to accept him as their king and their eagerness to become the vassals of Queen Elizabeth. It made a good story to tell in London. The Indians very likely believed that their own ceremonies, which ran a gamut from the smoking of a pipe of peace to flagellation, were immensely impressive to the Englishmen and that the friendly response of the white men indicated their willingness to become good Miwoks. At any rate, there were no hostilities during Drake's stay.

The *Golden Hind* had some essential repairs made on her bottom, and apparently one or two scouting parties explored the adjacent country. That these men went very far inland is most unlikely, but they saw enough of what is Marin County today, and possibly some of the present Sonoma County which later marked the northern end of the Royal Highway, to describe it as "farre different from the shoare, a goodly country and fruitful soyle, stored with many blessings fit for the vse of man."

The chaplain of the expedition was Francis Fletcher, a nephew of Drake. Their personal relationship was rather odd. While it is not recorded whether Fletcher held any avuncular love or hate, Drake referred to his nephew as "Ye falsest knave that liveth." In spite of this family contumely, *The World Encompassed by Sir Francis Drake* is generally supposed to have been written by the scorned nephew. It was not published until 1628, or forty-nine years after Drake left California and thirty-two years after his death. Since it tells very definitely what life was like in that part of California in 1579 a few of chaplain-author Fletcher's descriptions are worth noting:

The 3. day following, viz. the 21, our ship hauing receiued a leake at sea, was brought to anchor neerer the shoare, that her goods being landed, she might be repaired. . . . when the people of the countrie perceiued vs . . . they came downe vnto vs; and yet with no hostile meaning, or intent to hurt vs; standing when they drew neare, as men rauished in their mindes, with the sight of such things as they neuer had seene, or heard of before that time: their errand being rather with submission and feare to worship vs as Gods, than to haue any warre with vs as mortall men. . . .

In recompence of those things which they had receiued of vs, as shirts, linnen cloth, &c. they bestowed vpon our generall, and diuerse of our company, diuerse things, as feathers, cawles of net-worke, the quiuers of their arrows, made of fawne-skins, and the very skins of beasts that their women wore vpon their bodies. Hauing thus had their fill this times visiting and beholding of vs, they departed with ioy to their houses, which houses are digged around within the earth, and haue from the vppermost brimmes of the circle, clefts of wood set vp, and ioyned close together at the top, like our spires on the steeple of a church: which being couered with earth, suffer no water to enter, and are very warme, the doore in the most part of them, performes the office of a chimney, to let out the smoake: its made in bignesse and fashion like to an ordinary scuttle in a ship, and standing slopewise: their beds are the hard ground, onely with rushes strewed vpon it, and lying round about the house, haue their fire in the middest, which by reason that the house is but low vaulted, round and close, giueth a maruelous reflexion to their bodies to heate the same.

Their men for the most part goe naked, the women take a kinde of bulrushes, and kembing it after the manner of hempe, make themselues thereof a loose garment, which being knitte about their middles, hanges downe about their hippes, and so affordes them a couering of that, which nature teaches should be hidden: about their shoulders they weare also the skin of a deere, with the haire vpon it. They were very obedient to their husbands, and exceeding ready in all seruices: yet of themselues offring to do nothing, without the consents, or being called of by the men. . . .

After that our necessary businesses were well dispatched, our generall with his gentlemen, and many of his company, made a journy vp into the land . . . to be better acquainted with the nature and commodities of the countrie.

It is unfortunate that the author did not state the length and time of this journey. It must have been of at least a day's duration and possibly may have been as much as three or four days. If we only knew more of this survey, we could estimate just how much of the area the Englishmen saw. But after praising the richness and fertility of the land, Fletcher continues:

. . . Infinite was the company of very large and fat Deere, which there we saw by thousands, as we supposed, in a heard: besides a multitude of a strange kind of Conies, by farre exceeding them in number: the head and bodies, in which they resemble other Conies, are but small; his tayle like the tayle of a Rat, exceeding long; and his feet like the pawes of a Want or Moale; vnder his chinne, on either side, he hath a bagge, into which he gathereth his meate, when he hath filled his belly himselfe. . . . the people eat their bodies, and make great account of their skinnes, for their kings holidaies coate was made of them.

This country our generall named *Albion,* and that for two

causes; the one in the respect of the white bancks and cliffes, which lie toward the sea: the other, that it might haue some affinity, euen in name also, with our owne countrie, which was sometimes so called.

Before we went from thence, our generall caused to be set vp, a monument of our being there; as also of her maiesties, and successors right and title to that kingdome, namely a plate of brasse, fast nailed to a greate and firme post; whereon is engrauen her graces name, and the day and yeare of our arriuall there, and of the free giuing vp, of the prouince and kingdome, both by the king and people, into her maiesties hands: together with her highnesse picture and armes in a piece of sixpence currant English monie, shewing itselfe by a hole made of purpose through the plate: vnderneath was likewise engrauen the name of our generall &c.

The Spaniards neuer had any dealing, or so much as set foote in this countrie: the vtmost of their discoueries, reaching onely to many degrees Southward of this place. . . .

The 23. of Iuly they [the Miwok Indians] took a sorrowfull farewell of vs, but being loath to leaue vs, they presently ranne to the tops of the hils to keep vs in their sight as long as they could, making fires before and behind, and on each side of them, burning therein (as is to be supposed) sacrifices at our departure.

And so, Sir Francis Drake sailed on around the world and never saw California—or New Albion—again.

One item quoted above in Fletcher's account became of sensational interest in 1937. The "plate of brasse" was found. The pros and cons and complicated ramifications of this story are beyond the scope of this book. But the question remains: is the plate, which is now on display at the University of California, a priceless treasure or is it a fake? All evidence points toward authenticity, but the ultimate and irrefragable proof is still sought by scholars and scientists. It may be Drake's plate; it probably is—but is it?

Drake's visit to California of only thirty-six days in the year 1579 had an appreciable effect upon history. It warned the Spaniards that they had better look to their claims; it served to show any freebooter that if one pirate got to be a knight, there was a wonderful future in piracy (provided you had the sanction of your monarch); it further served to show that the long-sought Strait of Anián was still farther from discovery and might turn out to be a myth after all; and it hastened the day when somebody was going to take California by physical possession, and made it clear that whoever did so would have to hold the land by occupation and not merely claim it and sail away.

But who?

Galleons From Manila { 4

THE right to make a profit has always been a prerogative for free men and strong nations. When that profit can reach 200 percent or 400 percent—or even more—the fact that there will be physical hazard means concomitantly less and less to the eager investor. Merchants, importers, businessmen, opportunists, call them what you will, were attracted by the Manila Galleon gamble as early as 1566. And by 1571 the investment was considered more than attractive. Some of the participants "cleaned up" and others were "cleaned out," and perhaps this fact that it would surely be one or the other lent a zest to the investment.

A man who had $10,000 could borrow $40,000 more. With this amount he could then buy $50,000 worth of space on a galleon. The merchandise brought from Manila to Acapulco in this amount of space would be worth about $200,000. Silk from China brought the most lucrative returns, but various types of goods from all over the Orient were assembled at Manila, and you could be assured of a handsome profit no matter what your space on the galleon was occupied with—spices, porcelains, damasks, musk, wax, gum, bamboo, or on down the line to such extraordinary commodities as edible birds' nests.

For a merchant the financial risk was high, and for the crew the physical risk was higher. And in order not to have the influx of goods ruin the markets for its domestic products, the Spanish government eventually limited the galleons to one 500-ton ship a year.

The galleon was a tall, clumsy, unpredictable ship. The westward crossing from Acapulco to Manila was not too difficult, the

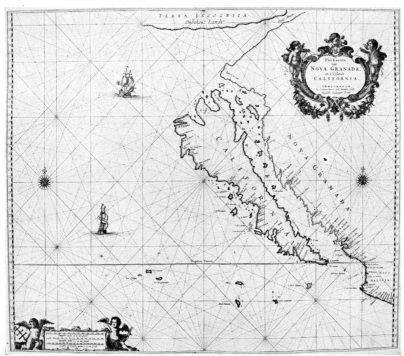

This old map shows California as an island

A typical *carreta*, or oxcart, first vehicle to travel the Royal Highway

Santa Barbara in 1840. The mission may be clearly seen in the background. Compare this with the modern view.

Modern Santa Barbara

route being directly across the Pacific with an occasional touch at Guam. The return trip was another story. Moreover, the vessel sailed west light and returned heavily laden, often dangerously laden, with its treasures from the Orient. All possible space was, naturally and greedily, devoted to the valuable cargo. Even food and water were sacrificed to make room for every last piece of merchandise. The crew accepted this as they were on a percentage basis. The skipper received about $4,000 for the trip; a deckhand, if one could be so designated on a galleon, received $25. But both skipper and deckhand could double or quadruple his money if the trip were successful. The hazards involved were storms, shipwreck, disease (particularly scurvy), boils, lice, dysentery, starvation—and worst of all, pirates.

The return course had to be made by following the great-circle route along the coast of Japan, across the northern Pacific Ocean often as far north as the Aleutians, and then on to the coast of North America, making landfall anywhere from Cape Mendocino to the Bay of Monterey in California, and finally, down the coast to Acapulco in New Spain. Since these galleons made annual voyages it is obvious that except for Cabrillo and Drake, they were the only ships to sight the California coast up to 1579; and they continued, year after year, on into and through the seventeenth century.

Drake's piratical forays made it plain to the Spanish that the long unguarded California coast line was a danger zone for the galleons. What is more, a port was needed far to the north where the galleons could put in, and find supplies and fresh water and protection. Francisco de Gali, who commanded the galleon of 1584, was instructed to explore as far as possible the California coast on his return trip. His reports were inconclusive. The viceroy of New Spain was now Pedro de Moya and he sent Gali back to the Philippines with instructions to try again. Gali died before he could lead another expedition, but his successor was Pedro de

Unamuno who, commanding a frigate called *Nuestra Señora de Buena Esperanza,* or *Our Lady of Good Hope,* followed the great-circle route and reached the California coast at what is now Morro Bay near San Luis Obispo in 1587. Unamuno took twelve soldiers and explored the interior, passed over part of what was to become the Royal Highway, went through the routine ceremony of claiming the land for Spain, tried to make friends with the Indians who fled at the sight of him, and built a cross and proclaimed the country Catholic.

Perhaps the Indians around Morro Bay and San Luis Obispo were a more warlike type than the majority of California Indians, for while they first ran away, they lived to fight another day and apparently attacked the Unamuno party with a rain of arrows. Unamuno was almost out of ammunition—or so his story was told—and he decided to live to fight another day, too, and thereby weighed anchor and sailed for Acapulco.

And if the need for protection of the galleons had been only a forethought up to 1587, it became a pressing reality with the fate of the *Santa Ana,* commanded by Sebastián Cermenho in that year.

This ship was the largest galleon yet—700 tons, with a cargo worth almost three quarters of a million pounds. A pirate and an Englishman named Thomas Cavendish had followed Drake's career and rounded the Horn and attacked, looted, tortured, burned and raped every Spanish port he could safely outman and outfight. Learning of the coming *Santa Ana* he lay in wait for her at Cape San Lucas at the lower end of Baja California. When she appeared she gave Cavendish quite a scrap before he was able to capture her, board her, loot her and finally burn her. Then this corsair further emulated Drake by running for England across the Pacific by way of China, India and South Africa, and became the third circumnavigator of the globe. Like Drake, Cavendish eventually got his final comeuppance, died and was buried at sea.

His death was small consolation to the robbed Spanish, but still they tried to protect themselves the hard way. Sebastián Cermenho, who had commanded the burned *Santa Ana,* was spared by Cavendish, and he was finally able to get the charred hulk back to Acapulco. Still the Spanish government did nothing about this outrage except instruct its ambassador to complain to the English crown. It is not on record that the ambassador's complaint ever gave Elizabeth a sleepless night.

And all the viceroy in Mexico City could do was to continue to instruct galleon commanders to look for a good and safe harbor where a galleon could find protection and a land base of supplies would be set up. San Francisco Bay would have been ideal. It was there all the time but no white man had yet seen it.

Cermenho commanded the galleon for the year 1595, the *San Agustín,* and again he turned out to be the hard-luck boy of the Manila-Acapulco run. In trying to follow orders to search out a good safe harbor somewhere along the California coast, Cermenho found Drake's Bay. Again white men scouted the area that was to become the northern end of the Royal Highway and again the Miwok Indians were friendly and hospitable. But Cermenho did not have Drake's luck. The clumsy overladen galleon was driven ashore by a storm and wrecked. All the precious cargo was lost and along with it, the remaining food supply.

Fortunately, Cermenho had part of his men building a small launch for reasons of local coastwise exploration. Abandoning his second wrecked galleon, Cermenho and his crew managed to make Acapulco in the makeshift launch after unspeakable privations and hardships. He arrived there with a great idea, and it is inconceivable that the viceroy hadn't thought of it before. It was simply this: Don't expect an overladen and inappropriate ship such as a galleon to serve explorative ends. Instead send an expedition up the California coast just as Cabrillo had sailed, but include enough maneuverable ships of light draught and enough food and equipment so that the job could be done right for the first time in over fifty years. By this time there was a new viceroy who was the Conde de Monterey. The idea seemed sensible and practical to him. He suggested it to the Council of the Indies and requested their recommendation for such an expedition with all possible speed. The Council approved but for one reason or another, political chicanery or personal graft, nothing happened for the next five years.

Then, in 1600, the Dutch freebooter, Olivier Van Noort, began pillaging the west coast of South America, and was ostensibly working his way north to capture the biggest prize of all, the Manila galleon for 1600.

Van Noort was either scared off or missed the galleon altogether, and he sailed on west across the Pacific. But his presence had so alarmed Spain at last that the necessary steps were finally taken in 1602.

The question of whom to put in charge of the expedition led to the usual politics and nepotism. And at last the "right" man was selected. He was Sebastián Vizcaíno and he was quite a different type of man from Cabrillo, the Little Goat. Vizcaíno had lost a fortune on the ill-fated *Santa Ana,* and he had made two trips to Manila and back. The latter, in 1590, earned him 2,500 ducats for an investment of only 200. In 1596 he had invested in pearl fishing off the coast of Lower California, and on the whole he was a man who dabbled in this and that and knew his way around and just whom to flatter and whom to insult. In short, he was a kind of political climber and opportunist, but of considerable energy, and the viceroy summed him up for the job as "of medium yet sufficient ability."

Vizcaíno was made "general" of three ships, all better-equipped and more seaworthy than those of any previous expedition. He was, however, definitely not "on his own" but had, instead, specific instructions which he was to follow on pain of death. He must make no changes in places already named; he must make a thorough examination of the coast from Cape San Lucas at the end of Baja California all the way north to Cape Mendocino. If weather permitted he was to go beyond Cape Mendocino but for not more than a hundred leagues. He was to make no settlements; he was to examine all bays and harbors but he must not spend too much time in any one of them; and he was to make friends with all Indians.

Vizcaíno listened to all this with half an ear, and sailed from Acapulco on May 5, 1602, "under the protection of Our Lady of Carmen," blissfully making his own decisions once under way and giving no heed to any instructions whatever.

A detailed account of his journey is unnecessary here as he closely followed the route of Cabrillo sixty years before. Instead of adhering to place names, he renamed almost everything he saw. It will be recalled that Cabrillo called the present San Diego Bay, San Miguel. It was Vizcaíno who changed it to San Diego, and he did the same sort of thing with all points up and down the coast. The Bay of Smokes became San Pedro, and so on. The place names used along the California coast today are largely Vizcaíno's and in spite of violating instructions he did a pretty good job of it. He sailed into an attractive harbor on December 4, Saint Barbara's Day, so to him the place was Santa Barbara and it has been called so ever since. A good-looking bay farther up the coast, with fertile lands beyond, he named in honor of the man who told him to make no changes. So what had had two or three names before became the Bay of Monterey, named for the viceroy, and this has held ever since.

And like every other mariner who preceded him, Vizcaíno missed the great San Francisco Bay entirely.

It is doubtful if he sailed farther north than the 42nd parallel, and even though the expedition had been well prepared in contrast to its predecessors, Vizcaíno began to run into trouble. Forty-eight men, or nearly half the complement of the three ships, died during the voyage. The explorations took eleven months, far more than had been anticipated, and of course food supplies ran out. Scurvy, the eternal scourge of the sea, attacked the crews. Some of the men became too weak to stand and had to crawl. Only two sailors on Vizcaíno's flagship were strong enough to climb to the main topsail. Realizing that he had certainly accomplished his aims as far as distance was concerned, for he had sailed beyond Cape Mendocino, this businessman-turned-explorer decided the wisest thing to do was to return to New Spain. That he made it at all was an accomplishment, and by all means it must be said that Vizcaíno, who had not been held in too high regard, had commanded a successful voyage. His most important contributions were his reports on the bays of San Diego and Monterey.

That San Diego offered an excellent harbor was now well understood in Mexico City. But in the description of the Bay of Monterey, the Vizcaíno report went overboard entirely with some wishful thinking and writing:

We found ourselves to be in the best port that could be desired, for besides being sheltered from all the winds, there is much wood and water, suitable for the masts and yards. . . .

And later:

. . . it is all that can be desired for commodiousness and as a harbor for ships making the voyage to the Philippines, sailing whence they make a landfall on this coast. . . .

And still later:

. . . this port is surrounded by the settlements of friendly Indians, willing to give what they have, and would be pleased to see us settle in this country. . . . It is in the same latitude as Seville and is almost of the same climate. . . . There are springs of good water; beautiful lakes covered with ducks and many other birds; most fertile pastures; good meadows for cattle, and fertile fields for growing crops. . . . Those who come from China in need of relief could very well resort to this port.

Monterey, then, would appear to have been exactly what the Spanish government needed. But the overflattering report was, strangely enough, not acted upon, Vizcaíno was more or less kicked upstairs by being handed the post of governor of Tehuantepec, and Spain, having at long last the port it was looking for, promptly forgot it and went searching for something else.

This curious farrago of motives was due to the fact that there was now another new viceroy, and he had not one jot of interest in developing the California coast. He was the Marqués de Montesclaros and he pooh-poohed all the efforts of his predecessor, the Conde de Monterey. The new viceroy declared that there should indeed be a port of refuge for the galleons, but that it should be near Japan where the worst storms were encountered. There were two islands—the Isle of Gold and the Isle of Silver—stated Montesclaros. The thing to do was to find them and utilize them and forget such things as Monterey—both the man and his bay. The fact that these two islands, Gold and Silver, had no more reality than the mythical Strait of Anián did not deter Montesclaros from recommending that they be found at once. And a fruitless expedition set out to do so and, of course, ended in a fiasco.

Thus, just when Spain was about to develop California, the whole history of the west coast was changed by the prejudice and whim of a man who is totally unknown to Californians today. The Marqués de Montesclaros was a blockhead, and his stupidity successfully retarded Spain's advance into California by 167 years!

After Vizcaíno in 1602, it was 1769 before the Spaniards made any efforts to develop their California claims again. By the time they did so, what had been the great Spanish Empire was utterly corrupt and tottering from within. The shoots that were eventually planted in California soon grew independently of the mother tree. But before those days came the incredible hiatus in her history—or California's long wait.

The Long Wait ⟨ 5

BETWEEN 1602 and 1769, during which interval not a single ship sailed north from New Spain to California, there were three men who kept the spark of colonial expansion alive. They were not explorers, although they perforce did some exploring; they were not businessmen, although they certainly had business ability; and they were not politicians, although they were entirely at home in political machinations.

They were Jesuits.

And they were the three who were indispensable during the long wait in bringing about the seizure of California by land, and in making essential an artery of transportation to be called the Royal Highway. Their names, known today by scholars and a few readers, were Eusebio Francisco Kino, Juan María Salvatierra and Juan Ugarte. Without their combined efforts, it might well have taken Spain another century to occupy California, and by that time it would have been far too late. In fact, the occupation was, to say the least, tardy in 1769. And even with the efforts of the three Jesuits, it took an even fourth and alien force to get Spain to move north and develop something she had claimed since 1542.

This fourth force was a foreign power. Her name was Russia. Her emissary was Vitus Bering. Her aim was California—and she achieved it. Her settlement was made by colonists coming across from Asia to Alaska, which was then Russian territory, and on down the Pacific Coast. Fort Rossya (today called Fort Ross) and the colony along the Russian River were hardly more than fifty miles north of the Golden Gate.

But this threat to Spain's ignored land of California did not come at once. Long before the Russian threat, the three gentlemen who were essential—Kino, Salvatierra and Ugarte—had done their parts.

In 1687 Father Eusebio Kino founded the mission, Nuestra Señora de Los Dolores or Our Lady of Sorrows, in what was known as Pimeria Alta and is now the Mexican state of Sonora. This mission is about 100 miles south of what is Tucson, Arizona, today. Thus began the first overland advance of New Spain's northern frontier toward her neglected California. It is interesting to note, in passing, that Kino was an Austrian whose name was Kuhn, sometimes spelled Kuhne, and its Spanish variation is either Quino or Kino. Few people realize that a Viennese had anything to do with the preparing of the way for the Royal Highway, but that is the fact in the case of this intrepid Jesuit priest.

Kino met Father Juan María Salvatierra in Mexico, and the two men were imbued with one idea—the colonizing of Sonora, Arizona and Baja California, with, of course, the eventual colonizing of Alta California, or what is the American state of California today. To their assistance came Juan Ugarte, whose Jesuit zeal was no less strong than their own. The Spanish government was interested, even sympathetic, and it wished the pioneers all success in their noble efforts to bring civilization to the frontier and an assurance of heaven to the souls of the aborigines but—the Spanish government declined to advance any money for the cause. That would have to be up to the Jesuits. The government would give them a very pretty license dated February 5, 1697, and with that—good luck, boys!

Difficult as it was, the Jesuits managed to finance the project, largely through the setting up of the Pious Fund of the Californias. It was something new in California history and was more than a straw in the wind. For now it was not the government that was boss, but it was the Jesuits themselves who were in full charge and control; not only of spiritual interests, but of the military, since they hired their own soldiers; of industry, since they hired their own workmen; of jurisprudence, since they administered their own laws; and of immigration, since they kept out of the project and the area all who were not Jesuits. The church became the state in these new lands, and this policy set up a precedent that eventually led to political difficulties and even to strife.

Salvatierra founded the mission and presidio at Loreto in Baja California in 1697—the first permanent settlement in the Californias. It is a quiet sleepy little town, basking in the sun on the Gulf of California today. Probably not one of its present citizens knows or cares that it was at one time the first capital of California and the very beginning of the Royal Highway, the first town on the road that was to open California to the world.

Kino, meanwhile, was devoting his efforts to Sonora and Arizona. He made numerous journeys over the land, founded many missions and settlements, and to his tireless energy may be credited the opening of this raw country, much of which is hot sandy desert and rocky inhospitable mountains. He brought cattle into the area, and European grains and fruits. He was an explorer, a historian, a geographer, a cartographer and an author, as well as a missionary who baptized more than 4,000 neophytes. He spiked once and for all the persistently fallacious idea that California was an island by riding on horseback from Sonora to the Gila River, down the Gila to the Colorado and across the Colorado to Baja California. He wrote a paper to prove it called *Cosmographical Proof That California Is Not an Island but a Peninsula.* He was easily the outstanding leader of Mexico's northwestern area. His physical endurance and his impeccable integrity made him a power far stronger than a small army. If there have been great men in the history of Spanish America, Eusebio Francisco Kino must be rated close to the top.

Salvatierra and Ugarte weren't far behind him when it came to earnestness and practicality. While Kino was in some respects more of a man of the field and more of a scholar, both Salvatierra and Ugarte were indispensable in founding and maintaining the Pious Fund of the Californias into which many an erring and aging sinner poured his gold in order to be assured of a place in heaven.

Salvatierra and Ugarte founded a number of missions in Baja California and their successors continued to spread this influence in both directions, north and south, from Loreto. Furthermore they brought in date palms and grapes, introduced the agricultural improvements of the time and stocked the mission settlements with domestic animals.

The choice of Loreto as the first settlement was accidental—or perhaps the story is apocryphal. At any rate, Salvatierra had a location in mind somewhat farther inland. But as the mule train started on its way, the animal bearing on its back an image of the Virgin collapsed. This mule could not be prevailed upon to get up. Here was proof enough, insisted Salvatierra, that the Virgin had selected this place to be her residence. So the mission was built on the exact site of the collapsed mule. This, and countless other stories of Baja California have a naïveté of their own. Even today it is a land of no railroads and impassable automobile roads; and an airport may be any flat land, even the top of a mesa. Max Miller has written an admirable and objective account of it called *Land Where Time Stands Still*. It is truly a country where a week may go by or a century may go by, and if you could conceivably return, you would not be able to say which interval of time it had been. For a good vivid close-up of life in Baja California there is another book, at once curious, spurious and delightful, written by a man who preferred to call himself Antonio de Fierro Blanco which was not his name (but we'll respect his privacy) and who called his book *The Journey of the Flame*. For those who like the picaresque and the highways and byways, this will provide a number of pleasant hours and inner chuckles.

During his travels in Sonora and Arizona, Kino realized that the crying need for the development of the frontier was a road. He strongly advocated such an artery of commerce to cross into California from Sonora and to be extended north into Alta California. Then the Manila galleons might make port, say at what Vizcaíno had called San Diego or Monterey, and the precious goods could, in part at least, be moved overland. This would help supply the new province of Alta California and would get the goods into the security of New Spain much sooner than would the long run down to Acapulco and its danger of lurking English and Dutch and possibly even French pirates. Moreover, Kino insisted, if Spain didn't get a good grip on California soon, somebody else might do so. The English already had claimed it through Drake, the French were in the great Mississippi Valley of North America and were moving west, and a few Dutch ships had made a feint or two at California from the Pacific. This situation could not go on forever. To Mexico City Kino recommended action. Of course there was none.

Years after this far-seeing Jesuit's death, however, the final impetus occurred that revitalized the spent and lethargic Spanish colonial strength. That, as has been mentioned, was Russia.

Bering and Chirikof made voyages to Alaska in 1741. The fruit of these explorations was the Russian fur trade and the establishment of Russian colonies in Alaska. And the bear had his eye on the attractive California coast.

Fortunately for Spain, she had the man for the occasion. He was forty-five-year-old José de Gálvez, a man of intelligence, energy and ability and a former student of law from the University of Salamanca. He saw the over-all picture at once, and while his enemies called him cruel and insane, there is in historical perspective no doubt that the long line of weakling and selfish and stupid executives such as the Marqués de Montesclaros came to an end with the arrival in Mexico City of Gálvez, appointed visitor-general of New Spain by Charles III in 1765. One of the first projects to catch the newcomer's imagination was an overland road to California. Gálvez' vigorous and expansionistic plans had the full approval of a new viceroy, the Marqués de Croix, who was one of his best friends.

Gálvez, among other plans for the welfare of New Spain, concentrated on one increasing purpose: Spain must take and hold the two Californias, both Baja and Alta, by sheer physical force. And it must be *Spain*—not the Jesuits. Certainly not the English or the French or the Dutch or the Russians. The seizure must be political, military, economic and of course must have the Christianizing power of Catholicism. The force to execute this maneuver must go both by land and by sea. From any Mexican west-coast port a naval force could be sent north. And in Baja California there was a town called Loreto. Let the land force start from there and let it never dare to stop until it had reached and seized that glorious Bay of Monterey which Vizcaíno had described so vividly those many years ago. Let the land force blaze the trail to become a royal highway—El Camino Real—and the sooner the better if this land was to be forever Spain's.

Gálvez' enthusiasm and foresight carried the plan to fruition. At last the Spanish were aroused. They went into action. It was 1769. The long period of gestation was over. The Royal Highway was born.

PART 〉 **2**

SPANISH ARCADY

1769 *to* 1821

Façade of Mission Santa Barbara, founded in 1786 by Padre Fermín Francisco de Lasuén

Photo courtesy of Edith Coulter and the University of California Press

Mission San Luís Rey de Francia in 1841. This mission was long considered one of the most beautiful architecturally. The artist is unknown.

Photo courtesy of California Mission Trails Association

Mission San Diego de Alcalá, the first of the twenty-one Franciscan missions of California, founded July 16, 1769, by Padre Junípero Serra

First, the Soldier

DON GASPAR DE PORTOLÁ became the first governor of an area he had never seen—California. There was a sprinkling of white men in what was called Baja California, but in Alta California, an area as large as Spain's bitterest enemy, England, there were only Indians. The capital city of both the Californias was Loreto. Few present-day citizens among the ten million or more people who make up California have ever heard of Loreto, much less realize that it was the first capital. And how many could name the first governor?

Looking down from my room in the St. Francis Hotel in San Francisco in November of 1948, at the Portolá decorations and lights in Union Square to commemorate the re-enactment of his arrival, I asked the colored chambermaid what they were for. "Celebrating the Gold Rush," she said.

Later when I asked a bellboy, he explained, "For some old bird called Portoley who got here early."

"Who was he?" I asked.

"Oh, the first mayor of San Francisco, I guess," said the bellboy.

These remarks are not quoted to show superiority or superciliousness on my part, for truthfully I did not know what the colors were for either. San Francisco was obviously celebrating something in a mild and civic and dispassionate sort of way. It turned out to be a festival and pageant, held a week before, to honor with parades and music and dancing the first governor's arrival in 1769 and his discovery of the long-missed and sorely needed San Francisco Bay. Some of the lights had blown out and some of the tinsel deco-

49

rations were falling down, and a few days later some trucks drove up and crews of workmen pulled the stuff down and hauled it away. Hail, Portolá!

Hail, indeed, to this capable and doughty Spanish soldier who was the first man to traverse the length of the Royal Highway—to blaze the trail—from Loreto to San Francisco Bay, a journey overland fraught with dangers from disease to starvation, a journey comparable in distance to one on the east coast from Miami to New York—by mule.

Shortly before this major undertaking, recommended and insisted upon by José de Gálvez and advocated by the viceroy, Marqués Francisco de Croix, an event of political and religious significance took place that set the Jesuits back on their heels. And Baja California, be it remembered, was virtually a Jesuit state. Charles III of Spain issued an edict expelling all Jesuits from the Spanish Empire. The reasons for this sweeping manifesto had nothing to do with conditions in Baja California; rather, it was the result of political peccadillos and greed and graft and corruption, coupled with the inflated ambitions of some of the men high in European circles of the Jesuit Order. This Society of Jesus was getting out of hand and was just a little too powerful within the Catholic Church. Most Royal Confessors were Jesuits; therefore, they had all the inside information and used it to their own advantage. The rise of deism as a philosophy in Europe after 1750 was definitely anti-Jesuit; men such as Voltaire and Diderot, the intellectualists, united with Pascal and the Jansenists to obliterate the Jesuit Order. They didn't quite do it, but they did rock the society to its very foundations.

So with one stroke of the pen by Charles III in Madrid the history of California was changed again. No Jesuits would be permitted to take any part in the seizing of this new land. The Jesuits were placed under arrest and sent to Vera Cruz and their personal property was confiscated. Unjust and unfair as was this suppression, it was a royal order and there could be no appeals. It was the end of the Jesuit influence in early California history. Their work was taken over by the Franciscans, who replaced them in the missions of Sonora and Baja California. A military man was sent to Loreto to see that all this was expeditiously carried out. He was General Gaspar de Portolá and, being a good soldier, he obeyed his orders. This was in 1767.

Gálvez, meanwhile, was urging the conquest of Alta California, and in 1769 he launched it. The Jesuits were gone, and the Franciscans only newly arrived when the California expeditions, one by land and one by sea, got under way.

The general in command of civil and military affairs was, of course, Gaspar de Portolá, a Catalan, a born soldier, courageous, loyal and tenacious, and now "governor" of California. His expedition left Loreto on March 9, 1769. It consisted of four divisions. The first, or advance guard, was led by Captain Fernando de Rivera y Moncado (hereafter referred to as Rivera), whose job it was to assemble a growing stock of supplies from foodstuffs to livestock, all of which must be contributed by the various missions along the way. Rivera nearly depleted one or two missions, and, as things turned out, it was a good thing for the expedition that he took all the supplies and equipment that he could muster.

The most northern outpost was the Mission San Fernando Velicatá. From this point on, about 300 miles below Tijuana on what is the international border today, the men were in unexplored country.

Two ships loaded with supplies were sent from La Paz, around Cape San Lucas and up the coast, with instructions to find the Bay of San Diego as described by Cabrillo in 1542 and Vizcaíno in 1602, and meet the land expedition there. The first ship to sail was the *San Carlos*. It was 110 days in reaching San Diego, being blown halfway to Panama and back. The second ship to sail was the *San Antonio,* and although it left a month after the *San Carlos,* it arrived in San Diego on April 11. On April 29 the *San Carlos* arrived. The latter ship was a shambles and twenty-four of her crew had died during the voyage. And on May 14 Rivera's overland party, the advance guard, arrived. General Portolá brought up the rear, and he reached San Diego on July 1, 1769. Thus was the first permanent city in present-day California founded.

Modern San Diego offers quite a contrast to the feeble little settlement of 1769 located at what is now the landmark called "Old Town."

When those on the *San Antonio,* who were the first to arrive, entered the bay they expected to be greeted by the crew of the *San Carlos* who, they presumed, would have had a full month in which to get a presidio under construction. But the only people to greet them were sullen and somewhat hostile Indians. When the *San Carlos* did arrive, its crew was ready for hospitalization; but there was no hospital, and the overland party was unreported. To add to the difficulties with most of the personnel ill, food was running low. After several weeks of uncertainty and anxiety, Rivera's advance guard arrived. The two crews were overjoyed; at last, here was relief.

Rivera's men, who had been on sharp rations for days, were overjoyed to see the two ships in the bay; at last, here was relief. So it was something of a let-down for both forces, and they made the most of it until July 1—six more weeks—until the governor of California arrived. Don Gaspar was not especially impressed with his constituency. But he was determined to carry out his orders; and with him was a man of courage equal to his own—if not surpassing his—a man of pious purity with an almost obsessed religious zeal, a scholar, a humanitarian, a gentleman, a mystic and a very capable executive, one of the greatest names in California history for all time—Padre Junípero Serra.

It is not necessary to trace here the long line of cause and effect that brought Serra from his birthplace in 1713, the Spanish island of Majorca in the Mediterranean Sea, to become the founder of the first Christian church in California, the Mission San Diego de Alcalá. There are a number of biographies of the man, notably the one by Padre Francisco Palou, one of his contemporaries, and a fair and lively twentieth-century account by Agnes Repplier.

But the exodus of the Jesuits resulted in the Franciscans taking over their labors and in Junípero Serra being more or less catapulted into the position of president of the Franciscan missions of California. The Franciscans of the College of San Fernando in Mexico City were given the Baja California area in 1767 when the Jesuits were forcefully expelled. The first to arrive in Loreto to try to save whatever good work the Jesuits had done was Junípero Serra. His seniority and his education (he was fifty-five years old, and had been educated at the Lullian University at Palma, and then for fifteen years had held the Duns Scotus chair of philosophy at the university) attracted José de Gálvez. He felt that Serra was the man to represent religious hegemony in Alta California, just as surely as Portolá was the man to command the military. And Gálvez made no mistake in either choice.

Serra was never blessed with a robust physique, but his will and determination seemed to enable him to transcend his debilities. At the time of the first overland journey from Loreto, Serra was suffering from an infected leg, and most of his life he seems to have been lame. Portolá thought that Serra should not try to make the arduous trip, and Francisco Palou even wrote Gálvez to that effect and asked that he himself go instead. Gálvez' answer was characteristic of Gálvez, and it put a quick stop to Palou's pleading. "I am happy that the Reverend Padre Junípero insists on accompanying the expedition," he wrote to Palou. "I commend his faith, and his confidence that he will improve in health, and that God will permit him to reach San Diego. I firmly believe he will get there."

Serra was delighted, for, leg or no leg, his great ambition was to be in the field and not behind university walls. An *arriero,* or mule-teer, approached him during the journey north from Loreto, a journey in which Serra was in constant pain. This muleteer believed he had a cure. It was a poultice and ointment made of fats and herbs, which, if the good Father would pardon him, always cured his mules of galls. If the good Father would only try it, surely no harm could be done, and possibly . . .

The result was an immediate easing of the pain and a decrease in the swelling of the leg. What did it matter if the president of the California missions arrived smelling strongly of mule ointment? He had safely arrived in San Diego, and this was all that counted. Immediately the first of the chain of California missions was founded. It is still there today, and the next time you are in San Diego, take a look at the building, The Mission San Diego de Alcalá—the odor of mule ointment has long since disappeared.

The founding of the first mission and the bringing of Catholicism to the Indians was only part of the assignment to Portolá. He had been directed to go to the Bay of Monterey and establish a presidio there. San Diego was only part way. Things were none too cheerful, even here. Of 300 men, his forces had been reduced by illness and death to 150. A third supply ship, the *San José,* was overdue, never did arrive, and to this day nothing is known of its fate.

Portolá had to make a decision and he had to make it in a hurry. Whereupon he wisely decided to split his forces three ways. The *San Antonio* would be manned by such sailors as could still function and would sail back to Mexico for more supplies. Padre Junípero Serra and the artisans, with some soldiers, would remain and hold the new presidio and mission of San Diego. And Portolá himself, with a company of sixty-three men, including his lieutenants, Costansó and Fages, Captain Rivera, Fathers Crespi and Gomez, Sergeant Ortega and thirty-two leather-jacketed soldiers, carrying mattocks, axes and shields, seven muleteers, two personal servants, and a number of Baja California Indians, would continue north by forced marches through the unknown country until they came to the Bay of Monterey, where, as Vizcaíno's account written one hundred and sixty-seven years before made it clear there was a horn of plenty—wild game, good grain, fresh water, friendly Indians, rich valleys, strong timber—and a little bit of California heaven on earth. It had never occurred to Portolá that Vizcaíno's report might be the wishful writing and thinking of a sagacious and somewhat romantic opportunist.

And so, on July 14, 1769, Portolá and his company left San Diego. Once again the pioneers were pushing the Royal Highway northward. And they counted it a goodly gain when they made from ten to twelve miles a day over country that no white man had yet seen.

If you should drive from San Diego to San Francisco today you would duplicate a good deal of Portolá's route as you followed U.S. Highway 101. Where the modern highway departs from the first governor's route, it is merely a matter of better engineering. For the most part, Portolá's trail blazing is still the main artery of transportation along the California coast today.

Since his objective was a bay some 500 miles north of San Diego, it is obvious that Portolá and his party followed the coast whenever and wherever practicable. At times they were forced inland by rugged and impassable mountain ranges that came down to the sea. Whenever these barriers proved insuperable, the Portolá expedition sought a side canyon and worked inland until they could find a valley that seemed to give access to the north. They followed this until it reached the coast, then they continued up the coast until they came to the next major barrier, and then they used the same technique all over again. The sound and sensible reason for this is that most of California's coastal rivers flow not west into the Pacific, but north parallel to it, forming long inland valleys before emptying into the ocean. Notable examples of this topographical configuration are such rivers as the Santa Ynez, the Santa Maria, the Salinas; and north of the Golden Gate, the Eel, the Mad and the Trinity.

After seeing his ship the *San Antonio* depart on July 9, 1769, a life line to New Spain carrying a report for Gálvez and a request for all possible supplies, Portolá bade a fond farewell to Padre Serra who was, literally, to hold the fort at San Diego, and with the ablest of his men, on July 14, after prayers and blessings, he marched north at four o'clock in the afternoon. When Portolá's party camped that night they were scarcely more than five miles farther north, but this Xenophon of Spain was off on a California anabasis that made history.

His route followed the coastal shelf exactly as U.S. 101 does today, turned inland to what was to become the site of Mission San Juan Capistrano a few years later, and shortly thereafter the party camped beside a stream that Padre Crespi called "the River of the Sweet Name of Jesus of the Earthquakes." Certainly Padre Crespi must have had some good reason for bestowing such a name, although a present-day Chamber of Commerce bulletin might describe it as "slight tremor felt." The river is known as the Santa Ana today.

Continuing northwesterly, and seventeen days out of San Diego, Padre Crespi recorded in his diary as translated by Professor Herbert E. Bolton in 1927:

We entered a spacious valley, well grown with cottonwoods and alders, among which ran a beautiful river from the north-northwest. . . . toward the north-northeast there is another river bed which forms a spacious water course, but we found it dry. . . . We halted not very far from the river which we named Porciúncula. The plain here is very extensive. It has good land for planting all kinds of grains and seeds, and is the most suitable site of all that we have seen for a mission, for it has all the requisites of a large mission.

No mission was ever built on this location. Not far away, however, to the northeast, San Gabriel Mission was eventually built. The actual spot that Padre Crespi described was the confluence of what is today the Arroyo Seco with the Los Angeles River. Instead of a mission finally being constructed on the site, a branch, or *asistencia,* is near by today. And it is completely swallowed up by a community known as El Pueblo de Nuestra Señora la Reina de Los Angeles de Porciúncula, which is now called by many people "L'Sangless," and by just as many, "L.A."

Since they were some distance from the coast (a two-day march at their pace), Portolá decided not to follow the Los Angeles River upstream, but to strike out toward the sea. This was sensible, for if there should prove to be a good coastal shelf, as there had been north of San Diego, this would be readily accessible country to follow north to the coveted goal, that rich and luscious Bay of Monterey.

Continuing west on a route that would be approximately Wilshire Boulevard in Los Angeles today, the party was surprised and pleased to note "natural vineyards of wild grapes, and an infinity of rosebushes in full bloom" (this was long before the days of "smog") and finally, "a number of large marshes of a substance like pitch that were boiling and bubbling." These were the now-famous La Brea Pits just south of Hollywood.

Another day and Portolá realized that the plan of following a coastal shelf was unfeasible, for there was no coastal shelf. What the men called the Santa Monica Mountains came down and met the sea. He had to turn inland or wade in the ocean, so he marched through Sepulveda Canyon to the present San Fernando Valley, thread-needled through the Santa Susana Mountains, found the Santa Clara River, and followed it to its mouth at what is today the small city of Ventura.

From here on, along the Santa Barbara Channel, they were among the Chumashan Indians—the people of Cabrillo's El Pueblo de las Canoas (Canoe Town) and they found them the highest type of aborigines they had met so far. These people even had some knives and one worn blade of a Spanish sword, gifts traded to their ancestors by Cabrillo exactly two hundred and twenty-seven years before. The Franciscan priests, Crespi and Gomez, were particularly pleased with these Indians: they were good fishermen, they grew a few crops, they lived in thatched huts, they didn't go entirely naked, they observed obsequies and had a burial ground, the women wove baskets, and on the whole they appeared generally healthy and intelligent. Here was a fine field of potential converts to Christianity.

On up the coast the Spaniards pushed their way, passing and noting the attractive site that was to become Santa Barbara and coming upon a number of other Chumashan villages. Vizcaíno had not named any of this country, and as there were so many creeks and canyons and points to be named, a colorful variety was given, almost all of which are still in use along the Royal Highway today: Refugio Beach, Paso de la Gaviota (Sea Gull Pass in English, but never called that, Gaviota being easy on the Anglican tongue), Laguna Graciosa (Graceful Lagoon), and El Oso Flaco (The Thin Bear). This last was near what is Pismo Beach on the highway today, and resulted from one of the party shooting a bear. Juicy bear steaks were anticipated, but when slaughtered and cooked, the animal proved to be so thin that it had hardly any meat on its bones. Turning inland, the party camped at what is now San Luis Obispo.

The modern highway climbs La Cuesta grade, curves through some especially beautiful country and finally reaches the head of the long Salinas Valley. Portolá was still adhering to his original plan of follow-the-coast-whenever-possible, and he went from San Luis Obispo to Morro Bay and on northward until the forbidding Santa Lucia Mountains, dropping from their peaks sharply down to the sea, made further progress impossible. Had they attempted to ascend and descend the corrugated canyons of the Santa Lucias (today's San Simeon Highway, or State Route 1, does it and still scares timid motorists) it would have taken them about another year to reach Monterey. They struggled on, barely making two miles a day, and at last they were all so exhausted that Portolá called a halt and a four-day rest. Padre Crespi, in a lugubrious mood, named the camp "The Wounds of St. Francis."

Portolá sent scouts afield to search for a better route, and they found that by veering inland the party would come into a long valley leading north with a good river in its bottom. This, of course, was the Salinas—although they named it El Rio Delfino. One of the soldiers wanted to call it the River of Chocolate for two reasons: one, because it was muddy enough to look like chocolate; and two, because he would have traded his shield and his deerskin jacket for a deeply craved taste of real chocolate. But at least they were out of the Santa Lucias and they were able to continue without any great difficulties. From here on, through San Ardo, King City and Soledad, the modern highway follows exactly Portolá's route. The Spaniards marched northward and downstream until the Salinas emptied into a bay.

They found it an unimpressive body of water and wondered how much farther it could be to Vizcaíno's glorious Bay of Monterey. They were, of course, standing on the very shore of the Bay of Monterey, but they did not know it.

It has been written into too many history books that Portolá failed to discover the Bay of Monterey, and this is a mistake. He discovered it from the land even as Cabrillo and Vizcaíno had found it from the sea, but because of Vizcaíno's glowing account, neither Portolá nor any of his men recognized it. Surely this shallow, unprotected, unproductive, unimpressive indenture in the coast could not be the object of their long search. Certainly they had not marched a thousand miles from Loreto to find *this* imitation of a harbor. This little *ensenada* shaped like a fishhook, where the ocean rolled in and winds whipped the waves and the whole surface was choppy sea, must be short of their real objective.

And where were the tall timbers and the friendly Indians and the rich valleys and the fresh waters? Of course there was a hill with some pines on it, and the muddy Salinas River did flow lethargically into the bay, and there were brush and chaparral growing in from the beach, and a few Indians did appear and at once fled— but none of these factors added up to the great Bay of Monterey.

Costansó, the engineer-lieutenant, checked his latitude with Portolá against Vizcaíno's records. It was very close. The Bay of Monterey must be somewhere near by, perhaps a little farther on. They decided that Vizcaíno's figures must have been erroneous and that the real Bay of Monterey must lie about a two or three days' march to the north. It had not yet occurred to any of them that there was nothing wrong with navigator Vizcaíno's figures and that they were in the right place after all, but where the trouble lay was in narrator Vizcaíno's adjectives.

So, with a few disparaging comments about this disappointing break in the coast line that should have been a real port, the party worked its way on to the north. They crossed another river, and on one of its banks they found the carcass of a large bird, stuffed with dried grass by the Indians. It must have been an eagle, for it measured over seven feet from wing tip to wing tip. Padre Crespi gave the river a holy name, as he was certainly bent and determined to do in nomenclature, but the soldiers called it El Rio del Pájaro—River of the Bird—and the Pajaro River it is today.

As they continued north they discovered a phenomenon far surpassing in wonder the great stuffed bird. They came upon a tree so huge that it made them seem like pigmies beside it. And soon after they found a whole grove of these trees. They were, of course, some of the famous California "big trees," or the *Sequoia sempervirens,* of the present Santa Cruz County Park. Lieutenant Fages recorded: "Here are trees of girth so great that eight men placed

side by side with arms extended are not able to embrace them."
Engineer Costansó recorded in a typically factual report: "They
were the largest, highest, and straightest trees that we had seen up
to that time. The largest of them were four to five yards in diameter." And Padre Crespi could think of nothing like them in this
world, so he described them solely in terms of what they were not.
"On October 10 we came on some tall trees of reddish colored
wood unknown to us, having leaves unlike the cedar and totally
without the odor of cedar." This is about the most negative description of a California big tree that is on record. But it was this
same Padre Crespi who gave the trees their permanent and popular
name. "As we knew not the names of these trees," he wrote, "we
gave them the name of *palos colorados* [redwoods]."

About that time—early October—in the year 1769, the fall rains
began. Since the Spaniards had no shelters, a state of being soaked
most of the day and night was added to their misery. They struggled on up the coast and finally camped, exhausted, at Half Moon
Bay. And it never occurred to any of the company that the scorned
ensenada, now far behind them, was the object of their search. All
they could agree upon was that somehow they must have missed
the Bay of Monterey altogether—or that Sebastián Vizcaíno was
the greatest liar ever born into the Christian world.

Portolá, himself now ill, sent Sergeant José Ortega on up the
coast with a small scouting party "just in case." And while he and
Costansó and Padres Crespi and Gomez rested, a deer-hunting
expedition was sent into the adjacent mountains to the east.

Both these secondary parties returned with surprising but unen-
couraging news. The deer hunters topped a range and looked
from it over the broad expanse of the lower part of San Francisco
Bay. And Ortega, marching north, was stopped in his tracks by
the southern portal of the Golden Gate. Across the water barrier,
and quite inaccessible to him, he was faced with what is today
Marin County; and far on the horizon as the coast curved to the

northwest, he could dimly make out Point Reyes and Drake's Bay. New Spain was staring for the first time at New Albion. It was November 1, 1769.

Both parties, the scouts and the hunters, returned to report the amazing find of this huge arm of the sea, which no navigator had ever seen, and which formed possibly the greatest landlocked harbor in the world—a port so great that "not only all the navy of our Catholic Majesty, but all the navies of Europe could take shelter."

Somehow this did not impress Portolá. He wasn't even sufficiently interested to go and take a look at this magnificent harbor that would put in the shade all that had been said of the missing Monterey. He had his orders to find Monterey and set up a presidio. He was sick, he was tired and he felt that he had failed. Like Columbus, he never realized that he (or his advance guards) had blundered onto something far surpassing that which they sought. He recorded that the scouts had "found nothing" and he decided to return down the coast to the useless and wave-washed and wind-whipped *ensenada* that should have been Monterey, but to him was not.

The men were limited now to five tortillas a day (hardly the equivalent of five pancakes) and whatever other food could be clubbed or shot or found among the rocks of the sea. Mussels gave them cramps, sea gulls were tough, deer were impossible to kill and the only meat available was the mules that carried the supplies (such as were left) and provided transportation for the sick who could not walk. On November 9 Portolá made the inevitable decision: they would have to try to get back to San Diego alive, and with God's will they might succeed.

On the southern shore of what was really the Bay of Monterey after all, the men built a large cross and inscribed on it: "Dig at the foot and you will find a message." This was done in case a relief ship had, by some chance, been sent up the coast since their departure. It was a chance in a thousand, but at least Portolá wanted to let any followers know that he had "with no provisions left except flour, set out this day for San Diego . . . at the Bay of Pines, December 9, 1769." And he buried this information in the sand at the foot of the cross.

The return trip to San Diego took less time than the journey north inasmuch as they could follow their own trail south—the second traversing in history of the Royal Highway. Food was the major problem and the party ate twelve mules during the tedious trip. As Portolá wrote later, "smelling frightfully of mules" they arrived at San Diego on January 24, 1770.

Padre Serra was happy to see the explorers, albeit Portolá counted the arduous journey a colossal failure. He had been farther north than even his orders from Gálvez had commanded him to go, and he could not, for the life of him, find that blasted Bay of Monterey.

Padre Serra smiled in consolation. Things had not been good in San Diego either. In all the time that the general had been away, over six months, the priest had been unable to make a single convert. These Diegueno Indians of the Yuman stock were willing to watch from a distance, but they refused to work and they refused to pray. When nobody was looking, however, they were eager to steal. Padre Serra found them a discouraging parish to say the least. But he had hope.

Portolá had none.

"Don't fret," said the priest. "You have merely been to Rome without seeing the Pope."

"I've been to hell," said the soldier, "and have shaken hands with the Devil."

Then, the Priest { 7

WHAT shall I do next? was the question in the mind of Gaspar de Portolá, and although he was the first governor of California to be so perplexed, he was not the last.

The settlement at San Diego was hanging on to its life by a hair. And the "settlement" at Monterey was nonexistent simply because the Bay of Monterey itself seemingly was a will-o'-the-wisp, a mere figment, in the mind of a man Portolá would cheerfully have throttled, Sebastián Vizcaíno, had not that worthy been dead for a century and a half in 1770.

Portolá had failed to execute his orders. In his own mind he felt he would be well justified in abandoning Alta California as a national fiasco in which it was his bad luck to have to report it worthless. But that was not what Gálvez, the visitor-general to New Spain, and the Marqués Francisco de Croix, the viceroy of New Spain, had instructed him to do. Find San Diego and Monterey, and fortify and hold them both, had been the essence of his orders. He was too good a soldier not to realize that he had failed to fulfill his command. So the military conferred with the church.

Padre Junípero Serra, while he had to admit that California was temporarily disappointing, continued to consider it most promising in the long perspective. And as they discussed it, the soldier and the priest decided there were only two courses to follow. One was to wait for the return of the vessel *San Antonio* which had been sent back to Mexico for essential supplies more than six months before, and then try again to locate Monterey; or, if the *San Antonio* were lost without trace as had been the ill-fated *San José*,

64

they would simply have to abandon San Diego and all of Alta California, and retreat as best they could with such survivors as could make the journey, back to the nearest outpost of New Spain, the northernmost mission in Baja California, San Fernando Velicatá.

January of 1770 went by, and those at San Diego waited, patiently or impatiently as their temperaments governed them, for the one remaining life line, the now overdue supply ship *San Antonio*.

Then February went by and things began to look hopeless. It has been written that Portolá was for packing up and giving California back to the Indians, although this was not exactly the case. And it has been written that Serra did not want to give up in any circumstances, and that was surely the case. But Portolá was in charge and Portolá's decisions were final. Serra urged him to wait until the end of March. Gloomily, or so the popular story goes, Portolá decided to wait at San Diego for a few weeks more. The attitudes of the discouraged soldier and the hopeful priest are well contrasted in their own words.

Portolá wrote:

Some of the cuirassiers were left with barely enough clothing to cover their backs. We planted a small quantity of corn in the best soil, but, although it grew well, the birds ate the best of it while it was still soft, leaving us bereft and disappointed of the hope we had cherished of eating the grain which our own hands had sown.

And Serra wrote:

Flowers there are many, and beautiful as I have noted before ... we have the queen of them all, the rose of Castile; when I write this I have before me a branch of rose bush, with three roses open, others in the bud, and more than six impetaled. Blessed be He who created them!

The contrast in attitudes is all too evident.

The story is told, or perhaps it should be called only a legend without credence, that Portolá reached the end of his patience, and in spite of Serra's pleadings, decided to abandon Alta California. His deadline was March 24, 1770. Serra, as the legend goes, made a novena and his prayers were answered. The *San Antonio,* with a cargo of necessary supplies and equipment, hove into view on the twenty-third of March, and Serra's faith had thereby saved the conquest of California and turned defeat into victory. It is a very nice story, but it has no historical evidence whatever to back it up.

The truth of the matter is, Portolá, although deeply discouraged, was not a quitter. He had sent Captain Rivera back to the Mission San Fernando Velicatá in Baja California, with instructions to go on to Loreto and return with an overland caravan of supplies. This can be authenticated. So it is obvious that Portolá would not have called a retreat from San Diego and that he intended to try once again to fulfill his orders. This fact does not detract from Serra. The courage of his efforts and the success of his exploits need no apocryphal furbishings.

At any rate, on March 24, 1770, the *San Antonio* arrived back in San Diego with its hold loaded with supplies for the little eleven-month-old presidio-mission. This was a cause of great rejoicing, for now the tiny colony was reasonably secure. In another few months at the most, Captain Rivera should get back overland from Loreto with additional supplies and personnel. Portolá decided to make a stab at Monterey again and, if it could not be found, to establish a presidio at the nearest place that offered any chance of permanent settlement. Serra was delighted. Between the two of them they arranged it so that Portolá would again go north over the Royal Highway to that worthless *ensenada* he had found at about the latitude where Monterey should be, and Serra would go north on the newly arrived *San Antonio* with supplies to meet the land party at that same *ensenada.*

This plan was acted on with all possible speed. Serra sailed on the *San Antonio* on April 16, 1770, and Portolá and his miniature army marched north for the second time the following day. This time it was not necessary to blaze a trail through unknown terrain, for the route was established and all they had to do was to follow their former tracks.

It was presumed that Serra on the *San Antonio* would arrive at the appointed destination first. Portolá and his men made their second northward march over the Royal Highway without untoward incident or major difficulty, but, when they again reached the disappointing bay, the *San Antonio* was not in sight. Adverse winds had held the ship back. Some days later, on June 1, 1770, her sails were sighted by lookouts, and later that day Junípero Serra stepped ashore at Monterey.

During the eight days of delay while Portolá and his men awaited Serra's arrival, they gave this bay a careful scouting. Father Crespi and Lieutenant Fages, walking along the beach and checking landmarks against Vizcaíno's descriptions decided that this must be the identical place because of geographical and topographical features, even though the rich and lush values of Vizcaíno's superlatives were not to be found. Portolá himself admitted that "this must be it" but added that Vizcaíno would have made a very poor witness. So Monterey, which had been found all along, was officially recognized at last. The huge landlocked harbor to the north, the Bay of San Francisco, would have been a much happier selection for a permanent settlement, but Portolá had been given instructions to seize, hold and fortify Monterey, and, if this were it, the order would be carried out to the letter.

On June 3, 1770, on what must have been the exact site of Vizcaíno's landing, an altar was constructed; over it was placed an image of the Virgin, and from a branch above two bells were suspended. Padre Serra sang the Mass, sprinkled a huge cross with holy water, and watched the erection of the cross by the soldiers.

Then the entire company knelt in prayer before it. Serra then sprinkled the earth, the beach and the harbor with holy water, to put to flight all powers of evil. He delivered a brief sermon, and then all sang the *Veni Creator Spiritus* and concluded the ceremony with the *Te Deum*. Thus was dedicated the Mission San Carlos Borroméo. And the baffled Indians stood by and watched.

When the religious services were concluded, Portolá went through the somewhat superfluous ceremony of taking political possession of the land—although that had been more or less accepted as a previous fact due to the visits of Cabrillo, Gali, Cermenho, and Vizcaíno—and after sufficiently impressive shooting had been completed to indicate to all and sundry, and to the further bewilderment of the Indians watching from a safe distance, that this land was now the personal property of his Catholic Majesty Charles III of Spain, Monterey was considered safely and adequately occupied. Portolá had his soldiers build a small fort of planks and sod, equipped it with some threatening cannon which had never been fired, and garrisoned it with twenty men. Then he breathed a sigh of relief. His job was completed. California? This first soldier-governor decided that the priest could have it. Possibly it offered a great opportunity for somebody, but that individual was not Gaspar de Portolá. Having found, settled and garrisoned both San Diego and Monterey, Portolá had carried out his instructions to the letter; now he was happily through. And he wasted no time.

On July 9, 1770, Portolá appointed Pedro Fages acting governor and military commander of California, and he himself cheerfully sailed away on the *San Antonio* to report to Gálvez and the viceroy in Mexico City. It was his personal intention never to see California again, and he never did.

When the news arrived in Mexico City that Alta California had been successfully occupied, it was an occasion of great rejoicing. Now let the rascally Russians or the grasping English try to get it.

The full might of New Spain was holding it (twenty men and some untried cannon on what had certainly been the Bay of Confusion), and in Mexico City bells pealed, flags were unfurled, salvos of artillery were fired and a special High Mass was celebrated. The viceroy, Marqués Francisco de Croix, was the hero of the day; and José de Gálvez was the man of the hour. Gálvez stood proudly watching the celebration in Mexico City, and at his side stood a happy, but a somewhat quixotic and quizzical Don Gaspar de Portolá.

The viceroy made the conquering soldier the governor of the province of Puebla in New Spain, and with that, Portolá passed from the annals of California history.

Hundreds of miles to the north, in Spain's newest and quiet little outpost of Monterey there was no simultaneous celebrating. The happiest, and perhaps shrewdest, man there was Junípero Serra, for he had achieved the goal of his fifty-seven years; he was president of the California missions, and albeit there were only two of them so far, many more would be founded in the ensuing years, and thus thousands and thousands of poor unbenighted heathen Indian souls could now be saved by conversion to Christianity. It was as rich a harvest for heaven as any missionary could pray for. And Padre Serra went to work.

Between Monterey and San Diego, countless times over the Royal Highway this tireless priest traveled. What had been an unknown land, with no trace or trail, gradually became familiar country to him in the next few years. And slowly the trail developed from the route established by Portolá until it was no longer a trail but was in actuality a road with each of the twenty-one missions approximately an easy one day's journey from the next. The Spaniards called this artery of communication El Camino Real.

Serra did not live to see the full flower of his missionary dreams, but his energy gave the project an impetus that carried it on to an even greater fruition after his death. The first five of the missions were founded by Serra: San Diego de Alcalá in 1769; San Carlos Borroméo in 1770; San Antonio de Padua, about seventy miles south of Monterey on July 14, 1771; San Gabriel Arcángel, just east of the present city of Los Angeles on September 8, 1771; and San Luís Obispo de Tolosa, on September 1, 1772. A glance at the map will show how these last three missions began the closing of the great gap between the first at San Diego and the second at Monterey. While traffic was not heavy over the Royal Highway, it was at least a road of sorts, and you could no longer travel for a week without meeting anybody but Indians.

For reasons which have been a moot question, and which have had an amazing variety of explanations, Serra moved the Mission San Carlos Borroméo, one year after its founding, from Monterey over the hills south down the coast to the Carmel River about five miles away. The new location was very beautiful (and so had been the first), but it is not likely that Serra made the move for reasons wholly aesthetic. It could not have been for any particular economic or political reason, for all the politics and economy of California were under the jurisdiction of the acting governor and military commander, Pedro Fages. Fages, at this time, was busy exploring and mapping San Francisco Bay. He went around its lower end and up the east side, passing over what are now Alameda, Oakland and Berkeley and continuing on to the Carquinez Strait. He was not at that time a source of trouble or annoyance to Serra, and yet Serra would not permit the second of the California missions to remain at Monterey. A small brochure, available at the mission today, says that for "obvious reasons" he chose the present site, and rechristened the institution Mission San Carlos Borroméo del Rio Carmelo. It is, of course, popularly known as Carmel Mission today.

But the "obvious reasons" are not further elucidated. Piecing it all together, historians are pretty well agreed that while Serra was busy converting the Costanoan Indians to Christianity, the soldiers in the Spanish garrison at Monterey were busy converting the Indian girls to pregnancy. So far, in the conquest of California, the Spaniards had brought no women. Therefore, the inevitable took place. Serra, realizing that just about every time he saved a soul another soul was damned, decided to remove the mission from the immediate vicinity of the garrison.

And while a move over the hills and five miles away did not exterminate the evil, it at least made it less opportune. Sin, decided Serra, like love, could be all too easily a matter of propinquity.

In May 1771 ten friars arrived in Monterey on the *San Antonio*. The ship also brought Serra's requested items: candles and candlesticks, incense and vestments, beads and bells. With this gain in personnel and property, Serra immediately founded the third of the missions along the Royal Highway—San Antonio de Padua—on July 14, 1771. With two of the newly arrived friars, Serra read the dedicatory Mass under a California live oak. One lone Indian turned up to see what was going on. The Spaniards gave him a friendly welcome, and, more important, a string of glass beads. This did the trick, and in a matter of days other Indians came to watch and wonder and get their beads. Before they quite knew what they were doing, they found themselves at work, under the guidance and instruction of the Franciscans, at building a church.

Serra remained fifteen days to be sure that all was well and that the work was going forward. The Indians seemed affable, even agreeable, and the walls of the mission rose with their labors.

San Antonio de Padua is some distance off the modern highway, U.S. 101, and if you wish to see its ruins it is best to take a secondary road south and west from King City. From a slow start it gained in momentum until in 1800 it had a population of 1,118 Indians. It was regarded as one of the best of the California missions and reached its peak of activity of births, baptisms and deaths between 1800 and 1810.

With this third mission successfully dedicated, Serra hurried south over the Royal Highway to found the fourth on September 8, 1771, San Gabriel Arcángel, near the present city of Los Angeles. So active was Serra in these days and weeks and months that it is almost impossible to follow him as he traveled the length of the road between San Diego and Monterey. "George Washington slept here" might well have its Western counterpart in "Junípero Serra slept here"—if and when the busy priest had time to sleep at all.

The Mission San Luís Obispo de Tolosa, or St. Louis the Bishop of Tolosa (nobody ever uses the English translation of the name even today), was founded by Serra on September 1, 1772. He left the day after the dedication, leaving a young Franciscan, Padre Cavaller, in charge, along with four soldiers, one corporal, and two Indians. Progress was slow at San Luís Obispo. First of all it was a long way from Monterey and even farther from San Diego. The reason for Serra's choice of the site was the fact that he wanted a mission somewhere about halfway between San Diego and Monterey. It was his way of getting a firm Franciscan grip on the country. The Indians at San Luís Obispo were not particularly interested in the mission, and one good reason was that they had better food than did the priest and soldiers stationed at this keystone spot along El Camino Real. Instead of the mission's raising the standard of living of the Indians, it was the Indians who contributed to the welfare of the missionaries. They were willing to trade their food for Spanish cloth, and San Luís Obispo struggled along until its first violence in 1776. Just what the source of trouble was is not clear, but the mission was attacked by Indians who shot burning arrows into its thatched roof, thereby destroying much of it by fire. This led one of the padres to suggest a roof made of tile, and that is how and why almost all the missions eventually came to have tiled roofs. The tiles looked better than tule rushes or straw, but more important than beauty, no enemy could set fire to the building by arching burning arrows onto it. Again necessity proved to be invention's parent.

A few weeks after dedicating San Luís Obispo, Serra sailed from San Diego on the ever reliable *San Antonio*. He had made amazingly good progress in the three years he had been in California. Believing that all would be well with the five missions until his return, and urging his fellow Franciscans Lasuén and Palou to keep up the good work and found other missions during his absence, Serra went to Mexico City to confer with the new viceroy, Antonio Bucareli. He had much on his mind, and his meeting with the viceroy was of immense importance to the immediate future of California.

In the first place, when Serra arrived at San Diego with Portolá and throughout Portolá's stay in California, the military was in full command. Serra's titular authority remained within religious activities only. This division of authority had been specifically directed by the government of New Spain to keep the Franciscans from running the whole show as the Jesuits had managed to do in Baja California. That was satisfactory with Serra as long as he could work with a man of Portolá's caliber. But after Portolá's departure, acting Governor General Fages began to get in Serra's way. Even Portolá might have done that had he remained. For now Serra had five missions to govern, and they were all of his creating, and Fages was a soldier and not a missionary. The military and the church did not run their offices in exactly the same way, and technically Serra was subject to Fages.

Apparently Junípero Serra and Antonio Bucareli, the new viceroy, struck it off very well from the start. Each seemed to have a high regard for the other's ability.

Serra had a number of requests that he wished the viceroy to grant. The first was to get rid of Don Pedro Fages. Actually the real governor of California was Felipe de Barri, who resided at the capital of both the Californias, Alta and Baja, the city of Loreto. Barri never traveled north and knew nothing of the country he presumably governed. And this man Fages, appointed by Portolá to take charge as a combination of acting governor and military leader, was, in Serra's eyes, incompetent. Serra needed soldiers, but he needed a military commander who would work with him in full co-operation with his religious efforts. Portolá's men had obeyed Portolá. But Fages lacked Portolá's capacity to discipline his men. Indian women were being seduced, even violently attacked. This aroused the Indians to hostility and the work of the Franciscans was impeded. Mission San Carlos Borroméo had to be removed from the vicinity of the Monterey garrison. Violence because of similar outrages perpetrated by the military had broken out at Mission San Gabriel Arcángel. There an Indian chief, furious at the ravishing of his wife by a group of soldiers who had lassoed her and ridden away with her, shot an arrow at a soldier. The soldier fired his musket and killed the chief. An Indian uprising threatened. Fages was responsible for his men and he could not control them. Moreover, Fages had permitted the unloading of two shiploads of supplies at San Diego when they were consigned to Monterey, and thereby delayed ecclesiastical activities and progress a whole month. So—off with Fages' head!

The viceroy agreed.

Serra wanted Sergeant Ortega made military commander. He had been a good man under Portolá, and it was Ortega who had worked his way on north until stopped by the Golden Gate and had thereby discovered San Francisco Bay. But Ortega was only a sergeant, and the proprieties of Spanish class consciousness could not permit a mere sergeant to become a military commander, no matter if he would have made an excellent one. Viceroy Bucareli pointed out these unfortunate but insuperable barriers to Serra, and they compromised on Captain Rivera for the job. Serra had some misgivings about Rivera, but at least he had got Fages sacked and that was something.

Next, Serra wanted the west coast port of San Blas in New Spain to be maintained as a supply base by sea for California. There had been some talk of abandoning the base.

Again the viceroy agreed. San Blas would remain.

Next, Serra wanted more funds for the exclusive use of future missions, and innumerable supplies of food, clothing, vestments, a forge and even a few luxuries—always good for morale—such as chocolate, olive oil, lard and a few barrels of wine and some of brandy.

And again the viceroy agreed.

Finally, as a last recommendation and something to consider for the future, Serra broached the idea of moving the capital of the Californias from Loreto in Baja California to Monterey in Alta California, thereby forcing the real governor to reside at the scene of all this new activity and progress and curtailing the existence of a military governor altogether.

The idea must have caused Viceroy Bucareli to smile. Here was a man who knew his business. This priest before him may have had his heart in the spiritual, but he had his brain in the temporal and practical. Here, decided the viceroy, was a very capable man. And while it was a trifle too early to switch the capital from sleepy Loreto to dynamic Monterey (dynamic mostly because of Serra himself), the idea was worthy of future consideration. Bucareli agreed he would, as might be said today, "sleep on it."

And then the viceroy had a question to ask the priest. It was an issue on which he would be happy to have Padre Serra's considered opinion.

Unknown to Serra, a man named Juan Bautista de Anza had a plan of connecting Mexico with California by establishing an all-land route. This was not new with Anza. It had been a dream of Padre Eusebio Kino, the intrepid and intelligent Jesuit, who had done so much to open Sonora and Arizona to Spanish civilization almost a hundred years before.

What, wondered Viceroy Bucareli, did Serra think of the feasibility of such an expedition?

Serra approved of it at once. He did more than approve; he declared that the opening of a land route from Mexico to Monterey would be a boon to California. Moreover, since he had established the Mission San Gabriel Arcángel in 1771, this location would be the ideal terminal for Anza's overland party. From there they could turn south to San Diego or north to Monterey over the now well-known and safe El Camino Real. Serra's quick reaction was a hearty indorsement of this scheme. While it is more than likely that Bucareli would have commissioned Anza to try it anyway, it is a certainty that Junípero Serra, by his presence in Mexico City at just that time, added to the viceroy's enthusiasm and thereby speeded up the founding of the cities of San Francisco and Los Angeles, and was indirectly responsible for the arrival in California of the colonists who became the first citizens of the many towns along the Royal Highway.

Serra was away from his beloved California for seventeen months—a trip that he would make by air today in a matter of hours—and got back to San Diego on the ever dependable *San Antonio* on March 13, 1774.

It is fitting and proper to say a word about this small ship that might be regarded as an unseaworthy fishing smack today. The vessel made numerous trips back and forth between San Blas and La Paz in New Spain to San Diego and Monterey in California. Its captain on every voyage was Juan Pérez and he has never had his just share of acclaim. Cabrillo was a navigator of courage, no doubt, and so was his successor Ferrelo. Drake was bold and daring, and the captains of the Manila galleons were not mollycoddles. All have their places in history, but Juan Pérez is scarcely remembered. Without him and his ability as skipper of the little *San Antonio,* back and forth from Mexican west coast ports to California, the entire history of the Royal Highway might have been quite different. Pérez never traversed the highway, but he provided a life line of supply that was indispensable. Moreover, he explored the Pacific Coast as far north as the fifty-fifth parallel, or the northernmost tip of Queen Charlotte's Island at the point where British Columbia and Alaska meet today. We properly salute Cabrillo for his courage, but Pérez should not be forgotten. He delivered the goods.

Back in California in March 1774, Junípero Serra was at the peak of his career. He had caused a new military commander to be appointed; he had won the confidence of the viceroy; he had got the supplies and equipment and funds that he needed; he had applauded the plan of an overland route; he had suggested Monterey as the future capital; and he had reached his sixty-first birthday. But what doubtless contributed to his happiness at this time was to learn upon his return that all five of his missions were functioning without any drastic difficulties, and that his co-workers in the field, Padres Francisco Palou and Fermín de Lasuén had not only successfully kept the spark of Christianity burning, but had added to the holy fire during his absence.

Serra had ten more years to live. Probably it was the happiest and surely the most fulfilled decade of his life.

Three new missions were founded and dedicated in the next three years. Serra did not act as the founding father himself, but gave that honor to the men who had done such good work in his absence. Mission San Francisco de Asís, named for the leader of all Franciscans, was founded in 1776 by Padre Francisco Palou, and Mission San Juan Capistrano by Padre Fermín de Lasuén in the same year. In 1777 the Mission Santa Clara, the eighth in the growing chain, was founded by Padre Tomás de la Peña.

Also in 1776, a garrison, or presidio, was constructed at San Francisco by Lieutenant José Moraga, and a pueblo, or "town," was founded at San Jose by a few colonists who had come overland with the first Anza expedition.

Serra's California was growing.

Also in 1776, on September 15, Don Felipe de Neve, governor of the Californias, residing at Loreto, was advised by the viceroy of New Spain that he would forthwith take himself to Monterey which would henceforth be the capital of both Alta and Baja California. Neve was none too pleased about it. Now whose idea could it have been to move the gubernatorial office from sunny, quiet, comfortable Loreto, where nothing ever happened, to this wild outpost he had heard of but had never expected to see? Neve grumbled—and moved. And Captain Rivera, who had pleased Padre Serra no more than had Fages, was relegated to Loreto as lieutenant governor.

It would seem that with the arrival of Neve Serra's major troubles with the political and military elements would be over. But such was not the case. The church, the army and the state have rarely functioned happily together in history except in those cases in which one of the three included the other two. Unquestionably, as his field of labors increased, Serra would have liked to have the full power that the ousted Jesuits had once enjoyed in Baja California. Had he been able to be a kind of dictator of Alta California, he would have had the unchallenged position that he sincerely believed his efforts needed and warranted. But a man who is called "governor" is bound to accept the fact that he is there to govern. And a man who is called a military commander surely acts on the basis that he is there to command.

Serra felt that the interest of the missions was the interest of California, and that any other authority was a detriment to the spiritual and cultural and social progress. The immoral records of the army leave much to be said for Serra's argument.

Felipe de Neve felt that he would be a mere figurehead if he did not exercise authority over the land and its people he was ostensibly sent to govern.

The military element felt that neither the church nor the state could survive if it were not for the very real and punitive power of the army.

The sum total made for many differences of opinion, quarrels and occasional physical clashes. In substance, Neve gave Serra more trouble than any of the so-called "acting" military governors who had preceded him. And to Neve, Serra was a stumbling block. The worst difficulty of all was Neve's *Reglamento* of 1779 which set up a code of laws on which all decisions were to be based, including those of the missions. Even more outrageous to Serra was the plan of Neve to found a new chain of missions inland. With these new missions—under his political supervision—Neve decided to make some changes in mission policy, and these same changes were to be applied to the missions already founded by Serra and his colleagues. One friar at a mission would be enough from then on—no need for two. The missions must supply all their own animals and equipment. All supervision and maintenance would be governmental, and the lone friar could thereby spend more time at his religious devotions and orisons.

Serra flatly refused to found any new missions under such external regulations. Through his recommendations, the College of San Fernando in Mexico City refused to send any more friars to California to staff the new missions. Thus the clash of human temperaments and frailties was strongly felt in this new land.

During this bout of cross-purposes, however, there were other and more cheerful indications of the development of the land through which passed the Royal Highway.

The first of the Anza expeditions had been successful, and on March 28, 1776, the second overland expedition arrived to settle San Francisco. It numbered 240 colonists, both men and women, and many mules, horses and cattle. One person died during the journey and three babies were born. One of these was the first white child born in California, the other two having been delivered in Arizona. He was Salvador Ygnacio Linares, who arrived just before midnight on December 24, 1775, near what is now Warner's Hot Springs in San Diego County. Padre Pedro Font, who was with Anza, baptized the child and stated in his diary with proper objectivity:

In the afternoon they called me to confess the wife of a soldier who since yesterday had been suffering childbirth pains. She was very fearful of dying. . . . I consoled her as best I could, and at half past eleven at night she very happily and quickly gave birth to a boy.

And another member of the party recorded with complete impersonality: "She is the third that has done this thing." The mother was permitted one day of rest—Christmas Day—and then the march was continued.

The dispute between Serra and Governor de Neve dragged on; but as the issues did not seem to become any more hopeless of solution (in fact the governor was never able to get the missions completely under his rule), Serra founded what was to be his sixth and last mission in California, and was the ninth of the growing chain between San Diego de Alcalá and San Francisco de Asís. This newest and ninth church was the Mission San Buenaventura at what is the city of Ventura today. The sandaled feet and the plodding mules along the Royal Highway in 1782 went directly past its main door; and the sleek sedans and heavy trucks on U.S. Highway 101 are doing the same thing today.

This last of Serra's missions flourished well indeed, had fine herds of cattle, good fields of grain, a population of 1,297 neophytes by 1800 and a unique oddity, *wooden* bells. A bell made of wood is not a bell, but the dummy forms were carved from wood, and then metal bands inserted within the "bell" against which the clappers struck. The result must have been a metallic clank instead of a sonorous reverberation, but a bell by any name . . .

More significant for the future of California than the dedication of Mission San Buenaventura was the founding of a small colony of eleven families from New Spain's province of Sinaloa. They totaled only forty-four people, including men, women and children, were nearly all mestizos, or half-breeds, and it has been said that none of them could read or write. This last, very likely, was true. Among the forty-four, history records two Spaniards who had mulattress wives, four Negroes, seven Indians, several ex-convicts, a number of beggars and others unidentified. The colony was settled at the order of Governor Felipe de Neve who had his own way of doing things apart from the Franciscans. This village of the illiterate was called El Pueblo de Nuestra Señora la Reina de Los Angeles de Porciúncula; its population is approaching two million today, most of whom can read and write. The city of Our Lady the Queen of the Angels of Porciúncula is, of course, modern Los Angeles. It is mere chance that the city was called Los Angeles from the mouthful of words that make up its full name. It might just as well have been abbreviated to Pueblo, or Nuestra Señora, or La Reina, or Porciúncula—but for some reason the invading Americans eventually settled on Los Angeles. Today the Royal Highway runs directly through the middle of the city.

Governor de Neve selected another location for a settlement, a spot long cherished by Padre Serra and a site where the priest had personally hoped to found a mission. The mission followed four years later, two years after Serra's death. Governor de Neve's presidio, meanwhile, was called Santa Barbara because that had been the name given the harbor by Sebastián Vizcaíno on Saint Barbara's Day, December 4, 1602, after he had been specifically instructed not to bestow any new nomenclature. This small military outpost was established on April 21, 1782.

Serra's friend, Viceroy Bucareli, had died of pleurisy in 1779. His death was a source of sorrow and loss to Serra. He was replaced by Martín de Mayorga, and the replacement was not an easy one. Bucareli had been a man of great capacity, an intelligent and far-seeing leader at the time when New Spain sorely needed his sound executive ability.

The job of viceroy was no sinecure if it were to be properly administered. In order to ease the load, a new office was created called *Commandante-General para las Provincias Internas,* or what we might designate as Secretary of the Interior. The office had full charge of eight provinces, two of which were Baja and Alta California.

Three months after the founding of Santa Barbara in 1782, Viceroy Mayorga made a change that was a bitter pill for Padre Serra. Governor Felipe de Neve was to be relieved of his appointment. That sounded good at first blush. But what happened was that Neve was promoted to this new office commanding not only California but a number of other provinces. It was a plum that gave him even broader powers; and of *all* people to take his place and be booted back to governor of California, was Serra's old anathema, that incompetent ex-soldier, the man he had demoted, Don Pedro Fages! It must have given Serra a bad turn. He was sixty-nine years old at the time, and it is not impossible that this event shortened his life.

Fages had had little success and considerable failure with every office he had occupied. After leaving California he had been sent to Sonora and Arizona and had botched up the relations between the Spaniards and the Yuman Indians. This was a great pity, as the Yumans lived on the road Anza had pioneered. As friends they had proved helpful and valuable, but as enemies they could virtually make impassable and impossible the new overland road to California. Stupid policies and a highhanded seizing of their agrarian wealth had made the Yumans enemies of Spain. Fages was sent to punish them for defending their own property. He accomplished little, except perhaps to antagonize them further. After that Mayorga appointed him governor of California, and back to Monterey came the very man Serra had successfully ejected a few years before.

With Don Pedro Fages, and with great protestation over the annoyance of having to take up her residence in such a distant outpost as Monterey, came Fages' new wife, Doña Eulalia. She was the first "lady" to arrive in California over the Royal Highway

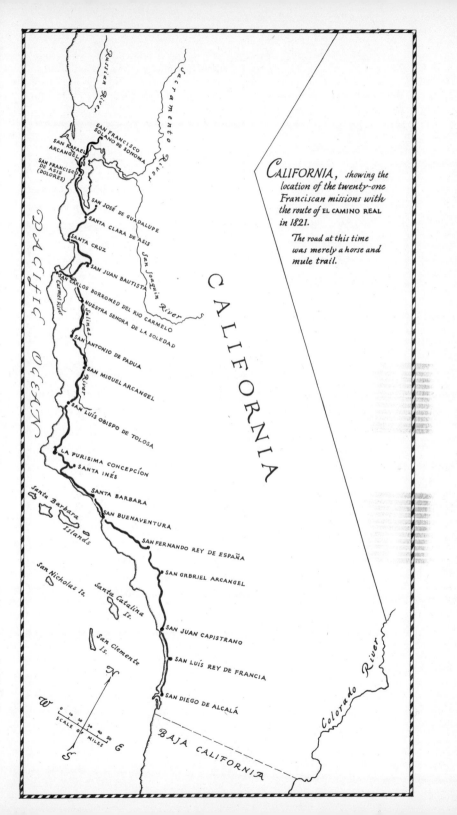

CALIFORNIA, *showing the location of the twenty-one Franciscan missions with the route of* EL CAMINO REAL *in 1821.*

The road at this time was merely a horse and mule trail.

PACIFIC OCEAN

CALIFORNIA

Pudden River

Sacramento River

SAN FRANCISCO SOLANO DE SONOMA
SAN RAFAEL ARCANGEL
SAN FRANCISCO DE ASIS (DOLORES)
SAN JOSÉ DE GUADALUPE
SANTA CLARA DE ASIS
SANTA CRUZ
Carmel River
SAN JUAN BAUTISTA
SAN CARLOS BORROMEO DEL RÍO CARMELO
Salinas River
NUESTRA SEÑORA DE LA SOLEDAD
San Joaquin River
SAN ANTONIO DE PADUA
SAN MIGUEL ARCANGEL
SAN LUÍS OBISPO DE TOLOSA
LA PURISIMA CONCEPCÍON
SANTA INÉS
SANTA BARBARA
Santa Barbara Islands
SAN BUENAVENTURA
SAN FERNANDO REY DE ESPAÑA
SAN GABRIEL ARCANGEL
San Nicholas Is.
Santa Catalina Is.
SAN JUAN CAPISTRANO
San Clemente Is.
SAN LUÍS REY DE FRANCIA
SAN DIEGO DE ALCALÁ

N
W   E
S
0 10 20 30 40 50
SCALE OF MILES

Colorado River

BAJA CALIFORNIA

CAL.
SAN DIEGO
TIJUANA
ENSENADA

ARIZONA

NEW
MEXICO

Pacific

BAJA

Gulf

SAN FERNANDO
VELICATÁ

Cedros Is.

of

CALIFORNIA

SANTA
ROSALIA

MEXICO

GUAYMAS

LORETO

Pacific

CALIFORNIA

LA PAZ

Ocean

California

Cape
San Lucas

N

W
SCALE OF MILES
0   100
E

S

BAJA CALIFORNIA
showing the route of PORTOLÁ
from LORETO, *the southernmost*
town on the ROYAL HIGHWAY,
to SAN DIEGO *in* CALIFORNIA.

from Loreto, as the other women who preceded her were merely wives of soldiers or artisans or were half-castes, and native Indian women, of course, could not be considered to be ladies.

Doña Eulalia took one look at Monterey and decided that this would never do for her. Life was dull and boring, she was unhappy and her husband should have been given a better appointment. Apparently she was very pretty, very spoiled and very determined to get back to Mexico City. Fages adored her.

Eulalia's particular brand of feminine wiles hit on a grand scheme that would get her husband transferred at once. With them was a Yuman Indian girl named Indizuela. Staging a big "scene," Eulalia accused her husband, in public, of carrying on an affair with the Indian servant. Eulalia refused to live under the same roof with Don Pedro Fages. Let him have his inamorata!

Nothing like this had ever happened in Monterey, and the reverberations were heard from California to Mexico City. Meanwhile Doña Eulalia took refuge in Mission San Carlos Borroméo.

Padre Serra nodded grimly. It all sounded quite logical and entirely within the character of the detested Fages and one more proof of the man's decadence of character. What manner of governor was this?

What Padre Serra was not schooled in, despite his many talents, was female psychiatry. He never considered that this pretty little termagant needed not sympathy so much as a spanking. There wasn't a word of truth in her charges against the bewildered Fages. She had simply striven to create a situation which would cause her husband to be recalled to New Spain. Padre Serra wished for the same objective, but it would never have occurred to him to employ such means.

The great scandal became gleeful gossip in New Spain's upper social crust and there were both civil and ecclesiastical investigations. Doña Eulalia, meanwhile, proved such a nuisance to the friars at San Carlos with her violent temper, her hurling and smashing of any and all loose objects, her shrieks and screams and tantrums (the first "lady" of California) and her vituperative insults, that they actually threatened this virago with a public whipping, a method of correction used on recalcitrant neophytes. Such corporal punishment of the governor's lady they would not have dared carry out, to their sorrow, and the lady told them so. More maledictions followed and the friars said a prayer that this sweet creature might be speedily removed to Mexico City. That, of course, was exactly what the sweet creature wanted.

When finally she was questioned and cross-questioned by state and church authorities, the Bishop of Sonora wrung from Eulalia the truth, namely, that the entire charge was a hoax, that Fages was innocent and that the Indian girl had been bribed to accuse the victim. Eulalia had pretty and tearful hysterics and begged forgiveness of church, state and husband. The baffled and befuddled Fages was delighted, and kissed away his wife's tears, exclaiming, "Again we dwell in union and harmony"—a statement the accuracy of which was extremely doubtful.

Padre Serra was disgusted. What was his California coming to? Weak and stupid governors, emotional and lying women—what next? And then suddenly, at the age of seventy-one, the good Franciscan was terribly tired.

In his last journey from mission to mission Serra concluded his travels at San Francisco de Asís, then and today popularly called the Mission Dolores. He was not entirely satisfied with the location and he suggested that it would be an astute idea to build other missions north of the Golden Gate. The presidio of San Francisco was all to the good; the great bay must be forever Spain's. But that land to the north—that was still California. Eventually his words were acted on and two more missions were built north of San Francisco. They were San Rafael Arcángel in 1817 and San Francisco Solano in 1823: the final efforts in the long project that Serra had begun in 1769, and the northernmost reaches of the Royal Highway. From San Francisco, Serra returned to his beloved San

Carlos Borroméo del Rio Carmelo. He lay on his crude bed of thongs under his one blanket and said, wearily and smilingly, to his friend and colleague, Padre Francisco Palou, "I have come home to die."

Palou stayed with him to the end. On August 28, 1784, at the age of seventy-one, after a lifetime devoted to what he considered the greatest cause on earth, with his final fifteen years filled with fruition, Junípero Serra closed his eyes, breathed his last and went to his just reward.

He was one of the first of the travelers along the Royal Highway, and surely the most important of them all throughout the eighteenth century.

In California there are monuments and peaks and avenues to recall his name. In 1913, in the little town of his nativity, Petra, on the Island of Majorca in the Mediterranean Sea, two hundred years after he was born, a monument to this native son was unveiled in the public square.

In the National Hall of Fame in Washington, D. C., California is represented by two of her heroes. The first, fittingly enough, to whom the state owes so much, is Padre Junípero Serra.

This great teacher and leader was buried before the altar at his own San Carlos Borroméo del Rio Carmelo in the only garb he had worn for years, a brown robe tied at the waist. The funeral was conducted with all the pomp and circumstance that his fellow Franciscans could offer. Ships standing off Carmel fired final salutes, while the bells of San Carlos tolled for their lost son.

Francisco Palou wrote: "On the 29th of August, 1784, in this church of San Carlos, in the sanctuary, before the altar of Our Lady of Dolores, the office of the dead having been recited, and a Requiem Mass having been sung, I gave ecclesiastical burial to the body of Father Lecturer, Fray Junípero Serra, President and Founder of the California Missions."

And all Franciscans everywhere agreed, "We now have an advocate in heaven."

And Then Feudalism { 8

In 1784 the Royal Highway, while neither royal nor yet a highway, was at least a vital artery of communication. It ran from the community of Loreto in Baja California to San Francisco in Alta California. And in passing it served the numerous missions of Baja California northward to the presidio and mission at San Diego. North of San Diego the highway passed through Mission San Juan Capistrano, Mission San Gabriel Arcángel, the tiny hamlet of Los Angeles, Mission San Buenaventura, the presidio of Santa Barbara, Mission San Luís Obispo de Tolosa, Mission San Antonio de Padua, the small capital of Monterey and the adjacent Mission San Carlos Borroméo del Rio Carmelo, the infinitesimal hamlet of San Jose, the Mission Santa Clara, and came to an end at the Mission Dolores and the presidio of San Francisco.

Apart from Portolá who had blazed the trail, these missions, towns and forts were the sum total of the efforts of Padre Serra and his Franciscans, Governor Felipe de Neve and his soldiers, and pioneer and settler Juan Bautista de Anza and his colonists. The forts, or presidios, while manifesting a militaristic front, didn't amount to much; the towns were clusters of peasant's huts and their existence was, at the best, precarious; but the nine missions were rapidly becoming self-sustaining simply because each had its clergy, its villeins and its serfs.

The white population of California was about 1,000, and the number of Indians was anybody's guess from 75,000 to 125,000. The Indians, for the most part, were two to three thousand years behind the Spaniards in socio-economic development. It was in-

86

evitable that with a small ruling class of a thousand whites, of which a good 50 percent were illiterate (perhaps 200 formed the educated governing body which controlled everything pertaining to the masses from their shirts to their souls), a civilization would evolve which was not only undemocratic, but was even more absolute in its dictates than the contemporary monarchy of Spain.

With the death of Junípero Serra in 1784, the office of president of the California missions went to Padre Francisco Palou. He was Serra's great friend and devoted Boswell, and it is due to his biography of the first of the presidents that Serra's career stands out in bold contrast to his contemporaries'. Palou spent his one year as president chiefly in writing Serra's story, *La Vida de Junípero Serra,* and he became thereby California's first author. About this work which he wrote at the Mission San Francisco de Asís, he apologetically and unnecessarily added: "I wrote this among the barbarian heathen at the Puerto de San Francisco in its new Mission, the most northerly of Nueva California, where books and the counsels of learned men are lacking: on account of this I beg you to pardon and overlook its faults."

While the book is a painstaking and creditable work, it is so strongly pro-Serra that the reader is bound to question the biographer's point of view. That Serra was a great man is unquestionable; that he was utterly infallible is open to at least a modicum of doubt.

Palou requested to be retired after approximately a year, and he returned to the College of San Fernando in Mexico City.

The third president of the California missions was Padre Fermín Lasuén. He held the office for eighteen years, and he carried on Serra's work with zeal and integrity. During this period the development of the Royal Highway and the development of California are one with the story of mission expansion. Save for the small and static presidios, or garrisons, and the struggling little pioneering communities, civilization in California owed its existence to the increasing number of missions, the total number of which reached twenty-one in 1823.

Padre Lasuén might well have been a Serra had he preceded the first leader. He was six years Serra's junior, and was sixty-six years old when he founded what later came to be called the Queen of the Missions—Santa Barbara—in 1786. During Lasuén's term of office, eight more missions were dedicated, bringing the total to eighteen. After his death, only one more was needed to fill the gap between San Diego and San Francisco, and that was Santa Inés, founded in 1804. The twentieth and twenty-first missions were constructed north of the Golden Gate, a northernmost expansion that Serra had recommended long before. These last two were dedicated when the period of decline had begun, and never attained the power of the earlier missions. They were San Rafael Arcángel in 1817 and San Francisco Solano in 1823. For the reader who wishes to see at a glance the order of the founding of all twenty-one, along with their founders, a list is appended at the end of this book.

California, then, was Franciscan, for the friars had in their possession the choicest and richest land in the territory; and the territory remained Franciscan until that power was finally broken by the Acts of Secularization on the part of the Mexican government, a process that began in 1826 but was not fully consummated until 1833-1834.

At its peak mission civilization in California represented the anomaly of being at once the only possible system in the given circumstances, and yet a system that never attained its professed ends and was foredoomed to destruction by projecting its inherent medievalism into what was certainly the unmedieval nineteenth century.

To the Franciscans the purpose of the missions was the saving of souls. To the Spanish government the purpose of the missions was the winning of the land for Spain. An eventual altercation and then finally open dissension were inevitable.

After the presidios of San Diego and Monterey were established, the great majority of the missions were founded in locations that would offer two values: (1) to attract the Indians; and (2) to fill in, by one-day journeys from mission to mission, the area between the two presidios. The Indians, who were of various stocks, but notably Yuman, Chumashan and Costanoan, were all lumped together and popularly called "Mission" Indians, and so they are known today. Or it might be more accurate to say that this misnomer has persisted even though the Indian himself has not. For with the purest intentions in the world, the sum total of the efforts of Serra, Lasuén and the Franciscan leaders who followed them, spelled just one thing to every missionized Indian, and that was death. Indian souls may have been saved but Indian lives were wiped out as ruthlessly as if the project had been devoted to that end.

It would seem on first consideration that the coming of the Franciscans with nought but love in their hearts for their fellow man, be he caballero or savage, would have been a boon to all California Indians. Each mission offered not only a sanctuary for the soul, but as the mission lands and facilities developed, it would seem likely that the Indian would develop too. It should have been a time of peace and growing prosperity, and if ever an Indian conceived of a "happy hunting ground" surely the missions provided it. First, the Indian was clothed; then, he had a sheltered life; and finally he was exposed to education. If not Latin, he could at least learn to read and write Spanish, and he was permitted and encouraged to embrace the Catholic philosophy of life. There were fields of grain, orchards, vineyards, many fat cattle and thousands of sheep. Men were taught farming and crafts; women learned to spin and weave. There was a contented agrarian security along the Royal Highway, with its chain of gray red-tiled missions, blending into the rolling California hills, amidst oaks and alders, and surrounded with roses of Castile, olives, oranges and sunshine. It was a bit of heaven on earth. That was one aspect.

Then what went wrong?

Probably it might best be summed up by saying that not even a Franciscan could make a thirteenth-century Spanish peasant (that was about the true standard of living offered) out of a Mongoloid race whose development was comparable to that of the natives of the Iberian peninsula at 2000 B.C. In short, the Indian didn't want it, he couldn't take it, he was forced to take it, so it killed him.

Unpleasant as it must be, to sweep away all the romantic glamor of the mission days in California, there is nothing like a firsthand eyewitness report. In 1786, just two years after the death of Padre Serra, there arrived at Monterey Jean François de la Pérouse (usually spelled Laperouse), commanding two frigates in the service of France. He was in port only ten days; and history records that he introduced the potato to California, although one or two historians have contested this. At any rate, Laperouse was made welcome in Monterey—any outsider was a cause for celebration at what was then a lonely outpost—and he wrote a good account of all he saw. His book—*Le Voyage de la Pérouse autour du monde*—was published in Paris in 1797 and an English translation appeared in London in 1799. This is how mission life looked to the visiting Frenchman:

The Indian population of San Carlos consisted of seven hundred and forty persons of both sexes, including children. They lived in some fifty miserable huts near the church, composed of stakes stuck in the ground a few inches apart and bent over at the top so as to form oven-shaped structures, some six feet in diameter and the same in height, and illy thatched with straw. In such habitations as these, closely packed together at night, they preferred to live rather than in houses such as the Spanish built, alleging that they loved the open air which had free access to them, and that when the huts became uncomfortable on account of fleas and other vermin they could easily burn them down and in a few hours build new ones. The condition of the neophyte was that of abject slavery. The moment an Indian allowed himself to be baptized that moment he relinquished every particle of liberty, and subjected himself, body and soul, to a tyranny from which there was no escape. The Church then claimed as its own himself, his labor, his creed, and his obedience, and enforced its claims with the strong hand of power. His going forth and his returning were prescribed; his hours of toil and his prayers fixed; the time of his meals and his sleep prearranged. If he ran away and attempted to regain his native independence he was hunted down by the soldiers, brought back, and lashed into submission. His spirit, if ever he had any, was entirely broken, so much so that in a short while after the establishment of a mission anything like resistance was almost unknown, and its three or four hundred or a thousand neophytes were driven to their labors by three or four soldiers like so many cattle. . . .

They were roused with the sun and collected in the church for prayers and mass. These lasted an hour. During this time three large boilers were set on the fire for cooking a kind of porridge, called *atole,* consisting of a mixture of barley, which had first been roasted and then pounded or ground with great labor by the Indian women into a sort of meal, with water. . . . Three quarters of an hour were allowed for breakfast. Immediately after it was over all the neophytes, men and women, were obliged to go to work, either tilling the ground, laboring in the shops, gathering or preparing food, as might be ordered by the missionaries, under whose eyes, or the eyes of other taskmasters appointed by them, all the operations were performed. At noon the church bells announced the time for dinner. . . .

At about two o'clock the Indians were obliged to return to their labors and continue until about five, when they were again collected in the church for an hour of evening prayers. They lived on porridge, but on rare occasions meat was given them in small quantities. This was eaten raw. When a cow was slaughtered the poor wretches who were not at work would gather round like hungry ravens, devouring with their eyes what they dare not touch with their hands, and keeping up a croaking of desire as the parts for which they had the greatest avidity were exposed in the process of dressing. . . . In rainy weather they were kept at hard work indoors, and on Sundays, although they were allowed an hour or two of games, they were driven for the most part into the church to pray.

Since Laperouse was kindly received by church and state authorities in Monterey, his matter-of-fact account, with no personal ax to grind, can hardly be discounted. The truth is that there are far more grim accounts in print than his description of life at San Carlos Borroméo del Rio Carmelo where the neophytes were probably better treated than at other missions, many of which had stocks, irons. and whipping posts.

Stories have been told of homesick Indians being permitted to return to their camps in the hills. But almost at once the soldiers were sent to round them up, returning not only the neophytes, but all the unconverted Indians they could find in the native camps, thus often doubling the neophyte population and greatly increasing the slave labor.

Except for maintaining the presidios the Spanish soldiers had little to do, and slight use for their meager military equipment. Apart from capturing runaway neophytes, they passed their time exploring the country, engaging in bear hunts and staging bull and bear fights, carrying the mail over the Royal Highway, carrying on flirtations and, when possible, love affairs with the few ladies of quality who came to the new land, gambling, drinking and overseeing Indians who were farmed out to them by the missions for the purpose of working the fields that provided provender for the garrisons. Apparently it was an easy, if somewhat boring life, and as long as you remained at the top and the Indians did all the work you were the basis of a new aristocracy.

The years 1805 to 1810 may generally be considered the peak of mission culture. All the missions had been established between San Diego and San Francisco, and only the two north of the Golden Gate remained to be founded. Mission prosperity and population were at an all-time high. Considering the territorial wealth as a whole, the missions were rich.

San Juan Capistrano, for example, thirty years old in 1806, had fifteen leagues (more than thirty miles) of fields of grain extending along the coastal slope. This mission was also rich in herds of stock. Santa Inés, too, was particularly well-known for its vast herds of cattle and its superior horses. Mission San Gabriel Arcángel was the richest in agrarian produce, its fields and orchards burgeoning with beans, wheat, grapes, figs, oranges, peaches, apples, limes, pears and pomegranates. Mission San José was noted for its production of wheat and at one time boasted of 62,000 head of cattle. At Mission Purísima Concepción the cattle were so numerous that the friars granted permission for a free slaughtering, and thousands were killed for their hides and tallow, the meat being left to rot for the natural scavengers such as the buzzard, the coyote and the poor Indian. Mission San Luís Rey de Francia, near San Diego, was the richest in sheep, having over 30,000 head. Mission San Buenaventura was said to be one of the richest of all, possessing not only huge herds of stock but numerous gardens, orchards and ranchos.

At Mission Santa Barbara, Indian labor developed extensive irrigation ditches, constructed a gristmill, an aqueduct, fountains and pools, and diverted the water into well-drained fields.

With more than 20,000 Indians bound to the nineteen missions established up to 1805, there were plenty of hands to do the work. And there were no salaries to pay. No Indian ever received a cent in wages.

Also, by 1805, with their immediate security guaranteed and their survival assured and a pool of slave labor to draw on, all the missions were steadily improved architecturally.

At first, in Serra's day, and even into the rule of Padre Lasuén, the early buildings were crude huts made of mud, clay and sticks with tule-thatched roofs. Only the altars and church furniture were distinguished, ornate and rococo. As the years went by, enforced Indian labor built the permanent structures that we see today, or which with the passing of the previous century have become ruins, only to be restored. In some cases this restoration has been done out of all semblance to the original edifice.

The architecture of the missions along the Royal Highway was developed from practicality rather than from tradition. The cathedral of tall spires, the Spanish *churrigueresco,* the great tower of Seville, were not suited to the California scene. What was needed, instead, was long, low, rambling buildings with massive walls. One sound reason for this was the occasional and unpredictable earthquake. California missions, therefore, do not stand out against the landscape as does, say, Mission San Xavier del Bac in Tucson, Arizona (Santa Barbara is something of an exception), but are more inclined to follow the contour of the land and blend into it. They have evolved from the original Moorish and Roman concepts and have established their own "California mission" type of architecture. The characteristics are an open courtyard, long cloisters or colonnades, arches, heavy-set and somewhat squatty bell towers, long corridors, heavy buttresses and of course the attractive red-tile roof which was evolved not for its beauty but because of the fact that an attacking force could not set it on fire.

No two missions were identical or even similar. Often the result came off extremely well, and among the most beautiful of all are, or were, San Luís Rey de Francia, San Juan Capistrano, San Gabriel Arcángel, San Fernando Rey de España, and the favorite of most tourists, the "queen" of them all, Santa Barbara.

But with all of the physical beauty, the spiritual intent and the commodious goods, there are admittedly seamy sides to the era of the missions.

San Juan Capistrano, for example, baptized 4,404 Indians and buried 3,227 up to 1834. The mortality rate for Indians was simply staggering, and never during the mission period did the Indian birth rate equal the death rate. Extermination was the end result.

Actually, the converted Indian was the property of the mission at which he professed his faith. Since the abysmal ignorance of the Indian precluded his understanding of what he was doing or what it all signified, he was in reality a serf. At first, under Serra, the Franciscans used friendliness and gentle persuasion. These efforts became more harsh as time went by. Obviously the Spaniard couldn't reason with the Indian, and in time the Spaniard became impatient. If the Indian was incapable of understanding that all this was for the good of his body and soul, then it was the duty of the Spaniard to take him over, body and soul.

As to the Indian: at first he was curious, then he was willing, later he was wary, later still he was unhappy and finally he was reduced to the state of an animal or he rebelled with violence. If he ran away he might escape to the hills; if he were caught, it meant a flogging and irons. The story has been told, through the research of Dr. S. F. Cook of the University of California, that 45 percent of the decrease in Indian population under mission rule was attributable to disease. Naturally, the Indian was vulnerable to the communicable ailments of the Spaniard. Measles, influenza, smallpox and syphilis led the attack. Infant mortality was 75 percent up to the age of two! Small wonder, indeed, the Indian wanted to avoid the missions. His own manner of life before the white man came may have been crude and unsanitary, but at least he survived. Miscarriages and abortions increased to such an extent that the Spaniards believed the Indians might deliberately be practicing this type of infanticide (most unlikely, however), and they thereby declared that any Indian woman who suffered a miscarriage was guilty of a criminal offense. The penalty for this crime was determined by Padre Zalvidea at Mission San Gabriel. The next Indian woman who was "guilty" was flogged at a given interval for fifteen days, had irons put on her feet and was forced to attend church with a dummy baby of wood held in her arms. These are not pleasant stories to come out of the mission era, but so much romanticism has been presented about the period that the cruel truth, even in a small part, should be told.

The fact that the Indians revolted is proof enough that their conditions were intolerable. On November 4, 1777, some 800 of them organized and attacked Mission San Diego de Alcalá. These were people of the Yuman stock and they were more prone to resentment and belligerence than were the Chumashan and Costanoan farther north along the Royal Highway. Perhaps half of the attackers were unconverted Indians from the hills back of San Diego. They came silently by night, set fire to the mission, burned it to the ground, and yelled and whooped and danced. When the eleven Spaniards tried to escape death by fire, they were showered with hundreds of arrows. Padre Luís Jaime was dragged from the mission and beaten to death, and thereby became the first Franciscan martyr in California. The Spaniards fled from the burning mission and barricaded themselves in an adobe storehouse near by. All were wounded in flight, and two more died. Once secure in the storehouse the remaining Spaniards held the Indians at bay with their guns, and by morning there wasn't an Indian in sight. The soldiers at the presidio, four miles away, who were there to guard the land and maintain order, blissfully slept through it all.

Later a number of Indians were caught and "punished." Others were granted clemency.

The revolt had a twofold effect: it caused the Spaniards to take proper precautions, and it seemed to indicate to the Indians that these alien people could not be ousted. There was no subsequent attack at San Diego and no concerted efforts made elsewhere. One or two individual and sporadic outbursts occurred at the Missions Santa Barbara, Purísima Concepción and Santa Inés, and there was an incipient revolt at Mission San Juan Bautista. But apart from these disorganized yet violent protests, the normally peaceful California Indians bowed to the inevitable. The case for the villeins and the serfs was hopeless.

This state of Franciscan feudalism, however, could not continue. In spite of the fact that the church did not want individual land grants in this new territory, private ownership of property began as early as 1784.

That thorn in the side of Padre Serra, Governor Pedro Fages,

Bell tower of the Mission San Carlos Borroméo del Rio Carmelo. The body of Padre Junípero Serra was buried before the altar.

San Francisco in 1806

Modern San Francisco, with the Bay Bridge to Oakland beginning in the foreground, and the Golden Gate Bridge in the background

that incompetent ex-soldier with the intractable wife, made the first of the land grants to individuals. They were three of the leather-jacketed soldiers who had blazed the trail with Portolá. They appealed to the governor for the right to run cattle in the area of the Los Angeles River. On his own initiative, Fages granted them this right. Later the grant was substantiated by the viceroy in Mexico City.

Trivial as it may seem, this event was a straw in the wind for the future of California and for this, if nothing else, Fages deserves a place in the history of the Royal Highway.

Each grantee was required to build a substantial house, stock his land with cattle or sheep or both, hire a sufficient number of *vaqueros* (cowboys) to care for the stock, identify all stock by branding them and prevent them from running wild. Thus developed the private "rancho," a social and economic contribution that was soon to make history along El Camino Real. For certainly if one person could own land, apart from the church, so could others. Fages' move, no matter what ecclesiastical authorities thought of it and thought of him, was the first indication that the grip of the Franciscans on the land might some day be broken.

Once Mexico City had empowered Governor Fages to make such grants at his own discretion, he proceeded to make another. This one was momentous, and it went to a man named José Verdugo. It covered all of what is now the California suburban cities of Glendale and Burbank adjacent to Los Angeles. Here was a huge, privately owned California estate, and Verdugo called it Rancho San Rafael.

Throughout the first quarter of the nineteenth century the private landholders of California increased. They could not, of course, be granted any property that belonged to the church, and many a covetous eye must have been cast on mission lands that were among the most desirable in the territory. Land meant wealth.

True, there were three independent villages quite apart from the presidios—Los Angeles, San Jose and the ill-fated Branciforte. But these were colonies of poor people and not huge estates of the landed gentry.

Even Branciforte (virtually unkown today) was protested by Lasuén. It was a feeble colony founded by Governor Diego de Borica in 1797 on the northern arm of the Bay of Monterey, all too close, insisted the church, to the Mission Santa Cruz which Lasuén had founded (the twelfth of the chain) in 1791. Branciforte, settled by convicts from Mexican penal institutions, was unable to sustain itself. The small group of felons drifted to San Jose or traveled the highway to Los Angeles, and Branciforte was no more.

That left only the two independent villages of Los Angeles and San Jose, and, as their development was hardly noticeable, the Franciscans were not too concerned.

But this business of land grants—something had to be done about it. Padre Zalvidea of Mission San Gabriel entered a protest against the holdings of Manuel Nieto who had received about 300,000 acres from Governor Fages. In time the church succeeded in having this grant substantially reduced. It was claimed that it conflicted with the interests and priorities of the mission holdings. Doubtless this was true. But whether the church, which had seized the virgin land, or a private citizen, who held title to it from his government, had the stronger claim to final ownership was a debatable and delicate question.

Again, as throughout history, church and state were moving toward a major dispute. As the first quarter of the nineteenth century went by the church was able to keep the total number of land grants down to less than thirty. Then, in 1826, the contest reached a crisis and a climax. And it meant the end of Padre Serra's dream and the end of the Franciscans as a power in California.

My House Is Yours (But Not My Land)

"THIS is a great country," wrote Diego de Borica, the seventh governor of California, from his home in Monterey to a friend in Mexico City. He seems to have been the first of the governors who was genuinely fond of the land he had been sent to govern. "To live well, and without care, come to Monterey," he urged.

Borica, who was a Basque, arrived in 1794 and remained until 1800 (a complete list of the governors of California, Spanish, Mexican and American, is appended at the end of this book), and apparently he was one of the most convivial travelers of the Royal Highway. His term of office established a note that is usually associated with California's Spanish days: comfort, culture, luxury, ease, gaiety and charming hospitality. All of it was true of the period from 1800 to 1821—with reservations.

Borica goes on:

The climate is healthful, between cold and temperate, good bread, excellent meat, tolerable fish, and *bonne humeur* which is worth all the rest. Plenty there is to eat, but the most astonishing [element] is the general fecundity ... the climate is so good that all are getting to look like Englishmen. This is the most peaceful and quiet country in the world; one lives better here than in the most cultured court of Europe.

This was no faint praise, in view of the fact that most Spanish diplomats and politicians alike considered an appointment to California much as we would look on an outpost at, say, Point Barrow, Alaska, today.

99

Governor Borica's term in office was one of general progression on all fronts. He and Padre Lasuén were good friends. The hiatus between church and state did not materially widen. Five important missions were founded by Lasuén, tightening the Franciscan grip on the country; meanwhile Borica established the short-lived colony of Branciforte (named for the viceroy of the period), laughed off Lasuén's protests that its criminal populace was too near Mission Santa Cruz, attempted to organize an educational system which he said was advisable at the time and would be essential later, and did a great deal of entertaining assisted by his attractive wife and popular daughter. He received guests with gracious courtesy and sent them away with lavish gifts; and he poured down an immense amount of wine and brandy. He was unquestionably one of the happiest governors in California's history.

During Borica's office, and for the two decades that followed it— up to 1820—Spanish Alta California moved slowly but steadily forward. The Franciscans ran their missions up to twenty, with only the final northernmost and relatively unimportant San Francisco Solano yet to be founded. The towns of San Jose and Los Angeles developed slightly. The presidio settlements, or military towns—San Diego, Santa Barbara, Monterey and San Francisco (first called Yerba Buena)—developed considerably. The twenty missions flourished to such an extent, thanks to enforced Indian labor, that some of their outlying lands very nearly met from mission to mission. And all during this time there was an occasional land grant, frowned on by the church and eagerly accepted by the grantee.

A traveler over the Royal Highway in 1820 would have had an easy time of it compared to the hardships suffered by Portolá and his men. Most of the route was still little more than a horse trail, but in places it was developing to a real road: between San Diego and Mission San Luís Rey de Francia, and between Mission San

Gabriel Arcángel and the little town of Los Angeles, the trail was well traveled by horses, footmen and oxcarts or *carretas*. North of Mission San Buenaventura you might have to ride your horse into the surf at high tide as the mountains came down to the sea and left little or no beach between Ventura and Santa Barbara. As late as the 1920s the road was still tricky at that spot and was built of planks which were forever being washed out. Even today along what is known to motorists as "the Rincon" the surf will occasionally break over the sea wall and wash over the four lanes of U.S. Highway 101.

It is a long drive from San Diego to San Francisco today, approximately 600 miles, but by steady driving, not necessarily speeding, it can be done in something over twelve hours, perhaps allowing fourteen for comfort. That is good, but not record time. In 1820 if you made it in three weeks on horseback you were doing equally well, and it would be better to allow four weeks for comfort. That would be good, but not record time.

There wasn't a single inn or tavern on the road in 1820 and none was needed. Once you left San Diego you would stop each night at either a mission or a rancho and you could be assured of being welcome. In fact, you would be a treat in the nature of a pleasant surprise to your host, be he a mission padre or the owner of a rancho, and he would probably urge you not to ride on the next day but to stay and rest and visit and relax for a day or a week or as long as you wished. The expression was *"Mi casa es suya,"* or "My house is yours." There was no charge for anything; you could make the trip without its costing you a cent. If there was any one characteristic of the social customs of the time in California, it was hospitality.

The reasons why this custom existed and persisted are twofold: first, the host lived in a lonely land without newspapers and with hardly a book, and to have a stranger from the outside world come to his door meant news of the times, good conversation, exchange of ideas and perhaps the beginning of a lasting friendship; and second, almost all who traveled the Royal Highway were gentlemen, and they knew how to use and not abuse the hospitable welcome. Moreover, they might, in good time, find themselves at home to the host when he himself was traveling.

No "lean and hungry look" of suspicion was cast on any traveler; and the traveler, although passing, perhaps, through a strange country, needed have no fear that he might be rebuffed or robbed or in any way molested. Crime was unknown, people were instinctively honest and a word was as good as a bond, if not better.

Suppose you were the owner of a rancho near San Diego. You had business that necessitated your seeing the governor in Monterey. You turned the full charge of your rancho over to your foreman and you rode leisurely north. There was no hurry, and no need to try to make it to Monterey in fifteen days or twenty days or a month. Monterey would be there when you got there, albeit, perhaps, the governor might not. He didn't know you were coming and he might be in San Francisco or elsewhere. It didn't matter. If he were in San Francisco, you'd live in his house in Monterey until he came back. If he happened to be traveling on the Royal Highway in your direction, you'd unquestionably meet him at some mission or rancho on the road, for there was no other road in all of California on which he could be traveling.

North from San Diego you might spend the night at Mission San Luís Rey de Francia. A second night possibly at Mission San Juan Capistrano—or you might spend two or three nights at each mission. The Fathers would be happy to see you; an Indian servant at the door (usually kept there day and night) would take your horse; a table would soon be laid with the best food and drink available; you would be offered the very best bed. With all this you might not be exactly comfortable according to modern standards. The rooms were damp and dank, there was little or no heat, there was no glass in the windows, and the floor was usually hard-packed earth or rough boards. There was scanty furniture, plumbing was unknown and the only light came from tallow candles. The very best bed might turn out to be a cowhide fastened to a frame on four legs, and fleas were abundant. But it was better than sleeping on the ground along the road and at least there would be a roof over your head in case of rain.

Unless you were fatigued or ill, or wished to peruse the few books pertaining to the Lives of the Saints in the mission library, or unless you could read Latin, there was little to induce you to stay on the following day. Whereupon the Fathers would wish you well and send you on your way with a sack of provisions containing possibly a whole broiled chicken, bread, cheese and hard-boiled eggs, and surely a bottle of wine and a flacon of brandy. An Indian would saddle your horse for you when you were ready to depart. And if by any chance your horse had gone lame or had a saddle sore, the host would give you another horse. When you returned you could retrieve your own animal which would be cared for during your absence. If something happened to alter your plans and you didn't get back or if some accident befell you—Hail Mary and Joseph, such calamity cannot be!—why, the exchange of horses mattered not at all. The mission had scores of horses. In truth, it was a pity you weren't traveling by oxen in a *carreta,* for then you could take a side of beef and a boiled tongue as a parting gift, and two Indians would be sent along to escort you to the next mission.

Your road on to the north would take you to such ranchos as La Zanja and Los Feliz near Los Angeles, or Rodeo de las Aguas which covered all of what is today Beverly Hills; or farther north the ranchos El Conejo near Ventura, El Refugio north of Santa Barbara and Las Salinas near Monterey. These and a number of others offered a happy haven to any and all travelers. And the degree of luxury far exceeded that of the missions where the Franciscans took pride in ignoring physical comfort.

The ranch house, indeed, would be yours, and your presence was the host's pleasure. In most instances all of his family would be happy to meet you. If you should happen to be an eligible bachelor and at the same time a gentleman of means—*caballero* was the word—you might well be attracted by a marriageable daughter of your host. More than one romance was so begun along the Royal Highway, and more than one marriage was eventually arranged. In such cases the economic factor was not without significance, for two ranchos might thereby come into the ownership of one family.

Nevertheless, *"Mi casa es suya,"* while literal up to a point, was a condition of graciousness, and beyond it there was a barrier. The Spanish had an inherent instinct for the protection, and even seclusion, of their women. This may have been a Moorish inheritance, for the status of morals and manners in which the distaff side was held had something of an Oriental propriety. Sometimes the traveler never saw the females of the house—Indians not taken into consideration, of course—and Don So-and-So might be happy to have you as a guest, provide you with his finest bed and board, and regale you with conversation over neat brandy after dinner until the late hour of eight o'clock, or even nine, at which time an Indian servant, ordered to be yours and to look after your needs, would light you to bed. But Doña So-and-So and the daughters of the family might be unmentioned by the host and unseen by the guest. And in such a case the polite and tactful guest would make no inquiries. If your business and travels should bring you to the hospitality of this same rancho again in a year or two or three, it is possible that the host might be pleased to introduce you to his wife and daughters, and in that case it would never occur to you to comment on the fact that you had not had the inestimable pleasure of kissing their hands before.

Then, into this land so sufficient unto itself in both economy and amenity, came the stranger, the outlander. Sometimes he was the blue-eyed, fair-haired, quick, businesslike and gruff northerner, in whose blood ran none of the Castilian manner and by whose aggressive behavior the Californian was surprised, baffled and, in the final analysis, displeased.

He was not at first a highway traveler, this foreigner, for the first of his kind came by sea. Not always were the strangers crude and gauche, and the first of them were happily welcomed.

The previously mentioned Jean François de la Pérouse, a gentleman and a scholar from France, was the first to arrive. He had been sent by the French government on a voyage of scientific exploration, to examine flora, fauna and aborigines, and was further instructed to investigate the possibility of establishing a French colony somewhere north of Monterey with an eye toward the new and lucrative fur trade. He was in command of two ships, the *Astrolabe* and the *Boussole,* which rounded Cape Horn and put in at the Hawaiian Islands. From there he sailed to the coast of North America and reached it at a point somewhat north of what is Sitka, Alaska, today, and then proceeded down the coast until he put in at Monterey on the fourteenth of September, 1786.

Laperouse received a hearty welcome from Governor Fages and Mission President Lasuén. And as *"Mi casa es suya"* was the custom, the French scientist lived in the governor's house. His stay must have been a welcome break in the monotony of life in this dreadful outpost to Doña Eulalia, the governor's lady, for nowhere in Laperouse's journal is there any mention of her tantrums, smashed furniture and hurled dishes. Very likely she raised her particular kind of hell the day after he left.

The Spaniards refused at first to accept any pay for the supplies that the two French ships required, but after professed courtesies on both sides, a token sum was agreed on. By some historians it is said that Laperouse made payment not in French money, which would have had little value in Monterey, but in seed potatoes which he had put on board in Chile, and that this is how the potato came to California. Other historians refute this, and the issue, ridiculous as it seems, has even been hotly disputed. It all comes down to a Swiftian argument comparable to the little-endians and the big-endians, and if the reader is further interested it is suggested that he search down a comprehensive history of the potato.

The Laperouse account of the life of the Indians under mission rule has already been quoted. While he sympathized with their piteous plight and understood the folly of trying to make Spanish peasants out of people totally unequipped to accept such a regime, he rated the highest of the Indians he saw as being no more than six years old mentally.

After ten days of Spanish hospitality Laperouse sailed away never to return. His visit was important (apart from the contested potato), for he brought news of Russian settlements in Alaska, he wrote the first scientific descriptions of California to appear in print, and his behavior and his courtesy made the Californians all the more eager to welcome the next visitor to their shores.

He was not long in coming as time was measured in those days, although it was actually another six years before a foreigner arrived again. This time he was an Englishman—Captain George Vancouver. Like Laperouse, he had been sent to explore the northwest coast, but unlike Laperouse, he habitually referred to the land as New Albion. Hadn't Sir Francis Drake so named it in 1579? Hadn't the land been English ever since the days of Good Queen Bess? Who were these Spanish upstarts? Vancouver did not consider himself to be in a foreign country. New Albion had always been English. But, being an English gentleman, he was gracious to these Spanish interlopers; and the Spaniards, happy to have a new visitor, were gracious to this English outlander. Neither race considered the fact that the mentally six-year-old (at best) Indians had a prior claim.

Vancouver made three visits to California ports between November 14, 1792, when his sloop-of-war *Discovery* put in at San Francisco Bay, and December 2, 1793, when he left "New Albion" for the last time. During the interludes between these visits he was exploring the coast to the north, along with his second in command, Peter Puget. The names Vancouver Island and Puget Sound remind us today of their eighteenth-century explorations.

During his first visit Vancouver was well received by Commandante Hermenegildo Sal at the presidio of San Francisco and by the Franciscan fathers at the Mission Dolores. He expressed an interest in the land, which, although he kept it to himself, he considered English. The Spaniards were proud to show off the land, which, without even saying so, they considered Spanish. A journey on horseback down the Royal Highway resulted, and George Vancouver was the first Englishman after Drake to leave the California littoral and make a visit to the interior. Along with some of his men he was escorted down El Camino Real (he might have called it the Dover Road) from San Francisco to the Mission Santa Clara, some forty miles. Apparently he was impressed with the country, for he described, in his subsequent publication, *A Voyage of Discovery to the North Pacific Ocean and Round the World,* the land of the Royal Highway, in somewhat euphuistic prose, as follows:

The stately lords of the forest were in complete possession of the soil, covered with luxuriant herbage and beautifully diversified with pleasing eminences and valleys; which, with the range of lofty, rugged mountains that bounded the prospect, required only to be adorned with the neat habitations of an industrious people to produce a scene not inferior to the most studied effect of taste in the disposal of grounds.

This is the area today known as the San Francisco peninsula, and certainly the towns of Burlingame, Hillsborough, San Mateo, Redwood City, Atherton, Menlo Park and Palo Alto bear out the visiting Englishman's opinion.

After returning overland to San Francisco, Vancouver sailed for

Monterey. His ship, the *Discovery,* had been met by a second
English vessel, the *Chatham,* under the command of William
Broughton. Both Vancouver and Broughton agreed that the Bay
of San Francisco "offers as fine a port as the world affords."

At Monterey the two English captains were royally received.
Again *"Mi casa es suya"* was the policy, and the English and the
Spanish fraternized for almost two months. A third English ship,
the *Daedalus,* made port, and there were three Spanish ships in at
the same time under Captain Juan Bodega. The result was a series
of balls (or *bailes* in Spanish) and dinners and picnics and protestations of undying friendship. The English entertained the Spaniards with a dinner on board their ship the *Discovery,* and the
Franciscans entertained the English at the Mission San Carlos, and
life was all one happy party. There was even a display of fireworks
set off as a touching climax on the beach. And again the bewildered and now browbeaten Indians looked on in wonder. Meanwhile Vancouver noted the "inferior and poorly placed cannon"
and the pusillanimous garrison, fat with soft living. The Spaniards,
on their part, noted the inability of the English to establish a land
base without their help and the fact that these foreigners could not
even have remained in port without the courteous silence of Spanish guns.

So everybody was everybody's friend, and the Spaniards refused
to accept payment for supplies generously donated to the English
ships. After all, the Indians did all the work. The *Daedalus* was
stocked with a cargo of longhorn Spanish cattle, which were a gift,
of course, and she sailed for Australia with these animals which
were the first of their kind to arrive in the antipodes.

But all good things must come to an end, and Vancouver could
continue his pleasant visit no longer. With speeches and embraces
the English and the Spanish parted. After another journey to
Hawaii, Vancouver returned to California almost a year later. This
time all was not love and kisses, for Governor José de Arrillaga was

in office and he had been told by Mexico City to distrust all foreigners and keep them at formal arm's length, or he would not remain governor.

Arrillaga might easily have "looked the other way" in this case, as the English were obviously not bent on conquest. But he was a man of literal mind, no imagination, a pipsqueak who feared authority, and in a pompous and picayune way he limited Vancouver's right to remain in port. One of Arrillaga's chief annoyances was the fact that on his former visit Vancouver had been allowed (really invited) to ride down part of the Royal Highway and thereby see some of Spain's precious California interior.

Vancouver, justly or unjustly irked, made short shift of his second visit to Monterey, and sailed on down the coast, touching land wherever he pleased, and going ashore at Santa Barbara, Ventura and San Diego. At these ports the Spanish authorities were happy to welcome him and some of the ire caused by Arrillaga's stupidity was assuaged.

Once more, after leaving San Diego, Vancouver made the trip to Hawaii, then Alaska and again down the California coast. When he arrived on his third visit, Arrillaga had been retired in favor of a man who greeted the Englishman with open arms and wine and brandy, the happiest of all governors, the man who loved California and even got along well with the Franciscans, Diego de Borica.

Again it was a case of "my house is yours," and, as far as Borica cared, Vancouver could travel the length and breadth of California if he so wished. Apparently the Spanish governor and the English captain were instantaneous friends. Both Vancouver and Puget were jolly good fellows according to Borica, but they were no more so than was he himself after all three had partaken of a dozen beakers of wine apiece.

Borica took Vancouver to the Mission San José, much farther over the land than he had traveled before, and the Englishman made mental notes of the rivers, valleys and general topography. Each mission, as has been pointed out, was known for its particular specialty, and at San José the chief craft was weaving. The looms were made by the Indians under the guidance of the padres, and all work was, of course, done by the Indians. Mission San José had five looms and could turn out 150 blankets a week. Vancouver was impressed, and he wrote: "Though they were rudely wrought they were well contrived. I saw some of the cloth which was by no means despicable, and, had it received the advantage of fulling, would have made a very decent sort of clothing."

After a month's visit Vancouver sailed away from Monterey and the hospitality of Governor Borica, and again scouted the California coast. As the land was part of England to him, he bestowed names on two headlands that were prominent landmarks from the sea, but he courteously named them for two of the Franciscans he had especially liked. They were Padre Fermín Lasuén and Padre Francisco Dumetz. The names have held through history with only a slight variation of the latter: they are known today as Point Fermin and Point Dume.

In his summing up of his California observations in his book published in London in 1798, Vancouver's thoughts turned from the hospitality to the land. Some of his comments bore a prophetic note.

Should the ambition of any civilized nation attempt to seize upon these unsupported posts, they could not make the least resistance, and must inevitably fall to a force barely sufficient for garrisoning and securing the country; especially that part which I have comprehended under the domination of New Albion, whose southernmost limits lie under the thirtieth degree of north latitude.

In other words, New Albion was everything along the Pacific

Coast from Baja California to Alaska inclusive. How Drake's claim had expanded over two centuries!

The Spaniards, in doing thus much, have only cleared the way for the ambitious enterprises of those maritime powers, who, in the avidity of commercial pursuits, may seek to be benefited by the advantages which the fertile soil of New Albion seems to afford. They stocked the country with cattle, demonstrated the fertility of its soil, showed by experiments what an unusual variety of vegetable products could be grown, and to a certain extent weaned the savages from an uncivilized life. . . . By the formation of such establishments, so wide from each other, and so unprotected in themselves, the original design of settling the country seems to have been completely set aside, and, instead of strengthening the barrier to their valuable possessions in New Spain, they have thrown irresistible temptations in the way of strangers to trespass over their boundary. All these matters would be valuable considerations to new masters, to whose power, if properly employed, the Spaniards would have no alternative but to submissively yield. That such an event should take place appears by no means to be very improbable, should the commerce of the northwest America be further extended.

Vancouver's analysis of things Californian at the dawn of the nineteenth century was not translated into Spanish. Had it been, the Spanish authorities might have been surprised at the conclusion of their guest. But even so, far too many ships began to put in their appearance in Pacific waters, and Spain decided to tighten her foreign policy. *Mi casa es suya,* yes, but at the same time *la tierra es mia,* or the land is mine.

More Guests Arrive 〈 10

THE first American ship to put into a California port was the *Otter* commanded by Captain Ebenezer Dorr, and she dropped her anchor at Monterey on October 29, 1796. Governor Borica did not find the phlegmatic New Englander quite so gay a guest as had been Vancouver and Puget. This *yanqui* didn't care for wine, and wasn't a drinking man at all. Fie on him! But at least the Californians did learn something of the new republic on the east coast of North America called Los Estados Unidos.

Borica considered it an odd name—the United States—the United States of what?

Captain Dorr told him.

"The United States of America," he explained.

"But this is America," protested Borica.

The Yankee captain merely snorted.

It was all news to Borica and the people of Monterey. They had heard that some kind of insurrection had taken place on the Atlantic seaboard among the English colonies. The only name they knew was Boston, and they had presumed the whole East Coast was called Boston. Borica wanted to know the name of the United States of Boston's governor.

"Our *president,*" snapped Captain Dorr, "is George Washington."

Borica, who couldn't even pronounce such an unusual name, explained that California's president was Padre Fermín Lasuén, not comprehending the political rather than the ecclesiastical use of the term by this tacit American. Actually John Adams had been inaugurated during Dorr's absence at sea, and Washington had

Mission San Gabriel Arcángel, showing its unusual outside stairway and
one of the commemorative mission bells

Los Angeles in 1853. This is the first known sketch of the city and was made at a point where José Flores' troops forced the surrender of Captain Gillespie and his men on "Fort Hill."

Monterey, the capital of California, in 1842

retired to Mount Vernon. Borica suggested that Dorr should meet Padre Fermín Lasuén. Dorr was uninterested. He had business to attend to, not priests to meet.

The business that Dorr had in mind turned out to be an affront to Governor Borica and all of Monterey. For on the *Otter* were ten men and one woman, English convicts from Botany Bay, Australia, who had somehow contrived to stow away. Dorr didn't want them and he landed them at pistol point on the Carmel beach. That was that, and good riddance. Then, without so much as a by-your-leave, he sailed for China. He was unimpressed with California. It would never measure up to New England. The Spanish! If only the United States had California, then watch. . . .

Governor Borica never permitted any problem to furrow his brow for long. The gruff American from Boston States, or whatever it was called, had gone, thanks be to God, and the eleven ex-convicts were on his shores and on his charity. So he put the ten men to work as carpenters and blacksmiths (history does not record the disposition of the lone woman, but doubtless Borica found some employment for her, perhaps as a domestic) at the munificence of 19 cents a day for wages. The former prisoners were so happy to be placed in a position of any kind, instead of shackles and irons, that all ten worked hard and well. Borica declared that they were more eager to work than the Spaniards and more intelligent than the Indians, and he wished that he could make permanent Californians of them. Unfortunately, by law, he was required and obliged to send any stranded foreigners to Mexico City. From there the eleven English wretches were shipped to Cadiz, and there history loses them. It is to be hoped that they did not finally get sent back to Botany Bay. But the episode, as a whole, left Governor Borica a bit uncertain about the wisdom of welcoming any more of the terse and taciturn people who called themselves Americans from the United States of Boston. What a tasteless country it must be, that Boston!

Captain Ebenezer Dorr was never heard from in California again. But in 1799 another of his sort, Captain James Rowan commanding the *Eliza,* put in at San Francisco. Borica, upon receiving this news, sent word to the commandante of the presidio that this ship from Estados Bostonios Unidos, or whatever its home port might be, was to be supplied without charge, regardless of its needs, but must be sent on its way with the imperative warning that it must not put in at any other California port. The *Eliza* sailed, to a destination unknown, and Governor Borica, upon hearing of this by a messenger who rode down the Royal Highway from San Francisco, relaxed and had an extra brandy. Now *that* was the way to handle these Boston Americanos. Why couldn't everybody be a Californian? These outlanders! More brandy, *por favor. Gracias!*

In 1800 Borica left California. He had been a good governor and it would be pleasant to record that he had a happy life in Mexico City. But unfortunately it cannot be done, and whether it was the potency of alcohol or the weakness of his liver, or a combination of the two, it must be stated with regret that this genial governor died at the age of sixty-four only six months after he left his California Arcady.

In that same year, a third American ship put in at a California port. She was the *Betsy* out of Boston (no wonder that to the Spaniards Boston and the United States were one and the same) and she dropped her anchor at San Diego. She was commanded by Captain Charles Winship. San Diego was not especially happy to welcome him, and Captain Winship cared not a hoot about San Diego. He wanted wood and water, he was willing to pay for it, and he was not interested in backward San Diego. The *Betsy* sailed away, and this news was speedily sent to the governor about six weeks after Captain Winship's departure.

Boston was represented again in 1803, and this time there was no welcome, but instead, there was shooting. Captain William

Shaler brought his ship, the *Lelia Byrd,* into the Bay of San Diego. He was formally welcomed by the commandante and the ship was inspected. But inspected and welcomed are two very different words. And what the ship was inspected for, nobody seemed to know. The commandante's Spanish nose was well up in the air, and Captain William Shaler's contempt was perfectly obvious. My house was not yours, in this case, and no basis of friendship could be established. The commandante left a guard of five armed Spanish soldiers on board this ship from the United States of Boston, and that proved to be unwise.

To Captain Shaler this was more than a port inspection; this was occupation. He made up his mind how he would handle *that.* When replenished with such supplies as he could get, and for which he was prepared to pay, and for which he very likely did pay, he suddenly ran up his sails, weighed his anchor and made a run for the open sea, taking with him the five Spanish soldiers who were "guarding" the ship. When a few miles out to sea they could walk back. They were landlubbers, weren't they? If they didn't want to do that, they could remain on board as his prisoners until such time as he decided to get rid of them on the coast of China.

But the Bay of San Diego is a landlocked harbor, and, in order to make the open sea, the *Lelia Byrd* had to pass under the raking guns of the Spanish fort.

After the first shock of surprise at seeing this Boston ship blithely sail for the entrance of the harbor with his own men on board, the commandante held his ears and ordered, "Fire!"

It is questionable whether it was more dangerous for those on the *Lelia Byrd* or those in the Spanish fort. For the Spanish guns were antiquated and had not been fired in anyone's memory. Nevertheless, the first shot between Spain and the United States occurred at San Diego in 1803. The fort fired six cannon balls and all six missed. The seventh tore through the ship's rigging. By this time the *Lelia Byrd* had almost made it and was directly under the guns of the fort. At that moment, Captain Shaler commanded his own gunners, "Fire!" and the *Lelia Byrd* opened up on the fort with her battery of six three-pounders.

The Spanish, at the time, were gingerly reloading their questionable cannon, when the *Lelia Byrd's* "thank you" arrived. The soldiers in the fort ran for cover and the *Lelia Byrd* ran for the open sea. Each made their objectives and the battle was over. There were no casualties.

But it was recorded in history that Spain had for the first time defended California by arms and that the dastardly would-be-invader was the United States of Boston. The commandante forwarded to the governor, who in turn forwarded to the viceroy, who in turn, presumably, forwarded to the king, the recommendation that Spain declare war on Boston and thereby exterminate it. Nothing more was heard of the issue.

Peace for California prevailed after this "war" until another ship from another nation sailed into the Bay of San Francisco and was challenged by the commandante of the presidio at the Golden Gate. It was in 1806 and the ship was the *Juno* and her commander, not knowing Spanish, could not tell if the hail from the shore were a welcome or a threat. So he yelled back, in his own language, which was Russian, and the commandante of the presidio, not knowing Russian, could not tell if the response were a greeting or a defiance. So both yelled again and each held his fire, and the Russian ship, under Nikolai Petrovich Rezánov, dropped her anchor in San Francisco Bay.

With Rezánov was Dr. Georg Heinrich von Langsdorff, surgeon, scientist and naturalist. When they were not fired upon, Rezánov and Von Langsdorff decided to go ashore. They were met on land on what is today San Francisco's *embarcadero* by Commandante Argüello and Padre Francisco Uría of Mission Dolores. The Spaniards, incredible as it may seem, did not have a single small boat to send out to "inspect" this invader. And none of the four could find a common language in which to converse.

The Spaniards tried Spanish and French but the visitors could not understand them. The visitors tried Russian and German, but the Spaniards could not understand them. None of the four could speak English. At length Dr. von Langsdorff and Padre Uría found a tongue they both could understand. It was Latin. All were so overjoyed at finding a medium of communication that they embraced one another and were friends at once.

So, by way of a classical language spoken by a German scientist and comprehended by a Spanish priest, a second defense of California was averted.

Rezánov was scouting for a likely site for a Russian colony in California, but he was far too tactful and diplomatic to say so. And, truthfully, his more immediate needs were supplies for the Russian colony of Sitka in Alaska which was in dire straits.

It so happened that the governor of California at this time was the literal-minded and feckless José de Arrillaga, now serving his second term. He had followed Fages and had alienated George Vancouver by his stupid dictates. Then came the jovial Diego de Borica and all was well again. Now Borica was gone and this dullard was back. He mistrusted everybody; and what is more he couldn't speak Latin and he could not tell what was going on even if present. This annoyed his little mind. He decided that Spain would not trade with these Russians.

Rezánov offered to make a journey down the Royal Highway from San Francisco to Monterey in order to discuss matters at further length with the governor. But, as before, Arrillaga was horrified at the thought of foreigners seeing the sacred California interior. He insisted on holding all discussions in San Francisco.

Then romance entered the picture, and in a few weeks Rezánov managed to have everything come into line just as he wished. He fell in love. The issue is debatable, and there are historians who think this handsome Muscovite, chamberlain to the Czar, privy councilor and one of the ten barons of Russia, forty-two years old, could not truly have been in love with Concepción Argüello, daughter of the commandante of the presidio of San Francisco, a beautiful girl of seventeen. History will never know. But this love affair, which was admittedly awkward due to religious variances, had great weight in San Francisco. Obviously the pair could not be married without the consent of the Czar and a dispensation from the Pope. But love in those days, as always, conquered all, and Rezánov declared his intentions of returning to St. Petersburg and placing his case before his ruler. He would then go to Rome and plead his cause to the Pope (by these means cementing an alliance between Spain and Russia that would never die), and return to California by way of Mexico to claim his bride. All this created great excitement in San Francisco, and the Argüello family and Rezánov tried to explain the tremendous international significance to the slow-witted governor. At length romance won, and Arrillaga agreed to accept the Russian goods on the *Juno*—mostly furs—in exchange for food supplies and clothing sorely needed in Sitka. Rezánov, having achieved his first and paramount objective, stocked his ship, bade his fiancée a loving farewell and sailed out of the Golden Gate never to return. Seemingly he intended to carry out his plans and come back to his California sweetheart, for he was on his way to St. Petersburg when stricken ill while crossing Siberia. In that wasteland Nickolai Petrovich Rezánov died. This news was years in reaching California and Concepción Argüello, her love unfulfilled, became a nun. Did the Russian intend to return? All the world loves a lover, and all the world says yes. Both Bret Harte and Gertrude Atherton have told the touching story of the Russian baron and the commandante's daughter, the former in poetry and the latter in her novel *Rezánov*. At any rate, so came to a sad ending the first great romance on the Royal Highway.

Rezánov's visit surely meant that the Russian bear was beginning to look to the south from Alaska, an eventuality that Spain had feared since the days of José de Gálvez.

In 1812 the bear moved. He sank his claws into the most favor-able location for a settlement he could find just north of San Fran-cisco Bay. The government of Spain was not consulted, and as for the English—who were they? Rezánov had dreamed of a Russian North America beginning at the north portal of the Golden Gate and extending to the Arctic Ocean. Ivan Kuskof founded Fort Rossya scarcely fifty miles from San Francisco near Bodega Bay. Adjacent there was a river which they called the Slavianska, and it is the Russian River today. The colony con-sisted of more than a hundred Russians and eighty Aleut Indians. The garrison was made up of a stockade of heavy timbers and two octangular blockhouses for the infantry. There were four twelve-pound cannon and four six-pound howitzers. Other buildings, to the number of sixty, were constructed. Let any Drake or Van-couver contest that. As to the near-by Spaniards, let them stay south of the Golden Gate. All the Russian ordnance was in good firing condition.

The Russian colony went about its business of sea-otter hunting and agriculture, and the Aleut Indians in the native canoes called *bidarkas* hunted otter up and down the coast and even under the very noses of the Spanish in San Francisco Bay. The colony wasn't interested in converting natives: this was a business deal.

Then Governor Arrillaga sent Sergeant Gabriel Moraga to Fort Rossya to investigate, and half feared that he might never see the soldier again, or that the Aleut hunters might bring back his head on a pole for a souvenir.

But no such thing. Moraga was courteously received, even though the language barrier made communication difficult, was taken on a tour of inspection—a case this time of my Russian house is yours but not my land—and was given to understand by sign language that the Russians would be happy to trade with their neighbors south of the Golden Gate.

When Moraga returned with the news that the colony was to

be permanent, was doing very well and wanted to open friendly trade negotiations, Governor Arrillaga was in an even worse predicament. Certainly it would be wiser to have these near-by outlanders as friends rather than enemies, and certainly the colony at San Francisco could benefit by trading with the Russians, but he had been expressly ordered to resist all foreigners, forbid them entry to California ports, and in no circumstances trade with them. Arrillaga, be it remembered, was a man who obeyed orders not intelligently but too well.

The year 1812 must have been a discouraging one for him, indeed, for not only had the Russian problem risen to confront him, but 1812 went down in history along the Royal Highway as *El Ano de los Temblores,* or the Year of the Earthquakes.

The shocks came intermittently over a period of many months. Mission San Gabriel lost part of its tower. At Mission San Juan Capistrano the entire bell tower collapsed on the roof of the church which gave way and crushed to death more than forty neophytes who were at mass. At San Buenaventura the entire façade fell from the church. Neophytes and priests alike fled to the interior to escape what they feared would be a great tidal wave rolling in from the sea. At Santa Barbara the tremors were so prolonged that nobody dared live indoors for weeks. Damage was great at Santa Inés, and at Purísima Concepción nobody could stand on his feet for twenty minutes, after which interval, an even greater shock brought down the entire church. To the childlike Indians, here was proof from the forces of evil that Christianity was a bad thing. In the confusion many seized the opportunity to flee to the hills and never returned.

First Russians and then earthquakes—what could a poor governor do then?

Supply ships from New Spain were long overdue at San Francisco. The people were in rags and tatters but had plenty of cattle and grain to trade. Groaning over the load of worry on his gubernatorial shoulders, Arrillaga, through Sergeant Moraga, made feeble and cautious overtures to the Russians for barter relations, and sent them fifteen head of cattle as a gift. Then it would be natural for the Russians to "give" the Spaniards something. Such could not possibly be considered trading, and the governor wanted everybody to know that he was strictly obeying his orders. Nowhere in the Spanish archives is there any record of trading with the Russians. Such could be done only on an order from the viceroy in Mexico City, and the viceroy had said no and meant "No!"

It is believed that about $14,000 worth of Russian goods were traded to the Spaniards at San Francisco for which the Russians received grain, meat and tallow. But if the commandante's wife happened to be wearing an new otter-skin coat, it must have been washed up on the beach, for certainly according to Governor Arrillaga, it could have got there in no other way.

Still in fear and trembling of Mexico City, Arrillaga was taken ill in his middle sixties and died while on a visit to the Mission Nuestra Señora de la Soledad in the Salinas Valley in 1814. He had served for fourteen years, following the happy Diego de Borica. Borica drank himself to death, and Arrillaga worried himself to death. José Argüello became acting governor until the viceroy could appoint a new man, or perhaps victim, for the office.

The body of Arrillaga was buried at Soledad Mission; and a few miles away, almost a century and a half later, the heavy traffic of U.S. 101 roars steadily and unknowingly by.

But if Arrillaga's worries were over, the problems of California had hardly begun. The fact that trade with the outside world was prohibited brought in its wake the inevitable smuggler. There were many good citizens of California who did not approve of the territory's trade restrictions. In a sense they were right, for it was a silly device, amounting to nothing more than a paper blockade, and to expect that type of legal and unenforceable legislation to keep foreigners out of California was, to say the least, shortsighted, while at the same time it was definitely injurious to the economy of the land.

Among those who were willing to defy the laws set down in Mexico City was the Ortega family. Sergeant José Ortega had been with Portolá and had been the first Spaniard to reach the Golden Gate back in 1769. He had been a capable soldier, and upon retiring, like most veterans, he wanted something extra for his services. He had applied for a land grant and he got it. Thus, in 1816, the Ortega family owned Rancho El Refugio not far north of Santa Barbara. There was a small bay at Refugio Creek, and while it offered scant protection, a vessel of slight draught could anchor with reasonable safety.

The second and third generation of the California Ortegas had no compunction about doing business with any ship that came to what was their personal and private port, for Mexico City was a long way from Refugio Beach. The modern highway has bridged Refugio Creek, but an old road curves down into the canyon and leads to the beach. But even from the present highway you can get a good view of the beach and the surf which look today exactly as they did when one Thomas Doak, an American, waded ashore from the smuggler ship *Albatross* under command of Captain William Smith from that pestiferous place called Boston.

Thomas Doak (a pity his name couldn't have been Joe Doaks), age twenty-nine, in the year 1816 became the first American settler in California. This young man from Boston liked California, and he traveled north over the Royal Highway to Monterey. He was baptized at Mission San Carlos Borroméo by Padre Mariano Payeras. In 1820 he married the daughter of Don José de Castro, a wealthy land-grant holder. Señorita María de Castro apparently was happy to become Mrs. Doak, or possibly the Bostonian changed his name to Don Tomas de Ok. Be that as it may, the first permanent American settler had arrived. Not only was *Mi casa es suya* the case for Señor Doak, but so was the girl and the land.

But conditions were moving toward a crisis, and the next visitor of importance helped, in a negative and destructive way, to bring that crisis about. He was a French pirate named Hippolyte de Bouchard who was not too particular about the flag he flew or how he changed the name of his ship between ports. He was said to be a large blustery man with a vicious temper and a brutal disciplinarian of his motley crew. When he arrived off the California coast in 1818, his ship *Argentina* flew the flag of Buenos Aires, and it has been said that she carried a crew of 266 men: Americans, Frenchmen, Portuguese, Negroes, Kanakas, Malays, Filipinos—the freebooters, pirates, ex-convicts and general riffraff of the seven seas—and twenty-eight guns. At Hawaii Bouchard met an English privateer named Peter Corney who was in command of a ship of equally bad repute, the *Santa Rosa* (she had several other names), with as rough and as tough a crew, and this ship carried thirty-eight guns. Bouchard and Corney considered themselves the "enemies of the King of Spain," which was to their advantage when looting Spanish ports. These two villains decided to have a look at California, and perhaps "liberate" it from the domination and tyranny of the bad Spanish king. They were sure the Californians would like that—and what is more, they had heard that the Californians were very rich and had many lovely women.

An American ship, the *Clarion,* sailing from Hawaii, brought the news of the coming of the "liberators," and Monterey, from the governor on down, was thrown into a panic. Against such ships and men the tiny capital with its rusted guns and paucity of ammunition would not stand a chance.

The governor of California was now Pablo Vicente Sola. He did what any other governor would have done: called upon all able-bodied men to organize a force to aid the forty-two ill-equipped soldiers at the presidio, sent all the women and children down the Royal Highway to Mission Soledad, and sent all movable valuables along with them. It was impossible for Governor Sola to call for soldiers from San Francisco or Santa Barbara or San Diego, as it was anyone's guess where the invading "gentlemen of fortune" would strike first. For almost a month California had a bad attack of the jitters, and then, on November 20, 1818, the two armed ships were sighted off Monterey.

Together the two vessels mounted sixty-six guns and probably close to 400 of the toughest *hombres* yet to touch the California coast. The defense consisted of the eight decrepit cannon at the presidio under the command of Sergeant Manuel Gomez, and three extra guns set up and concealed on the beach in command of Corporal José Vallejo. Governor Sola, of course, was military commander supreme.

Captain Corney, who called himself an "insurgent" voluntarily assisting the liberation of the Spanish colonies from the crown, brought the *Santa Rosa* into port at midnight and dropped anchor —no mean feat of navigation. The *Argentina,* under Bouchard, stood outside until dawn.

Historians differ as to what happened at sunrise. Some say Corney opened fire as soon as it was light enough to see, in order to let the Californians know that he meant business and that after a salvo (not a salute, mind you) he intended to open discussions for either their immediate alliance to his cause against the evil Spanish king, or, if they persisted in remaining loyal, to demand the immediate surrender of all of California on pain of extermination. Other authorities believe that Corney demanded a surrender first and fired later. At any rate he was not exactly an ideal guest of these shores and his behavior, in either case, was more than peremptory. It was dictatorial, insulting and outrageous.

It is to be regretted that a few ships from the "United States of Boston" under such commanders as the gruff Ebenezer Dorr, or the self-sufficient William Shaler, weren't in port at the time. It is highly probable that they would have given the invading privateers a little something to think about.

Regardless of historical differences of opinion, however, or a debate as to who fired first (and it would seem reasonably likely in the circumstances that it was Corney on the *Santa Rosa*) the shooting began shortly after dawn. Thus it would appear that not very much time had been given over to parley on the part of the invaders who were doing all this for the good of the poor Californians.

The duello between the ship and the presidio continued for two hours. Both sides scored hits and there were killed and wounded on both ship and shore. Meanwhile, Bouchard lowered six boats from the *Argentina* containing, in all, approximately seventy-five men who were an armed landing force, and at the same time he brought the *Argentina* into port and into position to bombard the whole of Monterey.

José Vallejo's three cannon concealed on the beach, silent thus far, opened up on the six landing boats as soon as they came within range. Since the invaders had expected fire only from the presidio, this supplementary Spanish strength surprised and disorganized the landing craft. Some hastily rowed out of range and others returned to the *Argentina*. Bouchard, whose temper was always on trigger edge, was infuriated at this turn of affairs.

Corney, on the *Santa Rosa,* then lowered his flag as a signal of surrender. Sergeant Gomez, not too intelligently, assumed that this meant a Spanish victory and he ordered the presidio to cease firing. Corporal Vallejo, most logically, assumed it to be a trick, and his battery continued firing. Governor Sola didn't know what to think and gave conflicting orders to an orderly who delivered them but got them confused in delivery, and the result was that Gomez was told to cease firing, which he had already done, and Vallejo was told to fire, which he was already doing! This opera-bouffe move confused all the Spanish soldiers, and meanwhile Corney sent an emissary ashore in a small boat to offer what Governor Sola thought were overtures for surrender on Corney's part, but which turned out to be Corney's demand for unconditional surrender on Sola's part.

Meanwhile Bouchard reorganized his men, and made a successful landing of at least five boatloads containing about sixty pirates on the beach out of Vallejo's range.

Sola, at a loss, arrested the "peace" emissary, who turned out to be an American named Joseph Chapman, and two escorting sailors along with him, and unceremoniously dumped them into the Monterey jail. Then Sola sent a small platoon overland to forestall a flank attack from the beach by Bouchard's newly landed pirates. Attacked by wild Kanakas with spears and pikes, knife-brandishing Malays and a few saber-swinging Filipinos, the outnumbered Spanish platoon fled pell-mell back to Monterey. Meanwhile Bouchard's six boats were landing more invaders and the *Santa Rosa's* guns were beginning to blast the presidio to pieces.

With the fort a ruin from the guns of the *Santa Rosa* and the town under fire from the guns of the *Argentina,* his own counter-offense routed and an overwhelming force of cutthroats advancing along the beach, Governor Sola decided that he knew when he was whipped. Knowing that surrender to this murderous mob would mean sure assassination, he called a full retreat, and all the Spaniards who could ride or run or walk or stagger fled inland and east and never stopped until they reached Rancho del Rey which occupied the site of the modern town of Salinas. Governor Sola had the forethought to carry the archives of the government along with him. If anyone thinks Sola was a coward he is greatly mistaken. For what he had to work with he put up a good resistance—far more than Bouchard anticipated—and if Sola had had only one good battery somewhere apart from but adjacent to the presidio, it might have sunk or set fire to the *Santa Rosa* which had the effrontery to stand in close to shore. That Sola did not have adequate defensive measures was not his fault. Vancouver had noted and recorded such a lack more than twenty years before, but the government of New Spain had done nothing to ameliorate this condition. Now, regrettably, Vancouver's predictions had come true.

With Monterey in their hands, these kindly "liberators" burned and pillaged everything. What they couldn't carry away, they destroyed. They remained in port six days but made no attempt to pursue the Spanish inland. It is uncertain whether or not they marched over the hill to the Mission San Carlos at Carmel.

As soon as it was known that Monterey was the object of attack, Sola had sent word to San Francisco and San Jose for reinforcements. Down the Royal Highway came most of the San Francisco garrison. A counterforce was organized at Rancho del Rey and advanced on Monterey to give battle. For this, history must give Sola his due; he was no quitter. He was determined to retake his capital and liquidate the enemy. This force arrived to find everything in ashes and the two pirate ships mere sails on the horizon. And where was their course directed next? South. Then look out Santa Barbara and San Diego! Down the Royal Highway went the best fighting men on the swiftest horses to assist these towns if the pirates attacked.

And attack they did, but not at the locations first expected.

Bouchard and Corney anchored off Refugio Beach, the private port of the Ortega rancho. They had heard that the Ortegas were especially wealthy. But the Ortegas had carried their valuables inland, and the women of the family had been taken to Mission Purísima Concepción. What is more, Sergeant Carlos Carrillo of Santa Barbara had ridden north with thirty men and was lying in ambush. There was a skirmish, and, in California *vaquero* fashion, the Santa Barbarans lassoed three of the pirates and tied them up in knots. The rest, not knowing how great (or actually how little) was Carrillo's strength, fled to the beach.

Enraged, Bouchard ordered the Ortega home burned, which was done. But first, of course, he carried off any objects of value.

Out of vile temper and plain cussedness, he had his men kill all the cattle they could find. Then he sailed for Santa Barbara.

Sergeant Carrillo and his men rode hastily to the town. It would have seemed a fitting gesture for them to erect a gallows on the beach in plain view from the bay, so that when Bouchard and Corney arrived, they might see the bodies of the three lassoed prisoners hanging by their necks.

Bouchard sailed over to Santa Cruz Island for wood and water and put in at Santa Barbara on December 6, 1818, just two days after Saint Barbara's Day for which Sebastián Vizcaíno had named the place two hundred and fourteen years previously.

Although it probably could not have defended itself much better than Monterey, if as well, Santa Barbara was ready to fight. The fact that the three prisoners were not hanged for Bouchard's edification may have saved the town, for after the *Argentina* and the *Santa Rosa* dropped their anchors in the roadstead, Bouchard sent word that he would spare the town if his three men were returned. If not, he'd wipe it from the face of the earth. He himself had a prisoner, captured at Monterey, and he would return this man for his own three—or else.

Seemingly there was a difference of reaction at Santa Barbara to this ultimatum. Sergeant Carrillo wanted to fight, but Commandante de la Guerra (whose name means "of the war") did not. Probably De la Guerra was wise, but it irked the younger men to have this highhanded murderer and thief dictate his own terms.

The exchange of prisoners was arranged. The three pirates were returned to the safety of their ships, and to the surprise of the Santa Barbarans, the prisoner returned by Bouchard turned out to be the Monterey garbage scavenger and town drunkard who had tried to join the pirates. This wretch must have regretted his fate; for Governor Sola ordered him to receive a hundred lashes, well laid on, and then to spend six years in chains at hard labor.

At any rate Bouchard sailed away from Santa Barbara without

attacking the town (very likely he thought it not worth the powder as everything of value and all the women would long since have been sent inland) and he gave San Buenaventura, farther down the coast, a few uneasy moments before his sails dropped out of sight.

He landed again, this time on the beach near Mission San Juan Capistrano. Here the pirates made a friendly overture, saying they would spare the town and the mission if they were equipped with provisions and whatever "other supplies" they might need. Bouchard received an answer to delight the heart: "We'll supply you all the powder and shot at our command and nothing else," which came from Sergeant Santiago de Argüello who had ridden up the Royal Highway with twenty men from San Diego just in case the invaders should chance to stop off the coast at Mission San Juan Capistrano. But the brave young Argüello was bluffing, and Bouchard was angered beyond control. That any lowly Californian *dared* say such a thing to this great protector of free men—and freebooters!

Bouchard sent his gangsters ashore (Sergeant Argüello didn't even have a single cannon to resist the attack), and what they did to San Juan Capistrano was plenty. The place was leveled, except for the walls of the mission which were not worth destroying. The pirates found a large stock of wine and spirits and many of them got roaring drunk while watching the little town burn. Argüello and most of his men escaped. Bouchard gave the most flagrant of the dissipated the cat-o'-nine-tails the next day. He had no time for drunkards; he wanted blood.

Back on their ships the following day, taking with them a few Indian girls for the amusement of the crews, the pirates felt quite well off. They had liberated California; they had collected a good haul of stolen goods; they had shown the king of Spain and his stupid loyal subjects a thing or two. California was a great place— they would doubtless come back and liberate it again next year.

And with that the two villains, Bouchard and Corney, sailed away, glutted and happy and bragging, and ignored San Diego where they suspected a goodly force would be waiting for them—figuratively thumbing their piratical noses at the garrison—and were never seen in California again.

The territory breathed a sigh of relief.

But a sigh of relief was not enough. That was not the answer. This last guest to the normally hospitable shores meant a turning point, not in the policy of Spain in Madrid or of New Spain in Mexico City. It meant that the Californians themselves could not and must not continue to live their lives in jeopardy through lack of defense against any nation, freebooter, imposter or pirate who happened to sail by.

Conditions were untenable. Even the growing issue between church control of the land versus control by individual land-grant holders lost its acute significance. With attacks from the outside, internal differences had to be deferred in favor of a united front for security and survival.

The administration by the Spanish government was utterly incompetent. Supply ships long overdue and eagerly awaited had never sailed at all; the military equipment was a farce; salaries of officials remained unpaid, first for months and then for years; the inquiries and pleas of the territory remained unanswered. The viceroy in Mexico City had problems far greater on his hands than the troubles of distant California. All Mexico was rumbling and grumbling against Spain. In California good and honorable citizens such as the Ortegas had been turned into smugglers by stupid legislation. For men who were capable and willing to fight for their land and property not to have the equipment they needed was exasperating and heartbreaking. Something had to happen. It had to be immediate. And it was. It was a word well known throughout history—revolution.

PART 3

MEXICAN
MAZE

1821 *to* 1846

Revolution!

THE commandante at the presidio of San Diego was awakened shortly before dawn. An orderly brought him the news that a messenger had arrived from the south, had, in fact, ridden up the Royal Highway all the way from Loreto in Baja California, stopping at mission after mission and making the trip in a record number of days.

Commandante Santiago Argüello (he who had had the courage to defy Bouchard the pirate at San Juan Capistrano) received the weary horsemen at once. The news seemed impossible, incredible, a dream—and perhaps a dream come true. For the messenger, who was a sergeant wearing a strange uniform, saluted the commandante in the name of their new emperor, Agustín the First.

Argüello had never heard of him. The king of Spain was Ferdinand the Seventh. Who was this Agustín?

"New Spain has ceased to exist," the messenger explained. "We are no longer subjects of the Spanish crown. We are now the subjects of Emperor Agustín Iturbide of Mexico. There has been a revolution. Mexico City has gone wild. The Empire of Mexico has been born. Long live Agustín the First!"

And again he saluted.

Argüello returned the salute. It was the first formal recognition in California of the Mexican Empire. It was January 10, 1822. California was no longer Spanish; it was Mexican.

Some months before this news reached San Diego, the chaotic political conditions of New Spain achieved some slight harmony when a Creole upstart, with a record none too impeccable with

133

regard to graft and bribes, formerly a colonel in the Royal Spanish Army named Agustín Iturbide, merged his forces and followers with those of another insurgent, Vicente Guerrero, at the town of Iguala. The plan of Iguala resulted. This called for a new and independent state, having no allegiance to Spain, but setting up, on its own volition, a limited monarchy to be known as the Empire of Mexico, its ruler the Creole opportunist, Emperor Agustín the First. The new ruler's first move was to recognize the Roman Catholic Church as the established church of Mexico. His second was to send the viceroy of the king of Spain scurrying for home. Mexico City had emerged from the Spanish yoke and was at last free of Madrid. Agustín I, with the support of the army and the church, settled down to be a benevolent and wealthy despot. With the spontaneous acclaim of the people, as well as the military and the hagiocracy, the new empire got off to a fine start. Juan O'Donoju, the sixty-second and last viceroy, recognized the futility of opposing this new and strong coalition, formally recognized its existence, and got back to Spain with his head still on his shoulders. There was never a viceroy in Mexico City again.

Commandante Argüello sent one of his own soldiers north over the Royal Highway from San Diego to relay the news to the capital at Monterey. The messenger took an unconscionable time in getting there, for he stopped at every mission and dallied at every rancho on the way. He was the bearer of the most amazing tidings yet carried along El Camino Real and he enjoyed his sensational assignment no end. Doubtless it was the first time in his life he had ever been a person of importance. He stayed three full days at Rancho Los Feliz relating the news time and again and answering questions, the replies to which he made up. Then he spent most of a week at Rancho El Conejo, and by this time he had embroidered a pretty story. He began to consider himself an emissary, not of Commandante Argüello, but of Emperor Agustín himself whom he had never known existed before. By the time he reached

Rancho Salinas he was just about the new emperor's best friend. And at last in mid-February he rode into Monterey with the great news.

Governor Sola was incredulous and not at all pleased, for it most likely meant that Governor Sola might soon be out of a job. "It is the dream of a dreamer," said the governor. He couldn't believe that California was no longer a province of Spain. He therefore did nothing whatever about it except to send the bearer of the news back the way he had come, and Monterey continued to bask in the California sunshine.

To the church it was not particularly pleasant news either. Father José Señan, the fifth president of the California missions, wrote to Commandante de la Guerra in Santa Barbara, "May God have mercy on this province, which seems at present to lie between Scylla and Charybdis."

But to the Californians themselves, and it is estimated that the territory had a white population of 10,000 to 12,000 in 1822, it was welcome news indeed. The people looked forward to better trade relations and a more up-to-date and vital foreign policy.

When a month went by and no further news came from Mexico City, Governor Sola was justly puzzled. He had received no formal instructions of any kind and the yellow and red banner of Spain still flew over the capital. So in March he called a meeting, or junta, of the captains of the four presidios—San Francisco, Monterey, Santa Barbara and San Diego—invited Fathers Payeras and Sarria of the Franciscans and presided over what amounted to the first California congress to consider the clouded political scene.

The junta "considered" without reaching any drastic decision, but at last word came from Mexico City that the canon of the Cathedral of Durango would visit Monterey as a representative of His Highness Agustín I, and would carry out the technical details of changing California from Spanish to Mexican allegiance. The *canónigo* of Durango did not arrive until September 26 of 1822, or just one year after Agustín Iturbide had assumed power. When his ship entered the Bay of Monterey it stayed well out of range of the guns of the presidio. The *canónigo* was none too sure just how he would be welcomed. The colors of Spain were still over the garrison and the red, white and green of the Empire of Mexico flew from the ship's masthead.

But all went well. The *canónigo,* a genial and jovial epicurean, shocked the Franciscans with his love of gambling, drinking and women, but he only wanted his Californian friends to know that under the great and good and kind and wise and benevolent Agustín I, things were going to be different.

A great occasion was made of the lowering of the Spanish flag. The Spanish lion came down and the Mexican eagle on his field of red and white and green went up and waved in the breeze. The power of Spain was gone forever. This was the signal for a great fiesta. There were rolls on the drums and bugle calls, and salutes from the presidio artillery answered by the guns of the ship in the bay. Everyone shouted, *"Viva la Independencia Mexicana! Viva el Emperador Agustín el Grande! Viva! Viva! Viva!"*

After the political acknowledgment, all the leading participants crowded into the Mission San Carlos Borroméo del Rio Carmelo, where the great and dignified and celebrated canon from Durango read a solemn Mass and delivered the *Te Deum.*

This was followed by games and feasts and fireworks and a bull-and-bear fight, and a parade of soldiers from the presidio and of sailors from the ship, and visiting rancheros in their gayest clothes riding their prancing and caparisoned horses.

Again the amazed Indians looked on and wondered what it was all about.

Governor Sola remained in office pro tem until Agustín I could appoint one of his supporters or relatives to be governor of California. Sola, then, would not be ignominiously kicked out, but instead, having been a good man and shown himself a loyal subject of Agustín, would be kicked upstairs to a newly created office, deputy from California to the Cortes (Congress) in Mexico City. At last California would have a representative at the seat of government.

Messengers were sent up and down the Royal Highway, and all Spanish flags were hauled down and the flag of the new empire went up. San Francisco, Santa Barbara and San Diego swore allegiance and each had its own fiesta to celebrate the great event. *Vivas* were yelled from one end of the highway to the other, and all ended with cheers for the mighty Agustín I whom nobody had ever heard of before. What a man! What an emperor! All hail Agustín!

But of course news was slow in those days, and ships were still an event in Monterey or any California port. What was going on in Mexico City at the same time would have astounded the Californians and might well have given the *canónigo* of Durango apoplexy.

For it was not so very long after all this fanfare that another messenger rode up the Royal Highway from Loreto in Baja California, even as had the sergeant who brought the news to Commandante Argüello of the birth of the Empire of Mexico.

When this emissary arrived at San Diego he was wearing a uniform unknown to the former Spanish soldiers who had only recently become soldiers of the Mexican Empire. They challenged him in the name of the empire as loyal subjects of Agustín I.

This newcomer seemed unimpressed. He was *not* a subject of the emperor they named. *He* was a soldier of a new nation. Hadn't they heard? Of course they hadn't, for he was bringing the news. And the news was this: *Viva el Republico de Mexico!*

"The what?" the bewildered commandante wanted to know.

"The Republic of Mexico!" shouted the soldier. He was, in fact, a major. There were more majors than sergeants in the new army.

"What new army?" the commandante wanted to know.

"The Army of the Republic of Mexico!" shouted the major.

"But the Empire?" asked the commandante.

"Is gone!" exulted the major. "Mexico is now a republic! Mexico is free! California is now a part of the great new Mexican Republic! *Viva! Viva!*"

"But the emperor—Agustín the First?"

"Oh, that imposter," said the major, "that traitor. Ha! Ha! He was taken out and shot."

Brief Honeymoon

12

THE position in which Governor Pablo Vicente Sola found himself might be described as the titular head of a state of utter confusion.

He, a native of Spain, had been appointed the governor of a province of New Spain by the viceroy in Mexico City of the king, who was in Madrid.

The viceroy had been sent packing.

The king had been denounced.

New Spain ceased to exist.

A new government had been set up called the Empire of Mexico under Agustín I.

After some thoughtful hesitation, Governor Sola had recognized Agustín I as Emperor of Mexico and had pledged him California's allegiance.

Even while this was being done, Agustín I was deposed and then executed.

The Empire of Mexico ceased to exist.

A government calling itself the Republic of Mexico had been organized under a general named Santa Anna, who was military leader and provisional president.

Governor Sola, meanwhile, had accepted a new appointment under Agustín as deputy from California to the Cortes in Mexico City.

That particular Cortes had ceased to exist.

So Governor Sola was a traitor to the Spanish king and a traitor to New Spain and a subject of an emperor who had been shot by a firing squad and no longer a governor yet still in office—and an enemy of the new Republic of Mexico.

It was hardly an enviable position.

While it left him well schooled in the ephemeral polemics of Spanish-American politics, it also left him in political jeopardy if not actual physical danger. Whatever he did, he was sure to be in trouble. But Governor Sola was not lacking in courage and tenacity, as was shown in his defense against the pirate Bouchard, and he was not lacking in political science. Such a situation would have driven the late Governor Borica to drink and the late Governor Arrillaga into a strait jacket, but Pablo Vicente Sola was a man who could meet the occasion. His place in California history has been somewhat slighted and he has been described as "weak" and "inept." Such was not the case. Governor Sola did exactly what any capable executive would have done—he ignored the Mexican hurly-burly and he organized his California. He did it expeditiously and well.

First—and a smart move it was—he declared that he was no longer governor. And he maneuvered into that questionable post one Luís Argüello, formerly commandante at the San Francisco presidio, who already was "acting governor" in view of Sola's new position as deputy under the short-lived Agustín I. Argüello was *elected* governor. It was the first time in California history that the territory chose its own leader. Moreover, that leader was California-born. He was not, of course, elected by the people who lived up and down the Royal Highway, but he was, nevertheless, elected by a group of presidio captains, Franciscans and ex-Governor Sola himself. The territory was no longer looking to Madrid or Mexico City; it was beginning to express its own political consciousness. For that the Californians could thank Sola.

The position that the *canónigo* of Durango found himself in was none too pleasant to His Worship. It was not fitting for the canon to be the personal emissary of an emperor who had been liquidated. Therefore the canon promptly decided, while still in Monterey, that Agustín I had been an upstart and a pretender after all, an emulator of Napoleon, and perhaps it was all for the best that he had been "taken out and shot." Whereupon the *canónigo* expressed his undying loyalty to the new Republic of Mexico.

Between ex-Governor Sola, provisional Governor Argüello, and the now-I'm-right-now-I'm-left canon of Durango who might have stepped out of a Gilbert and Sullivan operetta, a plan of government for California was set up in Monterey. The territory expressed its allegiance to the Mexican Republic. But the *Plan de Gobierno* went ahead on its own without waiting for instructions or advice from Mexico City. In a sense, the *Plan de Gobierno* was California's first constitution. It was a formal document and it provided for the raising of money (the local government started penniless) by the welcoming of foreign vessels which would now be free to trade; levying import and export taxes; and placing a tax on mission products since these were raised or manufactured without cost to the Franciscans by Indian labor. The Franciscans resented this, at first in gentle protestation, and soon vigorously and bitterly. The government pointed out that except for about twenty private ranchos scattered along the Royal Highway, the Franciscans with their twenty-one missions and vast holdings owned the majority of the wealth of the land. It would not be fair, therefore, to exempt the church and make the private rancheros carry all the tax burden. The Franciscans couldn't see it that way; their reason for being was the saving of souls, and that should be above the monetary level. Again the breach between church and state was opened and widened. To make matters worse, the government wanted to declare all Indians free citizens!

The *Plan de Gobierno* set up a judicature with civil justice to be administered by alcaldes (judges), *ayuntamientos* (town councils), a superior court and the right of appeal to the commandante of the presidial district.

It further set up a legislature with representatives from each presidio and each pueblo. The latter was important as it meant that the legislature would not be composed in its entirety of military men. A few private citizens from such towns as Los Angeles and San Jose would be present. The church looked askance at this as there was no provision for any Franciscans to serve in the legislative body. Many things were happening that boded no good and the Franciscans didn't hesitate to make that plain.

But the *Plan de Gobierno* went right ahead on no authority except that of the few men who made it up. Governor, judiciary and legislature were now in existence, and tax machinery to support these departments was put into action. A permanent militia was organized of 290 men who were a kind of police force as well as a military unit.

One more bone of contention arose between church and state; ex-Governor Sola insisted on some form of education. He could not bear to see children growing up in ignorance and illiteracy. To pupils who had learned to read this governor even distributed copies of Cervantes' *Don Quixote,* and promised them other stories if they would but read this one. He wanted to revive former Governor Borica's abortive attempt to set up some means of education for the young.

The Franciscans had considered education to be part and parcel of their duties. But education in the missions amounted mostly to the instructing of the Indians in religion, farming, herding, weaving and various crafts. That was not the kind of education Governor Sola meant. He wanted—of all things—a public-school system. The Franciscans frowned upon that. They would take care of the education of the young. Again church and state disagreed.

Again the *Plan de Gobierno* went ahead on its own. Funds were pitifully small, but in spite of the difficulties a few teachers were hired and a few crude public schools were opened. To the teachers Sola said, "Do not accept any excuse from parents who refuse to send their children to school; for, if the young are not educated, California, in place of making progress, will necessarily be forced to retrograde, a thing which it is our duty to prevent at all costs."

And historians have called Sola a "weak" governor! On the contrary, his importance to California ranks with that of Portolá and Serra.

With some form of government established and functioning and, best of all, a government built on the spot at the time to administer the immediate needs of the people and the land, Pablo Vicente Sola and the *canónigo* of Durango left Monterey for Mexico City to report what they had done to General Santa Anna, who, as far as anyone in California could tell, appeared to be running the Republic of Mexico. Governor Luís Argüello, thirty-eight years old, was left in charge at Monterey.

Sola never returned to California. The young and struggling Mexican capital needed his abilities far more desperately than the far distant territory of California. Withal, he seems to have been swallowed up in the political confusion of the new government, for little more is known about him. It is possible that he left Mexico and returned to Spain, although this cannot be substantiated. The truth is, Sola might have made a good president for the new republic which sorely needed capable leadership and whose history is one long series of plots, intrigues, insurrections, revolutions and counterrevolutions. At any rate, California could thank Sola for a government, and that was something it had never enjoyed before.

It was now the year 1824.

Life along the Royal Highway continued, on the surface, much as it has been described in previous chapters. The new government functioned with reasonable smoothness with only a jolt now and then. An Indian uprising of oppressed neophytes resulted in bloodshed at Missions Purísima Concepción, Santa Inés and Santa Barbara with casualties totaling eleven whites and twenty-five Indians.

Governor Argüello was forced to send the militia into action. Against overwhelming forces the Indians were routed and fled to the hills or were forced to surrender and face punishment. At Purísima Concepción they managed to entrench and fortify themselves within the mission, destroying church property and turning two rusty cannon on the soldiers who tried to oust them. The Indians held the mission for a month before superior forces could overcome them. For this crime seven Indians were tried and executed and others sentenced to long terms of hard labor.

This uprising, which was not against the government but against the church, was the only blot on the record during Governor Argüello's administration.

In May of 1825 the young and capable Argüello suspended the first meeting of the California legislature, or what was known as the *diputación*. The record was good, and Argüello wrote a report which summed up the gains made by California during the past year and a half.

His report stressed the miserable conditions of the Indians and the fact that slavery under a republican form of government could not continue. The day was coming, and coming soon, when the Franciscans could no longer utilize the feudal system. He recapitulated Sola's pleas for education and he even went so far as to say that the Indian child should be allowed an education at public expense even as the white child. This, of course, caused ecclesiastical reverberations.

The report further mentioned the advantages to all Californians of the lifting of the long-throttling trade embargo as imposed by New Spain. This embargo had been instigated simply to keep the foreigner out. All it had done was make the Californians smugglers and deprive the territory of an income from import and export taxation. Now foreigners were landing at California ports and were welcome. And since they need not be underhanded about it, a finer type of foreigner who was a boon to California was arriving. The days of the freebooter had given way to the days of the respectable settler. Men such as Abel Stearns (whose name is still preserved in Stearns Wharf at Santa Barbara), William E. P. Hartnell, Daniel Hill, Thomas Robbins and John R. Cooper came to California and married the daughters of California families. The English firm of John Begg and Company had signed a trade contract under which they would send at least one ship a year to California. It would bring a cargo of much-needed supplies for which it would take in return to England hides, tallow and wheat. A number of ships from "Boston States," came to trade and brought many useful and essential commodities. Californians began to look forward to these ships flying the red, white and blue—ships called the *Sachem,* the *Orion* and the *Rover.* No longer did the Ortega family have to smuggle in goods at Refugio Beach, and should another Bouchard put in his appearance, the militia was ready to deal with him.

The Russians at Fort Rossya were not enemies but friends, and to refuse to trade with them was ridiculous. Argüello was inclined to like the Russians anyway since his family had entertained Baron Rezánov, and his sister Concepción was pledged to become the baron's bride. From now on there was overland and water contact between San Francisco and the Russian colony. In fact, the Russian colony, so far removed from its seat of government—St. Petersburg!—wasn't doing too well. Its threat, now that California was taking strides forward, was negligible.

Any foreigner could settle in California provided he obeyed the laws of California as specifically stated in Sola's *Plan de Gobierno.* Security and personal property were guaranteed to any stranger who would become a good Californian. Mexican citizens (a Californian was, obviously, a Mexican citizen) were given preference in choice of lands, but this amounted to little, as any colonizer who wished to take up land had to restrict his selected area to approximately 15,000 acres which would be tax-free for five years, and must remain as a citizen of the Mexican Republic and live on his land.

These conditions had attracted many foreigners, mostly Americanos, willing to invest and work, and were certainly not the conditions to attract the "gentlemen of fortune" who wanted to loot, pillage and run.

This state of affairs, happy and progressive, continued until January 31, 1825. It was all too good to be true. Then, as usual, a new and disturbing element entered the picture. Governor Argüello had, from the start, been serving at Sola's instigation until the legitimate government, whatever that might turn out to be, in Mexico City, could send a new governor.

Mexico City should have sent an intelligent inspector to look over the situation and report back. Anyone with the sense that God gave a goose would see that the young Argüello was doing a splendid job.

But no, Mexico City didn't do things that way. A new governor was appointed without anyone in California even being consulted. He has been described as a "tall, thin, juiceless man," possessing but little enterprise, no force of character, and entirely obsessed with the condition of his health. His name was José María Echeandía, and he arrived by land over the Royal Highway from Loreto. Oceans made him ill. He doubted if the climate of Monterey would be to his liking or advantageous to his physical well-being. He thought best not to risk it at once. So when he arrived in San Diego he decided that for the best interests of his health he had better go no farther without a good rest.

A messenger was sent on up the Royal Highway to Monterey, and the alert and brilliant young Argüello was summoned to San Diego by this new authority who was his successor. Argüello was to come at once and "surrender" his authority. And the new governor wanted no dillydallying on the way. He was easily upset. So hurry.

The honeymoon for California was over.

"Double, Double Toil and Trouble"

13

WHEN, at length, Governor Echeandía cautiously traveled the Royal Highway from San Diego to Monterey, he found the small capital not so distasteful after all. In time, during his six years in office, he came to grow fond of it. Echeandía had arrived a Mexican; he left a Californian. His term of office, in spite of his personality, was not a retrogressive period for California, and if most of his work had not been immediately undone by his successor (typical of almost every change of gubernatorial office in California during the period of Mexican maze) the territory might have developed even faster. Instead, the end result was the Battle of Cahuenga Pass in 1831. Although opéra bouffe in character but nonetheless bloody, this battle was a more significant and determining factor in the history of the Royal Highway than many historians seem to be aware.

The 1820s were troublesome times throughout Mexico, and perforce these reverberations were felt in California. Echeandía handled some of them with capability approaching skill, and at other times went completely overboard on projects or efforts that had no meaning. One of his not-too-brilliant ideas occurred to him in 1827 when he decided to change the name of the whole territory. He persuaded the legislature that California was no longer a fitting name. It was tarred with the brush of Spain. Under the Republic of Mexico a name more suited to the land should be found, and at the same time it must be a name indicative of loyalty to Mexico. California was synonomous with things Spanish.

The Republic of Mexico had set up a sound government,

framed a constitution somewhat similar to that of the United States, and had elected Guadalupe Victoria as the first president of the republic. As a gracious gesture to this fine new government, Governor Echeandía of California, now a territory of the republic, suggested that the land be renamed "Montezuma." Why the use of an Aztec name should have been bestowed on a country that was never Aztec—the name of a chieftain who had been dethroned by Hernán Cortés three centuries earlier—was something that Echeandía never explained even if he gave it further consideration.

Furthermore, the new governor decided to make the capital Los Angeles, but to change the name of that pueblo to Villa Victoria in honor of the first president of Mexico. This pleased nobody in San Diego which considered itself the capital as long as the governor resided there, and pleased nobody in Monterey which considered itself the capital in spite of the chief executive's protracted absence. But Echeandía must have had a good time working out all these innovations, and he must have lain awake nights planning the territory's new coat of arms. It was to be an amazing monstrosity showing a half-naked Indian in feathered headdress, carrying a bow and a quiver of arrows, wading across a stream of water. The water symbolized the Strait of Anián, never found and now known to be nonexistent, and the whole shield was to be further embellished with an olive tree which somehow sprouted oak leaves. This, explained Echeandía, represented the original settling of the whole of North America. Fortunately, this governor's lack of talent in the matter of things artistic never produced his desired result. The California legislature, or *diputación,* passed the plan, accepted Montezuma as the territory's new name and sent all this information on to Mexico City for official approval. There some clerk filed it. Presumably the file was never opened again, for nothing more was ever heard of the great change in name. California remained California, and the state of Montezuma remained a governor's nightmare.

Had he succeeded in changing the name of his constituency, it would have remained only for Echeandía to think of changing El Camino Real, the Royal Highway, to the Republican Turnpike or some such alternative; but, discouraged over the lack of appreciation of his new state of Montezuma and its Great Seal, he turned to more pressing and difficult matters. In truth, he didn't have to turn; the matters landed in his lap.

His first problem, which would have been a major issue if not a great calamity, was a *sub-rosa* movement on the part of the more influential citizens of California (Montezuma!) to get rid of Echeandía posthaste. They wanted the capable and intelligent young Luís Argüello, whose interests were solely Californian and whose ability had been proved, to remain their governor. Had Argüello so much as nodded his head, the entire Monterey and San Francisco garrisons were ready to serve him and either "liquidate" Echeandía even as Agustín I had been liquidated, or at the very least pack him off to Mexico with a military escort the full length of the Royal Highway and a sharp warning never to come back.

All this would surely have meant more trouble and troops sent up from Mexico to replace in office the legitimate Echeandía or his successor, and would probably have resulted in a couple of Mexican sloops of war appearing in Monterey and San Francisco. Acting more wisely than Agustín de Iturbide, Luís Argüello rejected this bid for power, suggested that Echeandía be given a chance to prove himself and retired to his home near the Golden Gate. Unfortunately Argüello died at the age of forty-six in 1830, and his remains lie in the Mission Dolores in San Francisco. It is a pity that California had to lose him, for, with all the trouble that lay ahead, he would very likely have entered public life again and might well have been a great figure.

Among Echeandía's chief problems were foreign visitors who did not come by sea, but were the "mountain men," or trappers, pushing west overland, and were the first Americans to reach

California by the transcontinental route. The governor didn't know whether to receive them hospitably or eject them as trespassers. So he more or less welcomed the men of the first party—Jedediah Smith, Harrison G. Rogers and Thomas Virgin, who arrived in 1826—and ordered the men of the second party—James Ohio Pattie and his father Sylvester Pattie, who arrived in 1828—clapped into jail.

The governor stated that all these men had entered California illegally since they had no passports, and that his superiors in Mexico City would not permit such outlanders to remain in Mexico, so why should they be considered as "guests" in the Mexican territory of California?

The full import of the arrival of husky American trappers overland did not dawn on the average Californian, although it is possible that the ultimate significance meant something to Echeandía. It simply indicated that the vanguard of the United States, pushing west, had broken the mountain and desert barrier which had long been considered California's eastern and natural and impregnable defense. If one white American could travel overland from the Atlantic to the Pacific, so could two or two hundred or two thousand. California was open to traders in its various ports and to settlers who came by sea and took up land, and who obeyed the territorial law and embraced the constitution of the Republic of Mexico. But it was not open to the hunter, trapper or squatter who arrived exhausted on the life line of the Royal Highway at either Mission San Gabriel or at San Diego.

Jedediah Smith and Harrison G. Rogers, with the help of fellow Americans in Monterey, John R. Cooper, in particular, managed to rehabilitate themselves and their party and get out of California back over the deserts and mountain fastnesses.

But soon after their return to American civilization, Rogers wrote that "this Mission of San Gabriel, if properly managed, would be equal to a mine of silver or gold. Their annual income, even situated as it is and managed so badly, is worth, with Indians to do the labor, in hides, tallow, soap, wine, brandy, wheat and corn, from $55,000 to $60,000."

News like this taken back to the American frontier which had hardly jumped the Mississippi, meant simply that other Americans would surely be tempted to come and see.

This, at least, gave Governor Echeandía something else to think about nights instead of a change of name to Montezuma.

The Patties had a longer visit, and there was an extremely unusual aspect to it. Their story was ghosted by an editor in Cincinnati named Timothy Flint and published in that city in 1831. It is a most curious book. For almost everything in it is botched and mistaken and misdescribed. Dates don't jibe. James Pattie (or his ghost writer) barely mentions others who were in the party, although there must have been six or eight of them at one time. But he was certainly in California, surely came overland across New Mexico and Arizona, and obviously traversed the Royal Highway from one end to the other. He brought, of all things, vaccine to California for the first time, taught the Californians its proper use to counteract smallpox against which they had been helpless and, after being jailed by Governor Echeandía (during which incarceration his father died), was given the superlative title of "Surgeon Extraordinary to His Excellency, the Governor of Montezuma [still California]."

Some of this can be taken with a grain of salt, and most of Pattie's book would call for a pound of the chemical. He "recalled" his adventures for Editor Flint who wrote the astounding story with an eye to sales. When Pattie didn't exaggerate enough, Flint did. Pattie himself seems to have been a boastful, if not baleful, egoist. A present-day editor of a reissue of the book by the Lakeside Press of Chicago in 1930, Dr. Milo Quaife, has likened it to *Trader Horn*. In other words, it wasn't quite so, but it was something akin to the truth and made entertaining reading. It wouldn't be entirely out of order to place Pattie's book on a level with Joan Lowell's *Cradle of the Deep,* although that may be just a bit too much of a condemnation—of Pattie. But however scholars may attack the work with all justice, Pattie did, in the main and on a slightly lesser scale, everything that his ghost writer says he did. One of his achievements, which he tosses off in passing, was the vaccination of 22,000 Californians. To do that in 1828-1829 would have been possible, but it would have included 100 percent of the white population of the territory and a large number of Indians, and required perhaps two wagonloads of vaccine. Pattie wrote, with the help of Timothy Flint, that he did just that.

While being "Surgeon Extraordinary," James Ohio also helped foment a revolution against the governor, who, for some inexplicable reason, refused to pay his bill for the medical services. Ohio decided that the insurrectionists were not worthy after all and turned on them and helped quell the revolution, thus saving the governor's scalp. He engaged, on the side, in richly successful sea-otter hunting in San Francisco Bay, finally decided that California was beginning to become something of a bore and sailed away to Mexico to press his claim to the president for his surgical succor to smallpox-ridden Montezuma called California.

In his book Pattie and Editor Flint describe the trip up the Royal Highway from San Diego to San Francisco. It is worth quoting in part despite inaccuracies, garbled information and confused names of missions, simply because the trip was a reality; in spite of Pattie's narration by reflected light, and the narrative being further screened through Editor Flint, it does give a vivid picture of life along El Camino Real in 1829.

Pattie left San Diego on February 28 with a letter from an authority he calls the "General" (commandante of the San Diego presidio), granting Pattie his freedom from jail, but freedom only on parole, with the understanding that he was to vaccinate "all the inhabitants upon the coast" and "that horses and food and supplies" should be made available to him at the various missions. Traveling north from San Diego, Pattie arrived at Mission San Luís Rey de Francia. He states:

I reached it in the evening. I found an old priest, who seemed glad to see me. I gave him the General's letter. After he had read it, he said, with regard to that part of it which spoke of payment, that I had better take certificates from the priests of each mission, as I advanced up the coast, stating that I had vaccinated their inhabitants; and that when I arrived at the upper mission, where one of the high dignitaries of the church resided, I should receive my recompense for the whole. Seeing nothing at all singular in this advice, I concluded to adopt it.

In the morning I entered on the performance of my duty. My subjects were Indians, the missions being entirely composed of them, with the exception of the priests, who are the rulers. The number of natives in this mission was three thousand, nine hundred and four. I took the old priest's certificate, as had been recommended by him, when I had completed my task. . . .

The greater part of these Indians were brought from their native mountains against their own inclinations, and by compulsion; and then baptised; which act was as little voluntary on their part, as the former had been. After these preliminaries, they had been put to work, as converted Indians.

The next mission on my way was that, called St. John the Baptist.

This must have been San Juan Capistrano, and Pattie's memory slipped when relating this to Timothy Flint in Cincinnati two years later.

. . . The mountains here approach so near the ocean, as to leave only room enough for the location of the mission. The waves dash upon the shore immediately in front of it. The priest, who presides over this mission, was in the habit of indulging his love of wine and stronger liquors to such a degree, as to be often intoxicated. The church had been shattered by an earthquake. Between twenty and thirty of the Indians, men, women, and children, had been suddenly destroyed by the falling of the church bells upon them.

Again there is confusion. San Juan Capistrano is not on the ocean, but is a short distance in from the sea—perhaps three miles. Just what mission would fit Pattie's description of being adjacent to the sea is difficult to say unless he had confused Capistrano with San Buenaventura. Or possibly Pattie indulged in some of the priest's wines and spirits, too, and that might account for his discrepancy. For surely he was at San Juan Capistrano, as his mention of the earthquake casualties proves, and he could not have made that out of whole cloth. This was the disaster of 1812, and that it was well emphasized to a passing stranger in 1829 shows how indelibly the calamity had been recorded in the minds of the survivors. Pattie continues:

. . . After communicating the vaccine matter to 600 natives, I left this place, where the mountains rose behind to shelter it; and the sea stretched out its boundless expanse before it.

Continuing my route I reached my next point of destination. This establishment was called the mission of St. Gabriel. Here I vaccinated 960 individuals. The course from the mission of St. John the Baptist to this place led me from the sea-shore, a distance of from eighteen to twenty miles. Those who selected the position of this mission, followed the receding mountains. It extends from their foot, having in front a large tract of country showing small barren hills, and yet affording pasturage for herds of cattle so numerous, that their number is unknown even to the all surveying and systematic priests. In this species of riches St. Gabriel exceeds all the other establishments on the coast. . . .

My next advance was to a small town, inhabited by Spaniards, called the town of The Angels [Los Angeles, of course]. The houses have flat roofs, covered with bituminous pitch, brought from a place within four miles of the town, where this article boils up from the earth. As the liquid rises, hollow bubbles like a shell of large size, are formed. When they burst the noise is heard distinctly in the town. The material is obtained by breaking off portions, that have become hard, with an axe, or something of the kind. The large pieces thus separated, are laid on the roof, previously covered with earth, through which the pitch cannot penetrate, when it is rendered liquid again by the heat of the sun. In this place I vaccinated 2500 persons.

From this place I went to the mission of St. Ferdinand, where I communicated the matter to 967 subjects. St. Ferdinand is thirty miles east of the coast, and a fine place in point of position.

The mission of St. Buenaventura succeeded. Not long previous to my arrival here, two priests had eloped from the establishment, taking with them what gold and silver they could lay their hands upon. They chose an American vessel, in which to make their escape. I practised my new calling upon 1000 persons in this mission.

The next point I reached was the fort of St. Barbara. I found several vessels lying here. I went on board of them, and spent some pleasant evenings in company with the commanders. I enjoyed the contrast of such society with that of the priests and Indians, among whom I had lately been. This place has a garrison of fifty or sixty soldiers. The mission lies a half a mile N. W. of the fort. It is situated on the summit of a hill, and affords a fine view of the great deep. Many are the hours I passed during this long and lonely journey, through a country every way strange and foreign to me, in looking on the ceaseless motion of its waves. The great Leviathan too played therein. I have often watched him, as he threw spouts of water into the air, and moved his huge body through the liquid surface. My subjects here amounted to 2600. They were principally Indians.

The next mission on my route was that called St. Enos. I vaccinated 900 of its inhabitants, and proceeded to St. Cruz, where I operated upon 650. My next advance was to St. Luis Obispes. Here I found 800 subjects. The mission of St. Michael followed in order. In it I vaccinated 1850 persons. My next theatre of operations was St. John Bapistrano. 900 was the number that received vaccination here. Thence I went to La Solada, and vaccinated 1685, and then proceeded to St. Carlos, and communicated the matter to 800.

The last paragraph quoted above is a jumbled mess. St. Enos was Santa Inés. "St. Cruz"—and how he ever got that—must have been Purísima Concepción since the real Santa Cruz is north of Monterey and Pattie had not reached that capital yet. His "Obispes" is obviously Mission San Luís Obispo de Tolosa. St. Michael was San Miguel Arcángel. And his "St. John Bapistrano" sounds as if he had again indulged in mission wine and spirits. It could have been no other but San Antonio de Padua. His "La Solada" can be translated only as "The Sediment" or "The Dregs"—and perhaps that was the case. At any rate, he had reached Mission Nuestra Señora de la Soledad. And his "St. Carlos" is correct enough, for there he had arrived at San Carlos Borroméo del Rio Carmelo, the last resting place of the great Padre Junípero Serra.

From San Carlos Pattie says he "went on" to Monterey, although he doubtless reached Monterey first, went south to the mission on the Carmel River and then returned to Monterey. At any rate, the balance of his trip and its ironic conclusion are worth following:

From the latter mission I passed on to the fort of Monte El Rey, where [there] is a garrison of a hundred soldiers. I found here 500 persons to vaccinate. The name of this place in English signifies the King's mount or hill. Forests spread around Monte El Rey for miles in all directions, composed of thick clusters of pines and live oaks. Numberless gray bears find their home, and range in these deep woods. They are frequently known to attack men. . . .
From Monte El Rey I advanced to the mission of St. Anthony, which lies thirty miles E. from the coast.

This was Mission San Juan Bautista, Pattie having confused it with San Antonio de Padua.

. . . In it I found one thousand persons to inoculate. I had now reached the region of small pox, several cases of it having occurred in this mission. The ruling priest of this establishment informed me, that he did not consider it either necessary or advisable for me to proceed farther for the purpose of inoculating the inhabitants of the country, as the small pox had prevailed universally through its whole remaining extent. As I had heard, while in San Diego, great numbers had been carried off by it. I then told him that I wished to see the church officer who had been described to me by the first priest whom I had seen on my way up the coast. He furnished me a horse, and I set off for the port of San Francisco, vaccinating those whom I found on the way who had not had the small pox.

I reached the above mentioned place, on the twentieth of June, 1829. Finding the person of whom I was in search, I presented him all the certificates of the priests of the missions in which I had vaccinated, and the letter of the General. I had inoculated in all twenty-two thousand persons. After he had finished the perusal of these papers, he asked me, what I thought my services were worth? I replied, that I should leave that point entirely to his judgment and decision. He then remarked, that he must have some time to reflect on the subject, and that I must spend a week or two with him. I consented willingly to this proposal, as I was desirous of crossing the bay of St. Francisco to the Russian settlement, called the Bodega.

It was not called Bodega, but the settlement was located at Bodega Bay and up and down the coast from the mouth of the Russian River. Fort Rossya was the place Pattie wished to visit, and did visit.

The Russians treated him well and he continued his vaccination crusade among them. He seems to have liked these people better than the Spaniards (or Mexicans or Californians), although how he managed to converse with them is something of a mystery that he does not explain. He says that he was paid a fee of $100 for his services, but does not say in just what manner or medium this sum was paid, for it is unlikely that the Russians had any American currency. Nevertheless he appears to have been well satisfied with his visit and in a short time, which is not specified, he returned to San Francisco to collect the fee that the authorities had decided on for his medical services along the Royal Highway.

I soon saw myself again in the presence of the Spanish priest, from whom I was to receive my recompense for the services performed on my long tour.... He then demanded of me how I liked the coast of California? I answered, that I very much admired the appearance of the country. His next question was, how would I like the idea of living in it? It would be agreeable to me, I returned, were it subject to any other form of government. He proceeded to question me on the ground of my objections to the present form of government? I was careful not to satisfy him on this point.

He then handed me a written piece of paper, the translation of which is as follows:

> I certify, that James O. Pattie has vaccinated all the Indians and whites on this coast, and to recompense him for the same, I give the said James O. Pattie my obligation for one thousand head of cattle, and land to pasture them; that is, 500 cows and 500 mules. This he is to receive after he becomes a Catholic, and a subject of this government. Given in the mission of San Francisco on the 8th of July, in the year 1829.
>
> JOHN CABORTES

When I had read this, without making use of any figure of speech, I was struck dumb. My anger choked me. As I was well aware of the fact, that this man had it in his power to hang me if I insulted him, and that here there was no law to give me redress, and compel him to pay me justly for my services, I said nothing for some time, but stood looking him full in the face ... but before I made a movement of any kind he spoke, saying, "You look displeased, sir." Prudential considerations were sufficient to withhold me no longer, and I answered in a short manner, that I ... should rejoice to find myself once more in a country where I should be justly dealt by. He asked me, what I meant ... I told him ... [I] wished to be in my own country, where there are laws to compel a man to pay another what he justly owes him, without his having the power to attach on the debt, as a condition upon which the payment is to depend, the submission to, and gratification of, any of his whimsical desires. Upon this the priest's tone became loud and angry as he said, "then you regard my proposing that you should become a Catholic, as the expression of an unjust and whimsical desire!" I told him "yes, that I did; and that I would not change my present opinions for all the money his mission was worth; and moreover, that before I would consent to be adopted into the society and companionship of such a band of murderers and robbers, as I deemed were to be found along this coast, for the pitiful amount of one thousand head of cattle, I would suffer death."

When I had thus given honest and plain utterance to the feelings, which swelled within me, the priest ordered me to leave his house. I walked out quickly, and possessed myself of my rifle, as I did not know, but some of his attendants at hand might be set upon me; for if the comparison be allowable the priests of this country have the people as much and entirely under their control and command, as the people of our own country have a good biddable dog. For fear they should come barking at me, I hastened away, and proceeded to a *ranch,* where I procured a horse for three dollars, which I mounted, and took the route for Monte El Rey. I did not stop, nor stay on my journey to this place. I found upon my arrival there, an American vessel in port, just ready to sail, and on the point of departure.

Meeting the Captain on shore, I made the necessary arrangements with him for accompanying him, and we went on board together. The anchor was now weighed, and we set sail.

The whole thing is a most curious account of events that obviously happened and other events that stretch credulity to the breaking point.

In Pattie's book, the full title of which is *The Personal Narrative of James O. Pattie of Kentucky,* he claims to have returned to California and to have taken part in the abortive revolt against Governor Echeandía instigated by unpaid and dissatisfied soldiers led by General Joaquín Solís. The revolt was quickly put down. Solís was overpowered at Santa Barbara in January of 1830, attempted to flee to the hills, was caught, jailed, convicted and sent off to Mexico to prison. It was one of Echeandía's numerous head-aches, and Pattie, back in California after leaving in dudgeon, was first on the side of Solís and then indicates that he changed his mind and was instrumental in the defeat of Solís.

So this unaccountable frontiersman strutted his hour at least along the Royal Highway and his name cannot be ignored. His observations in other parts of his book on the mission system, such as: "I saw women in irons for misconduct, and men in the stocks . . . the priests appoint officers to superintend the natives . . . and are very rigid in applying the rod to those who fall short of the portion of labor assigned to them," may be quite true as Pattie is not alone in such criticisms. But he certainly was not pro-Catholic, and his editor, Timothy Flint, was an ex-Protestant minister. These factors may account somewhat for his rather consistently critical at-titude toward the Franciscans. On the other hand, it is all too true that fine men such as Serra and Lasuén were gone, and even the best of their successors, sincere, zealous and scholarly men such as Padre Mariano Payeras and Padre José Señan, had both died in 1823. The men who followed seemed to be less tolerant and often strict and unnecessarily cruel. Hubert Howe Bancroft, famous his-torian of the Pacific Coast, summed up the enigma that was Pattie as "a self-conceited and quick-tempered boy with a freedom of speech often amounting to insolence and an unlimited ability to make himself disagreeable." This is probably as equally just an estimation of Pattie as is his rather contemptuous attitude toward the friars.

Governor Echeandía held Pattie, and any and all Americans who came overland, with no great regard. But in spite of his cool and even hostile treatment of these "mountain men" they con-tinued to enter California and present a continual problem to the governor.

Ewing Young, a rugged Tennessean, who, his name being un-

The reception of Jean François de la Pérouse at Carmel in 1786. The French scientist was the first foreign visitor to reach Spanish California.

An Indian dance near Mission San José in 1806

How the caballero entertained his best girl—a spirited canter on a Sunday afternoon in the 1840's

A gold seeker, presumably a soldier deserting from the garrison at Monterey. The artist intended to imply that the following vulture would get first the mule and later the gold seeker.

pronounceable in Spanish, called himself Joaquín Joon for the benefit of the Californians, arrived in Los Angeles in 1830 with a man whose name is famous throughout the West—Kit Carson. With them were four or five rough and tough six-footers who were trappers and went by such names as Big Jim and Mighty Higgins. They crossed the Mojave Desert, came through the Cajon Pass and finally reached Mission San Gabriel. Illegal entry meant nothing to them and they trapped down the inland valley of the San Joaquin River all the way to San Francisco Bay, and then returned, up the same inland valley to the Tejon Pass and on to Los Angeles. Thus Young and Carson and their roughnecks did not traverse the Royal Highway but only touched it at certain places.

In Los Angeles they were told to produce passports or face a term in jail. To this insult to their dignity Big Jim and Mighty Higgins proceeded to smash the alcalde's office and hurl all his papers out into the street, and vowed to kick him four times around the plaza. The amazed alcalde wisely fled when violence broke out. The authorities in Los Angeles sent a plea to the governor. These Americans seemed to have no concept of Mexican law.

While Big Jim and Mighty Higgins and two or three others were roaming the streets looking for more blankety-blank Mexican So-and-So's who would *dare* tell them what they could and could not do—and if they found just *one* they'd cut his ears off and make him eat them—Los Angeles trembled and stayed indoors.

Young and Carson had no way of controlling these fellow trappers, for each was on his own, but fortunately for the security of the citizens of Los Angeles, Big Jim and Mighty Higgins decided to do a little drinking. They got roaring drunk and finally picked a fight with each other and Higgins shot Big Jim through the heart.

A day later, when some degree of sobriety occurred, the whole band rode away, leaving the body of Big Jim where it lay, and went on back across the deserts to Arizona and New Mexico. That such visitors were a problem hardly needs saying. It was one more gray hair for Governor Echeandía.

Not all of the trappers were so bad as this, and some who managed to stay made fine citizens. Names such as J. J. Warner, Job F. Dye, George C. Yount, Joseph Walker and Antoine Robidoux have a respected place in California and Royal Highway history.

Another long-stirring problem that faced Governor Echeandía was the mission question. In economy, the missions controlled California. In politics, the government controlled California. The two policies were not in accord. Something was going to have to give.

But both church and state were, in the final analysis, at loggerheads over one issue—namely, who owned the land?

Under Charles III of Spain, nobody owned the land except the king. He owned it all. California was his royal property, and note the name of its one highway—*El Camino Real*.

All persons or institutions who made use of such parcels of royal property that made up the whole of California, were permitted to do so only because of the benevolence and graciousness of the man who owned it all. The fact that the owner, Charles III, had only a vague idea of the land, and could not even have pointed out the area on a map, in no way refuted the fact that he owned all of California. More important was the fact that while final title belonged to Charles III, anyone who occupied the land had, at best, only usufructuary claim to it. In other words, the Catholic Church, under the Franciscans, had the "use" and "fruit" of the land, but the land *per se* was not theirs.

This was another great idea that occurred to Governor Echeandía, and it turned out to be far more momentous than changing the name of the territory to Montezuma.

For Charles III was gone. Ferdinand VII who followed him was gone. Spain was gone, as far as California was concerned.

Then who owned the land? Why, whoever took over the property from the king of Spain.

And who was that?

Agustín I, Emperor of Mexico.

But he had been shot.

The Empire of Mexico had been succeeded by the Republic of Mexico, and Governor Echeandía was that government's first appointed governor of California.

So it was obvious, in the sequence of historical events, that the Republic of Mexico—and that meant the *people* of Mexico—owned the land.

Therefore, the people of California were the true owners of California. And who were these people? About 20,000 Mexicans and possibly 50,000 Indians.

That was quite an idea to occur to Governor Echeandía. He thought so much about it that he acted on it. The mission lands should be secularized—that is, given in title to their rightful owners rather than held by ecclesiastical occupation. The missions were not to be done away with—perish the thought!—but were to take their rightful place in the communities as parish churches.

This move was one of the most significant in the history of California. And the situation was extremely delicate. Nevertheless, Echeandía had the courage to issue a decree which would, at the very least, begin in a gentle way the machinery of eventual and total secularization.

On July 5, 1826, the governor authorized the Indians (of *all* people!) of the districts of San Diego, Santa Barbara and Monterey, to form civil (as distinguished from clerical or military) pueblos and to take title to the lands of those areas under strict governmental supervision.

That caused the lighting of many candles and the counting of many beads.

But Echeandía was not highhanded about it, and he conferred

carefully with Padre Antonio Peyri, who was to a large degree sympathetic and understanding toward the plan. In that, Peyri was exceptional, for most of the Franciscans not only vilified the plan but declared that Mexico should never have been separated from Spain in the first place.

Of course, things didn't work very well. The Indians proved incapable of assuming the responsibilities of private ownership of property. The Franciscans were quick to point out that the whole scheme of secularization was a madman's dream.

And worse, in Mexico City, there was another political turnover which can be described only as the perennial Mexican revolution. A new president, Manuel Pedraza, was "elected" and he lasted just three days. The Mexican Congress declared his election null and void and on its own volition "elected" Vicente Guerrero president—he who had been the partner of Agustín de Iturbide in the latter's sweep to power as "Emperor!" Guerrero didn't last long. He was double-crossed by his own vice-president, Anastasio Bustamente, and Congress declared Guerrero mentally incapable of occupying his high office, thereby making Bustamente automatically president. Of course there was nothing wrong with Guerrero mentally, and he organized a counterrevolution, but it fell by the wayside and he became one of those who was "taken out and shot." Nor did Bustamente last long, for he was denounced as a usurper and booted out of office by Manuel Pedraza (the president who had lasted only three days) who had meanwhile organized an army as a counter-counterrevolution. Congress then declared the former three-day Pedraza was president after all. Pedraza, of course, didn't last long, but it is useless to continue the Mexican political confusion further. It is sufficient to show, however, that distant California could never be sure who was in power or if the people of the territory were loyal or not, and if they were—to whom?

In the midst of all this turbulence, Echeandía had begun the secularization of the missions. The man can safely be called an idealist.

Meanwhile, in Mexico City's seesaw for power, the clerical party got in, got out and got in again. Once in power for a brief time, it immediately "fired" Echeandía as governor of California and appointed in his place Manuel Victoria, loyal to the church and bitterly opposed to any and all secularization.

The incoming governor gave Echeandía much the same treatment he himself had served forth to Luís Argüello: he curtly told him to come down and meet him in San Diego and "surrender" his office.

Echeandía tried hard to force the secularization through. He refused to come to San Diego, stalled for time and sent word down the Royal Highway that he would meet his successor in Santa Barbara. In that interlude he arbitrarily and bravely issued a decree of total secularization of all mission properties to be effective at once—January 6, 1831. Then, having had that edict proclaimed as his last contribution to his office, he set off for Santa Barbara to surrender his power.

In a sideways glance it is equally interesting to see what California did for Echeandía, during his six years as governor, as it is to see what he did for California. He arrived a pompous, effete dilettante, chiefly concerned with his health and in thinking up new names and seals for his constituency. He left his office a capable and farseeing executive, much better equipped and experienced for the job than the newcomer to whom he had to surrender it.

The new governor's first move was tantamount to a slap in the face for Echeandía's administration. He immediately countermanded, abrogated and outlawed the decree of secularization.

Now what? All California wondered.

The Battle of Cahuenga Pass

14

THE job of being governor of California was not coveted by anyone in Mexico City. To receive this appointment meant that you had missed half a dozen or more finer plums and got California as a kind of consolation prize. The general pattern that followed, in almost all cases, resulted in a disappointed and disgruntled executive arriving under protest, only to get to like the place, to understand its particular problems in a way that nobody in Mexico City could possibly do, and to take such steps for the good of California that he ran into trouble, not with the Californians, but with the unstable political circus that was Mexico City. That was true of Pedro Fages, of Diego de Borica, of Pablo Vicente Sola, and of José María Echeandía. All four of these men arrived with misgivings, and yet all four made constructive contributions to the territory, and all four left as better executives than they had been upon arrival.

Then there came the exception to the rule.

Manuel Victoria was unquestionably the worst governor in the history of California, from Portolá up to the present, and that is a remarkable achievement in striking an all-time low. The man had an especially dark and swarthy complexion, and was promptly nicknamed *El Gobernador Negro* (The Black Governor). It is thought by many that he had a good proportion of Mexican Indian blood mixed with Jamaican Negro.

The first thing he did in Monterey, after scotching all efforts toward secularization, was to review the criminal code. He found it unsatisfactory and vague, and too open to individual interpreta-

166

tion. So he set up a new standard of punishments for criminals of all types no matter where the crimes were committed along the Royal Highway. This seems an odd obsession as California was remarkably crime-free, and a sharp and vigorous criminal code was not one of the most demanding of social necessities.

Governor Victoria declared he was going to see to it that any citizen could leave his purse, or even so little as his handkerchief, in the plaza at Monterey for a day or a week or more and return to find it untouched. To bring this ideal situation about he dealt harshly with the first offenders.

Two Indians stole a piffling amount of foodstuffs from the store-room at Mission San Carlos Borroméo. Ordinarily the local padre would have taken care of such peccadilloes. The two Indians might have had their food quotas cut off for a day or two, or have been given extra work for a week. But Governor Victoria insisted on having them shot. The mission padre put in a personal plea for the culprits, but Governor Victoria was adamant. He had ordered the death penalty and the death penalty they would receive. And they did. The Franciscans were aghast. This was the man who was the friend of the Franciscans and had put a stop, once and forever, to secularization of mission property.

A short time later an Indian boy was caught stealing some brightly colored buttons from the military store. The governor ordered the boy lashed and then shot. The order was carried out. This truly shocked the easygoing people of Monterey. What manner of monster was this who had come to rule their lives? If only Governor Echeandía were back!

But the sharpening of the criminal code was only the beginning.

The governor decided he had no need or use for the *diputación*. A legislature? What for? He was governor. He would rule. He refused to call a convention of the *diputación,* and when timidly asked why, he said that most of the legislature's members were illegally elected. Within a few months after taking office, Governor Victoria had scarcely a friend in California with the exception of the Franciscans. Since they were not represented in the *diputación* they cared not a hoot if that congress were never to convene.

But there were Californians who thought otherwise and who petitioned the governor to call the *diputación* into session. This made Victoria furious. Who were these swine who dared tell him how to govern? They had best see that their heads stayed on their shoulders.

The "swine" were some of California's leading citizens: José Carrillo, Pío Pico, Juan Bandini and Abel Stearns (who had married the beautiful Doña Arcadia Bandini). In San Diego ex-Governor Echeandía was about to embark for Mexico. These men urged him to stay. They felt that Governor Victoria would not remain governor for long.

Victoria, hearing of this, was again furious at such insubordination and handled it in his own dictatorial manner. He declared that José Carrillo and Abel Stearns were guilty of treason. Death, of course, was the penalty, but being a kindhearted man he decided to spare their lives. Instead, they were to be banished from California forever. All this was done without a trial of any kind. Carrillo and Stearns went to Baja California, and there they began to organize an army.

It wasn't much of an army, but it was made up of a few hundred discontented men who were willing to oppose the governor. In a few weeks the army marched north and seized San Diego. The fact that the army was made up of most of the San Diego garrison made it an entirely bloodless revolt.

Things were not long in coming to a crisis. The insurrectionists, led by Carrillo and Stearns, marched north over the Royal Highway, finding nobody who loved the governor sufficiently to oppose them, and "took" Los Angeles. This town was delighted, as a number of its prominent citizens were in jail—or were supposed to be—on Governor Victoria's orders. Los Angeles went all out for the down-with-Victoria movement, and Pío Pico, the local leader, added his weight to the rebellion.

Governor Victoria was not a man to stand for any insult such as this. Taking a few members of the San Francisco and most of the Monterey garrisons, he personally led his punitive force south down the Royal Highway to meet and defeat the upstarts. This time the death penalty would be carried out for all and sundry.

Hearing of this, Carrillo and Stearns moved their men north to meet the governor's forces. This meant business. Only one or the other would survive. The result was the Battle of Cahuenga Pass, fought on December 5, 1831. While the whole conflict had its ridiculous aspect (only two men were killed—one on each side), it had also a peculiarly colorful angle, and its final results were of inestimable importance to the future of the internal economy of California.

To citizens of Los Angeles, Hollywood, North Hollywood and other San Fernando Valley residents, the Cahuenga Pass is as familiar as Broadway to a New Yorker. Today U.S. Highway 101 funnels through it, as well as the double tracks of the Pacific Electric Railroad. Its eight lanes of fast freeways are ever teeming with traffic, and its overpasses, underpasses and ramp approaches facilitate this constant flow. It is unquestionably one of the busiest arteries in the world, for just below the pass, crossing through Hollywood and bisecting U.S. 101, is the U. S. transcontinental Highway 66.

While Don Gaspar de Portolá blazed the Royal Highway in 1769 he missed the pass and headed west, intending to follow the coast line north. Finding this impractical as he neared what is now Santa Monica, he turned through a more difficult pass (Sepulveda Canyon today) and came out in the San Fernando Valley. After his failure to recognize the elusive Bay of Monterey, Portolá and his weary soldiers staggered back to San Diego. It is probable that they located the Cahuenga Pass from its northern end, instead of returning through the mountains by way of Sepulveda Canyon, and thus were the first white men to go through it.

The Franciscans, on their way from San Gabriel to the next mission to the north—San Fernando Rey de España—invariably went around by way of the Los Angeles River through Ranchos Verdugo and Los Feliz, skirting the area that is now Griffith Park.

Eventually, as Los Angeles developed, the road through the Cahuenga Pass became more and more the main route. When the irate Governor Victoria led his miniature army south to mop up the rebels in 1831, he headed straight for the Cahuenga Pass. Lying in wait for him on the plain at the southern end of the pass at what would be approximately Hollywood Boulevard and Vine Street today, the heart of the movie capital, were the insurgents, several hundred strong.

It is to be wondered why José María Ávila, who commanded the rebels, didn't deploy his men and ambush the governor's army in the pass, and thereby wipe it out. And it is to be wondered why Victoria didn't attempt to come down on Los Angeles by following the Los Angeles River and the route the Franciscans used between missions San Fernando and San Gabriel. But both armies dispensed with subtlety and they met head-on.

Victoria's army was somewhat less than half the size of the insurgents, but he considered his opponents yellow dogs who would run at the sight of his show of power. The stage was all set for one grand scrap, but instead of a pitched battle it became a jousting match, much to every participant's surprise, and instead of this Hollywood fracas being played on a scale of D. W. Griffith's *Intolerance,* it turned out to be more in the nature of a Mack Sennett comedy.

Governor Victoria's army hauled up as it emerged from the pass and glared at the enemy a few hundred yards away, and the enemy glared back. Victoria demanded that all the insurgents surrender and come over to his side. They refused. Whereupon Victoria ordered his men to fire. The volley was returned by the rebels and the battle was on. But both sides had deliberately aimed over the heads of the other in the hope of scaring the other into submission.

At that moment the most incredible thing happened. Captain Pacheco, misunderstanding Victoria's commands in the noise and confusion, charged the rebels on horseback singlehanded. His weapon was a lance about six feet long.

Halfway between the two forces he realized that something had gone wrong, that he was alone, and he held back his horse.

But this display of defiance so incensed Captain Ávila of the rebels that *he* charged on horseback at full speed, *his* lance aimed for Pacheco.

Both armies stood with their mouths open at this unpremeditated turn of events, and Pacheco and Ávila went at it like knights of old. They charged, struck, parried, plunged past each other, wheeled their horses and charged again.

The whole battle had been reduced to a duello. Everyone instinctively understood that this was it, and this would be just about all of it, and the soldiers on both sides became not participants but spectators. Whatever would be the outcome of this engagement would be the outcome of the battle. Some sat down, some climbed trees to see better, and everybody relaxed and enjoyed it. As if it had been arranged beforehand, Captain Pacheco of the governor's forces was mounted on a black stallion and Captain Ávila's horse was pure white.

But Pacheco and Ávila were not in jest. Each sincerely wished to kill the other, and for a third time they charged, lances pointed, full speed. Both men were superb horsemen and the match was equal. On one side Monterey roared, and on the other Los Angeles.

Then King's Mountain versus The Angels came to an abrupt end. Pacheco on his black horse forced Ávila on the white to lose his lance. As again they turned Ávila was so infuriated that he pulled a pistol from his belt and shot Pacheco dead.

This unsportsmanlike gesture so enraged the watching Victoria that *he* charged Ávila. Captain Ávila, surprised at what he had done, paused for a fatal second, and Governor Victoria shot *him* dead.

This so incensed Captain Portilla of the rebels that he charged the governor with his lance and ran him full through the face with it, tearing off a goodly portion of the governor's features.

The governor fell writhing to the ground, fainted in his agony, and the battle was over.

None of the spectators, formerly combatants, had the slightest inclination to carry on the fight. If battles must be fought, it is a pity they can't all follow this pattern. Most of the participants enjoyed it, and while two men were dead and the governor gravely wounded, the bloodshed had indeed been held down to a minimum. Everybody went home.

The rebels fell back on Los Angeles.

The government troops repaired to Mission San Gabriel where the moaning and gasping Victoria received medical treatment.

Thus was the first blood shed between Californians and Mexicans and it must have created conversation for many days.

Governor Victoria, suffering from shock and loss of blood, released a statement of abdication as he lay recuperating in Mission San Gabriel. He wanted no more of California; he would return to Mexico as soon as he could travel. Knowing that former Governor Echeandía was still in San Diego, he sent word to him of his immediate abdication, and requested Echeandía to act as governor until the clouded affairs of state could be cleared. Echeandía accepted and at once called the *diputación* into convention. The members met in Los Angeles. A few weeks later ex-Governor Manuel Victoria sailed from the port of San Pedro never to return to California. As someone quite properly and literally put it, "He hadn't even been able to save his face."

It would seem that this lucky turn of affairs would keep California from further violence, and to a large extent it did, but it served only to complicate the local political scene until 1833.

Echeandía, quite naturally, assumed that he was again governor, even if only until a new executive could be sent from Mexico City. But the *diputación* that Echeandía had called appointed Pío Pico temporary governor. When the people of Monterey heard of this, they were indignant, and they arbitrarily appointed and accepted one Agustín Vicente Zamorano, a man who had been secretary to Echeandía and a citizen of Monterey, as the *real* new governor pro tem.

So, look at it as history will, California had three governors at once—and actually none. This chaotic state of affairs lasted until January 14, 1833. During that interlude from December 1831, San Diego with Echeandía, Los Angeles with Pico and Monterey with Zamorano, each considered itself the capital city on the Royal Highway. The reverberations of the Battle of Cahuenga Pass that ousted Governor Victoria were indeed felt throughout the territory. All this scramble for power came to an end, however, when the ultimate effect of the battle resulted in President Bustamente of Mexico (who was none too secure in his own office) sending José Figueroa to govern California.

Figueroa arrived by ship at Monterey, and that town was again formally the capital. As a contrast to Victoria, who had been the worst, Figueroa was probably the best of the Mexican governors.

The very first thing he did was to grant an act of amnesty to all who had taken part in the Battle of Cahuenga Pass. It was over; it was to be forgotten; and California was to start anew with a clean slate. Everybody liked that. This new governor, who was certainly not prepossessing to look upon—he was part Spanish and part Aztec, stoop-shouldered, thick-set, with black hair, piercing eyes and buck teeth—was somehow able to inculcate confidence wherever he went. He was polite, democratic and—don't overlook it—part Indian. Moreover, he had an excellent education. With all of this, he treated the most ragged Costanoan neophyte with the same courtesy he used for visiting officials. He made a trip to San Francisco and then down the Royal Highway to San Diego and back to Monterey. He was not an "indoor" governor; he wanted to see the land and the people firsthand.

With Figueroa on his ship had been eleven Zacatecan friars. These men had been sent to replace the aging Franciscans, and they took over the seven northernmost missions, or all those north of San Carlos Borroméo at Carmel. These men were of Mexican birth, rather than Spanish as had been the first of the Franciscans, and were men of inferior mental and moral stature. Immediately there was trouble and strife at all seven missions.

This served only to re-emphasize the old issue of church versus state. In 1833 the Mexican congress passed a bill ordering the immediate secularization of all the missions in California. As governor, it was up to Figueroa to do it.

It was Figueroa's major problem and he handled it judiciously. Some historians say that Figueroa was the man who "ruined the missions," but that is patently ridiculous. The mission system ruined itself and was well on the way to extinction under Governor Echeandía, only to be given a stay of execution by the incompetent Manuel Victoria.

Figueroa was a practical man and, even though Indian blood ran in his veins, he was quick to see that an immediate transfer of all mission properties, except the buildings and their contents, to the California Indians would not be feasible. A gradual evolutionary plan in slow stages, carefully supervised, was the only possible method that would bring about the desired results. The reason for this was all too obvious, and had been pointed out by visitors such as Laperouse and Vancouver—namely, the Indian was hardly more than six years old mentally and was not equipped for the responsibilities of full citizenship. It was an anomaly that Figueroa understood clearly. Strip the missions of their lands and deed them to the Indians, and most of the Indians would cease to work the lands. They would trade them for liquor or gamble them away to any unscrupulous scalawag who could manage to infiltrate his grasping desires into the Indians' naïve idiosyncrasies. It was a dual problem of how to emancipate the downtrodden Indian from the mission system, and at the same time save the Indian from himself.

Figueroa solved it with his famous document *Reglamento Provisional para la Secularización de las Misiónes de Alta California* and this edict was one of the first papers printed on the first printing press to reach California by the territory's first printer, Agustín Zamorano.

This is the same Zamorano who was secretary to Governor Echeandía, and who, in turn, became one of the three more or less simultaneous governors of California during the period after Victoria and before Figueroa. When a legitimate governor finally arrived at Monterey, Zamorano was happy to step down and be a secretary and printer again.

A word about Zamorano's press is in order. It was a sorry mess. It came from Boston, where it might well have been sold for junk. Zamorano had expressed a desire for a printing press as early as 1829 to a *yanqui* sea captain who promised to bring him one. The name of this Bostonian who is responsible for California's first press should not be overlooked. He was Thomas Shaw, and he stowed on board his ship, the *Lagoda,* this old relic which Zamorano received in 1834. It had two fonts of battered type, and was a press of the same kind used by Benjamin Franklin in Philadelphia a hundred years before. It would not be improper to estimate the age of Zamorano's press when he received it as about fifty years old, and probably more.

Zamorano printed a few handbills and some government documents, and among other incidentals a notice—*Aviso al Publico*—that he was offering printing service with "greatest punctuality and care" and hoping to find "gentlemen who may wish to start a periodical."

Unhappily, no gentleman did.

But Zamorano did have the job of setting up and printing the most important governmental statement in the history of California up to 1834, a pamphlet of 184 pages, and it was Governor Figueroa's edict secularizing the missions.

Those among the Indians who were of sufficient responsibility were given farms, seed, domestic animals and farming implements. Only ten missions of the twenty-one were to be secularized at once, and the others were to follow this pattern over a period of years. At no mission must more than half the land and livestock be turned over to the Indians. The other half must still be under control of the mission itself. The padres were to continue their religious endeavors with no change. In time the remaining half of the land and livestock would revert to the Indians provided they had proved their ability to utilize the first half properly. The Indian who accepted a farm could not sell it at once or give it away or gamble it away. If he took it, he had to use it. All this was to be executed by commissioners who would be appointed by the governor at the recommendation of the *diputación*. Each mission would in reality become a small town, or pueblo, with the parish church at the center and the outlying farms in the possession of the parishioners.

The plan was carefully thought out, and Figueroa tried hard to see that this great social and economic change from feudalism to private enterprise did not get out of hand.

He was in for something of a surprise in the field of Indian psychology. For these people were no longer the wild aboriginal type who lived for one thing only—escape. These Indians were now third and fourth-generation Mission Indians and they knew nothing better. Of the fifty-nine most intelligent Indians at Mission San Diego de Alcalá, only two wanted to take up land and

Photo courtesy of California Mission Trails Association

The Gaviota Pass, where the Santa Barbarans lay in wait for Frémont and his men—and waited in vain

Padre Junípero Serra   Don Mariano G. Vallejo

Agustín Iturbide, first emperor of Mexico,
and thereby the first and only emperor
of California

hold it as private property. The other fifty-seven were content to live in their virtual slavery.

At Mission San Luís Rey farms were offered to the Indian heads of 108 families. Only ten accepted.

In other words the Indian didn't want to be a farmer. If forced into it as a slave laborer, he would farm, but, if given his personal choice, he wasn't interested in agriculture at all. Figueroa was faced with the change-over from feudalism to private enterprise only to discover that those offered the opportunity of freedom and the right to practice private enterprise weren't even able to comprehend what it meant. It was a social anomaly indeed, but with infinite patience and careful administration and wise overseeing the actual secularization began. Figueroa would probably have been able to carry it out over a period of years without the evils of graft and corruption. But unfortunately, and to California's great loss, this capable governor dropped dead of apoplexy in Santa Barbara on September 29, 1835. He was mourned by everybody. His loss meant the loss of a wise and guiding hand and mind when both were sorely needed. Once his influence was gone chaos resulted. Californians seemed to sense it, and there were demonstrations of grief throughout the territory. Few Californians today, however, know or care that the remains of Governor José Figueroa lie under the sanctuary floor of the Mission Santa Barbara.

Thus the period between the arrival of Manuel Victoria in 1831 and the subsequent Battle of Cahuenga Pass, and the death of Figueroa in 1835, marked the end of any really constructive policy on the part of Mexico City with regard to California.

The power of the church had been broken. Land grants to individuals were increasing. The Indian was found to be an incompetent misfit. New governors arrived who had no knowledge of the territory's problems. And life along the Royal Highway was heading toward a condition of economic and political uncertainty that meant more trouble ahead, if not outright disaster. It was a state of affairs that could not continue. It meant the coming end of Mexican control of California. To the handful of Americans who were living in the territory, the sooner Mexico cracked the better. After Figueroa anything could happen. And scarcely ten years later came the end.

Adios

15

"IT WAS the best of times, it was the worst of times," might very well have been a description of the last decade of Mexican rule in California as well as the opening sentence of *A Tale of Two Cities*.

Certainly, in many respects, it was the best of times that California had known even if there wasn't an inn in which to spend a night or a physician to call in an emergency, the length of the Royal Highway. In the 1840s a traveler was still dependent on the hospitality of the rancheros, and if he fell off his horse and broke his leg, the host would give him a tumbler of brandy to drink while a ranch hand sawed his leg off.

There was plenty to eat and nobody had to worry about survival. In a market in Los Angeles or San Jose or Monterey, a dozen quail cost the equivalent of 25 cents. A pound of jerked beef cost 3 cents. Fresh beef was only 1 cent a pound and there was so much of it running around on the hoof that it was foolish to go to a market and buy it. Instead, simply rope a steer with your lariat and drag it home with you. Then it wouldn't cost even a cent a pound for your fresh meat and you had all the by-products as well, such as the tallow and the hide. And who owned the animal before you roped it? Nobody could say for sure; there were too many animals to count. A saddle horse would cost from $3.00 to $10 depending upon the age and fitness of the animal. The saddle, being more difficult to obtain, might cost as much as $14 or $15. Mules cost a little more than horses as they were beasts of burden and more in demand. A fancy petticoat for your wife or daughter might be as much as $1.50. You could buy a whole sheep for 75 cents, but fresh eggs were rare and outlandish in price at 20 cents a dozen. Fruit was something you couldn't find in the market. It wasn't worth the merchant's putting it in, as everyone had his own fruit trees and hence all the oranges and lemons and peaches and pomegranates he could use. But if you looked far enough you might find a basket of 100 or more oranges for 3 cents, including the basket. A hundred pounds of fine flour would be $1.25, and a bushel basket of beans would reduce your purse by 15 cents. Coffee and tea were rare and usually reserved for special occasions, but wine flowed freely. A *caballero's* typical breakfast might be some tortillas, a beefsteak, a few vegetables (probably beans or chick-peas) and a bottle of wine. He might have a fowl and some cheese for luncheon, and more beef and vegetables for dinner, with fruit and wine for desert or perhaps some brandy. Drinking for its own sake was not heavy and intoxicated people were almost never seen.

This same *caballero* might cut quite a dashing figure as he rode his horse along the Royal Highway. His shoes would probably be made of deerskin and embroidered with gold and silver thread. His trousers would probably be cut from black broadcloth, open at the sides below the knees, or might even be made of velvet. Around his waist he'd wear a sash of red satin. He'd have an open-necked shirt, largely concealed by a waistcoat of blue or gray or black velvet with gold or silver braid. On his head he'd wear a broad-brimmed hat, not quite the type we know today as a sombrero, but somewhat larger than the cowboy Stetson. This hat might have a cord around the crown of silver or gold thread, and would surely have a chin strap to prevent its being blown off in a hard gallop against the wind. Even the horse would be caparisoned, and at the pommel of the saddle there would be a lariat. Spurs were not the habitual custom, contrary to popular belief, but were worn at all times if the *caballero* happened to be wearing boots.

If you passed over the Royal Highway at any time between 1836 and 1846, you would be certain to meet this gentleman or someone very similar, just as you would be certain to meet a number of Fords or Buicks or Cadillacs along the highway today.

Should you spend the night at the *caballero's* rancho, which would probably include 40,000 acres of mountains, valleys, pastures, farms, creeks and woodlands, you'd live in his adobe ranch house, made of sun-dried bricks of mud and straw. The rancho itself would be entirely self-sustaining as an economic unit. All the rest of California could fall into the sea, but a good-sized rancho could survive on its own products.

The *caballero's* wife might be dressed somewhat more conservatively than her husband. In the California of the later Mexican period the males wore the plumage. But the dress of the wife would be none the less colorful by modern standards. She would have a gown of silk or crepe, with short sleeves, rather snug-fitting at her waist and falling in voluminous flounces to her feet. Under her dress there would be one or more petticoats. Corsets, brassieres and the general "foundation" garments of today were unknown. She had a figure and it was fat or thin as nature endowed, and there was no concealing it either way. A brightly colored sash was *de rigueur*. Shoes were made of doeskin, and every woman wore earrings and one or two necklaces. Hats were rare. The *rebozo,* or shawl, served as a headdress unless the lady were exposed to the sun for a day's horseback ride. In that case she would wear a broad-brimmed hat similar to her husband's. Or if she were on foot she would surely carry a parasol. Indoors, her headdress would be a large tortoise-shell comb, unless she happened to be quite a young girl, in which case her hair would probably be plaited in two long braids.

By this decade—1836 to 1846—or let's say, arbitrarily, the year 1840, the Spanish amenities and customs had been changed by a generation or two of local conditioning. These people were no longer Spaniards in their own eyes, and, while politically they were

Mexicans, they considered Mexico City as far away as Madrid. As for themselves, the expression was, "I, a Mexican? Señor, I am a Californian!"

The population began to increase geometrically. Almost everyone married; bachelors and old maids were virtually unknown. Girls were married quite young, sixteen being considered a normal age. All marriage arrangements were completed between the prospective bridegroom and the girl's parents, or between the parents of both families. During this period of consideration (nothing was ever hurried among the Californians) the young pair hardly ever met. Perhaps they might exchange quick and shy glances at church, or might converse through the language of flowers. The institution of the serenade was prevalent. At night the young swain would strum a guitar outside the window of his beloved, and she might, or might not, whisper sweet words of encouragement to him through the open, but barred, window.

Weddings were popular social events, and the celebrating often lasted for three or four days of music, dancing, games, food and wine. Most marriages were quickly blessed with children. Californians were prolific. The average family had eight to ten children, and it was not at all unusual for a couple to produce fourteen or sixteen.

Intermarriage was not frowned upon and occurred to such an extent that almost everyone was related to almost everyone else. Marriage of cousins was taken for granted; everyone called every one else "cousin" anyway, even if such a relationship did not exist.

Education, which the better run of governors under both Spain and Mexico strove to encourage, never made much headway. Lack of funds, incompetent teachers, indifference on the part of parents and discouragement on the part of the church made public education a weak and pitiful institution. Also the absence of books in the territory was a great misfortune. At the time of secularization, the twenty-one missions had a total of approximately 3,000 volumes, all on religious subjects and many in Latin. Books that might provoke thought seemed to be feared by the church. The Carrillo family in Santa Barbara bought a small library from one of the captains of a "Boston" boat, only to have the contents branded as seditious by the Franciscans and the books eventually burned in spite of a flat protest from Governor Echeandía.

When José Figueroa became governor there were only three small schools functioning between San Diego and San Francisco. He established six more schools and raised the meager salary of the teachers.

A number of books were smuggled into the territory and a few private libraries began to grow. At the time of Mexican collapse in 1846 William E. P. Hartnell had built up a small private library and he was willing to lend his books to his friends. Don Pablo de la Guerra, in Santa Barbara, collected several shelves of scientific and medical books which he wisely kept under lock and key. John Marsh, in Los Angeles, was said to have built up a sound library of history and literature. But it can safely be said that the average Californian of what Gertrude Atherton called "the splendid idle forties" never read a book in his life. Magazines and periodicals, of course, were nonexistent, and throughout the Mexican period there wasn't even a newspaper.

Medical science was in such a state that it would probably have been wiser to conceal an ailment than to announce it and seek treatment. The redoubtable and questionable James Ohio Pattie brought vaccine into the area for the first time and may—or may not—have done much to quell or retard the spreading of small-pox. Anesthetics and sterilization of instruments were unheard of. "Bleeding" was the first choice as a cure for almost anything, and various herbs were prescribed for complaints ranging from child-birth to senility.

For a toothache a certain cure was to place in the mouth of the sufferer the eyetooth of a black dog. To cure cancer boil rosemary leaves in red wine and take internally. For kidney ailments eat four ounces of fresh butter and drink half a pint of white wine without ceasing to swallow. Sinus sufferers were relieved by eating the white meat of a hen stewed in wine. For fever, powdered soot, salt and sage, mixed with the white of an egg, and placed in a sack and tied at the patient's wrist would relieve him in twelve hours—unless he died.

For jaundice the cure was a diet of radishes and sugar, accompanied by a poultice placed over the heart, but it had to be made of a cloth dyed with cochineal. This was also considered good for minor mental disorders such as melancholia, lovesickness and jealousy. To gain in wisdom, simply sniff powdered mustard seed three times a day and the intelligence quotient would soar.

Californians considered themselves far from being medically impoverished, but, on the contrary, to be living in a land of especial health largely due to such natural endowments as the leaves of the swallowwort which cured eye troubles; cascara which was good for the bowels; *yerba santa* (holy plant) which would cure respiratory complaints; stewed young ferns which would eliminate tapeworm; a compress of gray sage which would heal cuts and bruises; and the roots of wild cucumbers which were a soporific. Every rancho had its herb garden which was considered much the same as later generations came to accept the corner drugstore.

So life was good along the Royal Highway in the 1840s and to a Californian it was "the best of times" in many ways that were personal and intimate, and it was "the worst of times" only in the stress and strain of politics and religion. As for the Indian, he didn't matter because he didn't think.

During the eleven years between the death of Governor José Figueroa in 1835 and the end of the Mexican maze in 1846, California had *eight* governors. This, in itself, is enough to indicate the confused political state of affairs. It is useless to follow these men in the sequence and turmoil of their offices at Monterey, but it is better for clarity's sake to get an over-all picture of just what went on during this chaotic period when the Mexican administration literally came apart at the seams.

There were four events that were of indisputable significance to those who lived along the Royal Highway. The first was the completion of the secularization of all twenty-one missions, the second was the great increase in the number of private land grants, the third was the internal political fighting and jockeying for power by men of mostly second or third-rate abilities, and the fourth was the abandonment of Fort Rossya by the Russians and its purchase by a man named Johann August Sutter who was, unbeknown to himself or anyone else, indirectly destined to alter the course of California history.

The eight remaining Mexican governors vacillated between six or seven in favor of secularization and one or two who wanted to restore the mission system.

When the first official moves were made under Governor Figueroa to break up this feudalistic system, it was estimated that the twenty-one missions had under cultivation almost 200,000 acres of land, owned 245,000 cattle, 65,000 horses and 320,000 sheep, and had as slave laborers 20,000 Indians.

Meanwhile the number of private land grants which had been held down to less than fifty up to 1823, increased rapidly as the mission economy cracked wide open. The era of the mission, a Spanish institution, gave way to the era of the privately owned and usually equally feudalistic rancho, a Mexican institution. When the Mexican government lost all control of California in 1846 there were at least 700, and possibly closer to 800, private ranchos. And by that time the twenty-one missions were a shambles and many were abandoned ruins. It was a sorry end to Padre Serra's dream.

Yet the missions had never been intended, even by the government of Spain, to hold the land in perpetuity. They were to be a religious and colonizing force, and then to become parish churches while the Franciscans moved to pastures new. In fact, in the original Spanish plan the Franciscans were supposed to Christianize and civilize the Indians in ten years, and then move on. The patent impossibility of doing any such thing with the Indians in ten years (ten generations would have been a better estimate) was quickly apparent, and the mission system considered itself, *ipso facto,* the heir to the soil.

The long struggle between church and state finally was won by the state, and the ranchero—or don or *caballero*—replaced the padre as the outstanding figure in California.

What really wrecked the mission system by pulling the props out from under it was not only secularization, but the seizure by the Mexican government of the famous Pious Fund.

Years before the Franciscans were in power, the Jesuits, be it remembered, in Baja California under such men as Kino, Salvatierra and Ugarte, had been denied funds for their efforts by the Spanish government. So these three men—largely due to the efforts of Juan Ugarte—financed their project by means of private collections of money poured into a treasury called the Pious Fund. This money was given over to the jurisdiction of the Franciscans when Charles III of Spain so vigorously expelled all Jesuits in 1768. The Franciscans carried it on through the years, and the religious rich made constant donations to it in order to ease their road to heaven.

In 1842 the Mexican government removed the Pious Fund from church authority and incorporated it into the national treasury. It had no right to do so, but there was no means of stopping it. The government literally seized the money and "held it" for the church. Graft and corruption and theft and bribery followed, and in turn came litigation. The church sued for its rightful money. By the time all this got into the courts, California had passed from Mexico and had become the thirty-first state of the United States of America. The case went through Mexican and American courts, was appealed to an English referee, was complicated by cross complaints, countercharges and demands for accrued interest, made headlines in 1869, 1875 and 1891, and finally wound up at the Tribunal of Arbitration at The Hague in 1902. It was the first case to be tried by the World Court. By that time the accrued interest alone was almost $1,500,000,000. The court decided Mexico owed the church the accrued interest on the capital and that it should be paid in installments to the United States to give, in turn, to the Catholic Church in California. The court could make the decision but the court did not have the power to enforce the judgment. To this date the Mexican government has never paid one cent. Jesuit Juan Ugarte, when he conceived of the Pious Fund, could little have guessed the swathe it would cut through history. And it is not over yet.

At any rate, Mexico's seizure of the church's money in 1842, hardly an honorable move, was one more telling blow in the destruction of the mission system.

With the secularization under way, one of the last of the great Franciscans died on the altar at Mission Nuestra Señora de la Soledad as he delivered a sermon. He was Padre Vicente Francisco Sarría, a native of Bilbao, Spain. He was a fine man of the Padre Serra tradition, a scholar and an executive, devoutly religious and with it all tolerant and compassionate. His death epitomized the end of the entire mission system and the end of the type of men who had brought it to flower only to see it go to seed.

In 1845 Governor Pío Pico completed the secularization. By this time, instead of following Figueroa's carefully thought-out evolutionary plan, it was a scramble to see who could get what. Church property was simply stolen and carted away. The buildings themselves that Figueroa had intended to make into parish churches were sold outright. Two men, Forster and McKinley, bought Mission San Juan Capistrano for $710. Purísima Concepción was sold to John Temple for $1,110. Scott, Wilson and McKinley bought

Mission San Luís Obispo de Tolosa for $510. Nicholas Den and Daniel Hill leased Mission Santa Barbara for $1,200 a year, and a number of others also were rented, notably Santa Inés, San Buenaventura and San Fernando.

Padre Narciso Durán, the last president of the California missions, died in 1846. No other president was appointed. There was no need for one. The missions were history.

Meanwhile the political scene in the 1840s was as confused as ever. There were right and left-wing governors—and governors who were first one and then the other and who blew hot or blew cold as their personal advantages dictated.

What California needed was a strong and courageous leader who was a Californian at heart, a man who could say with Virgil, "The noblest motive is the public good," and proclaim an independent Republic of California. But such a man was not to be found on the Royal Highway in those troublesome times. Moves and feints were made in this direction but nothing really constructive was accomplished. There was a "home rule" movement that got nowhere, although it might well have done so had its sponsors had the courage to fight for it. Lack of unity among the Californians themselves was another deterrent. San Diego was jealous of Monterey and both mistrusted Los Angeles and her leading citizen Pío Pico, who wished that city to be the capital.

Among the governors who came and went was Manuel Micheltorena, who might have been a capable executive. Leading Californians, however, were not convinced of his integrity, and along with him, to see that he had the power to keep himself in office and not be unceremoniously booted out, Mexico City sent a small battalion made up of ex-convicts and banished felons. The governor was welcomed at San Diego, but that town breathed a sigh of relief when his "army" of thieves and cutthroats escorted him north over the Royal Highway. In spite of the felons, all along the road Micheltorena was made welcome, the people promptly forgetting ideas of home rule and seizing the arrival of the new governor as an opportunity for fiestas, dinners, dances, rodeos and bull fights.

Meanwhile the missions decayed and the plight of the Indian was worse than ever. Some took to the hills, but the majority hung around the missions, or worked now and then for food at the ranchos, or drifted to the towns of San Diego, Los Angeles and San Jose. Those that took up land soon abandoned it, or gambled it away for a pittance, or traded vast acreages for a few bottles of *aguardiente,* a cheap and fiery brandy. Rascals and scalawags soon had the Indian's inheritance and the Indian hardly seemed to know it.

Micheltorena managed to stay in office a little over two years, but it was a period of minor uprisings and near revolution. A second (and this time bloodless) "battle" of Cahuenga Pass occurred in which Micheltorena's soldiers engaged in a two-day artillery duel with insurgents from the south under Juan Alvarado and José Castro. Both sides carefully remained well out of range of the other until the ammunition was exhausted and then the battle was over. The casualty was one dead horse. The result of the issue was Micheltorena's promise to send his jailbird Mexican army—ostensibly present to keep order but which kept itself drunk, and looted and stole because it never was paid, and made the streets unsafe for women whom it was supposed to protect—back to Mexico.

But Micheltorena didn't dare send his soldiers back and when it was apparent he intended to do nothing but let *status quo* reign, there was more trouble. Foreigners began to take sides. Johann Sutter supported Micheltorena; Abel Stearns supported Alvarado and Castro, who, in turn, were supporting Pío Pico for a second try at being governor. When things got too far out of hand somebody suggested a fandango, and again there was music and dancing and wine and flirting and bullfighting and bearbaiting.

Micheltorena finally decided it was wiser to leave California to the Californians, for if someone were to shoot him, which might happen any day or night, it would certainly be done to music! So he "resigned" and left California to its own devices. This was in March of 1845. That was the moment for California to rise on its own feet if ever there was a moment, but instead everybody gave parties to celebrate the sailing of Micheltorena and his convict army, and nobody seemed to know what to do but install Pío Pico as governor pro tem until Mexico City sent a new and, to be hoped, capable man.

That man never arrived.

Something else happened.

Manuel Micheltorena was the last Mexican governor of California. When the Californians said *Adios* to him it was really good-by to all things Mexican, although at the time nobody knew it.

While it took California some time to hear of it, and a little while to digest it, the news, when it was eventually told and retold up and down the Royal Highway, was stunning and staggering. California, after all, was a part of Mexico. On May 13, 1846, a man unknown in California, named President James K. Polk, had asked the Congress of the United States of America, on the basis of unprovoked aggression, for a declaration of war on the Republic of Mexico. The American Congress acted on the President's message and declared war.

PART 4

AMERICAN INFLUX

1846 to 1850

T*he Gringo*

BEFORE the actual war between Mexico and the United States began in 1846, there was a strange preliminary incident in 1842 that had international reverberations with a seriocomic ending.

On October 19, 1842, Monterey was resting quietly as usual. The soldiers of the garrison were either asleep or in the town or drunk or making love. The ammunition was almost exhausted and not a gun or a cannon had been fired in months. Most of the ordnance was in such bad repair that to fire it would have been a great risk to those who did the firing.

Then, to the amazement of the town, all the citizens of which came down to the beach to watch, and to the utter consternation of the commandante of the presidio, who hurriedly put on his trousers and his medals, three warships sailed into the harbor, fired a salute and maneuvered themselves into position to destroy the town. They were the frigate *United States,* and the sloops of war *Cyane* and *Dale.* The commander of the squadron was Thomas Ap Catesby Jones, and he demanded the immediate surrender of the port, the presidio, the pueblo and the people in the name of the United States of America. He gave the commandante, who had his trousers on but was still pinning on his medals, just twelve hours to turn over Monterey in unconditional surrender or face annihilation. The trembling commandante surrendered at once, and felt much better thereby. Now nothing could happen—he hoped.

Commodore Jones sent a landing force ashore and occupied first the garrison and then the town. American sailors hauled down the Mexican flag and raised the Stars and Stripes. Nobody objected and everybody was polite and Jones cautioned his men to accept this quick victory with formal propriety. There must be no pillaging, looting or rape.

Mariano Silva was the commandante, and he ventured to ask why the Americans had come.

Jones explained that the United States and Mexico were at war and that California was now occupied by the fighting force of the United States. He demanded to see the governor at once and receive his formal surrender of not only Monterey, but the entire territory, including Arizona, Utah and Nevada as well.

Then Jones was told that there was no governor, but that, as far as they knew, the Californians were getting a new one who was at this time somewhere on his way up the Royal Highway and should arrive in a few weeks. His name was Manuel Micheltorena, and he would be most surprised, for, to the best of any Californian's knowledge, there was no war between the United States and Mexico, if you please.

After another twenty-four hours of careful investigation and questioning of such officials as seemed to be in office, Commodore Jones began to realize that he had acted too soon. What had touched him off had been the fact that Washington had sent him and his squadron to the Pacific to seize California in *case* of war or in *case* the territory was in danger of being seized by any foreign power. A British squadron under Rear Admiral Thomas was in the Pacific, cruising off South America and Central America. This squadron, with which Jones had made friendly contact, had suddenly sailed for a destination unknown. Jones had acted at once. He had been sent to the Pacific to grab California and he had no intention of remaining idle while somebody else did it. He had set a course for Monterey at full speed fully expecting to find the port bristling with defense, and perhaps the British squadron shelling it. Instead he had found the tiny capital utterly defenseless and thoroughly bewildered.

Jones then did the only decent thing. He apologized to the commandante; he sent a written apology by a Mexican messenger down the Royal Highway to meet the coming governor; he had his men haul down the American flag and restore the Mexican flag; he made a public statement of regret for this annoyance to the civilian population in behalf of President Tyler; and he had his flagship, the frigate *United States,* fire a salute to the Republic of Mexico.

The people of Monterey took no umbrage at Jones's premature seizure, but it gave Governor Micheltorena something to think about when he heard of it. For it certainly threw a clear light on the eventual intentions of the United States.

But Monterey smiled and shrugged it off, and Commandante Mariano Silva had a great idea. Why not give a ball and have a fiesta to celebrate the arrival of these Americans? For surely with them in port nobody else was going to take Monterey, and that was an occasion for a celebration. So again there were music and dancing and singing and a bullfight. And when all the tumult and shouting and protestations of undying friendship had died down, and the last bottle of wine had been consumed, Commander Jones said farewell and the American warships sailed out of the Bay of Monterey, leaving the town surprised, happy and probably a little heady.

The incident gave Mexico City pause, for it indicated how easily any foreign power could seize a defenseless California.

Some days later Governor Micheltorena and his ragged army of ex-convicts, called *cholos* (rascals) by the people along the Royal Highway, arrived in Monterey. Micheltorena made much of the incident. He reported the gross insult to Mexico City and embroidered it beautifully. According to his version, the cowardly Americans had fled when they learned he was marching up the

Royal Highway with his eager soldiers, spoiling for a fight and determined to drive the invading gringos into the sea. Jones, apparently, had left just in time to escape utter destruction. But let not these *yanquis* think they could get away with any such outrage! For Governor Micheltorena demanded not an apology but the payment of an indemnity. He wanted 1,500 new uniforms, $15,000 in cash and a complete set of military musical instruments! Needless to say, the demand is still resting in the limbo of unfinished business.

President Tyler was followed in office by James K. Polk, who, from a Mexican point of view, was the biggest gringo of them all. Polk was a combination of Jacksonian democracy, rabid expansionism and Scotch Presbyterianism. His temperament had little sympathy, accord or rapport with things Mexican. His foreign policy had one undeviating aim, and that was to make everything north of the Rio Grande to the Pacific Coast a part of the United States. He was not a warmonger but he certainly was willing to go to war if all else failed.

Polk's first move was an attempt to buy California and New Mexico—this latter included Arizona—from the Mexican government. This was not easy to do for two reasons: one, Mexico was still smarting over losing Texas which had broken away and become an independent nation only to join, almost at once, the United States; and two, no Mexican administration seemed able to stay in office long enough to accomplish anything constructive or even begin negotiations. Mexico had had seventeen revolutions in twenty-five years. No president could trust anyone around him, and no president knew if he would live to see the next sunrise or not. To make a purchase from a government like that was tenuous, to say the least, for the next administration might repudiate it.

Feeling that Texas had been filched from her and that the United States had backed Texan independence as a mere pretext for the ulterior motive of incorporating it into the Union, Mexico broke off diplomatic relations. President Polk's emissary for the purchase of New Mexico and California, John Slidell of New Orleans, who was well versed in Mexican relations and who spoke excellent Spanish, was rebuffed. President Herrera of Mexico refused to see him.

Herrera might gladly have sold the territory wanted by the United States, but he dared not do so, for it would merely invite revolution. The whole Slidell mission was supposed to be a secret in order to protect Herrera and to get the deal set before any other foreign power could approach Mexico for the purchase of California. The secret was soon public, and it was rumored in Mexico City that Slidell had landed at Vera Cruz empowered to bribe Herrera with $1,000,000 for his own pocket if he would sell to the United States the territories of New Mexico and California. While this was not the case, it effectually upset the Herrera administration. The Mexican president fled for his life—and made it. Slidell was unable to get anywhere with the new government under President Paredes, possibly because he did not produce the check for $1,000,000 as an opening wedge. Disgusted with Mexican politics, Slidell sailed for Washington and reported to President Polk that it was impossible to do business with Mexico simply because there was no such thing as a stable Mexican government. So Polk's first efforts came to nothing.

But that was just enough to rouse the Scotch in him, and he vowed that by one of four means, plus the coat of whitewash known as "Manifest Destiny," the United States should and would acquire California.

Since the first means, that of direct purchase, had failed, there remained three others. The Californians might revolt against Mexico's injurious and pusillanimous policies and set up an independent state. That was the Texas pattern. If the Californians wished to do that, the United States would, quite naturally, not be disinterested.

A third possibility lay in the power of the Americans who were already citizens of California and hence Mexican subjects. If the native Californians lacked the initiative and the courage to revolt, the gringo citizens might seize power and proclaim a government of their own which would be the true government of California organized by Americans for the protection of Americans and their interests. The United States would recognize such a government and would welcome it into the Union.

A fourth possibility was a declaration of war on Mexico and an immediate military occupation of the desired area.

That this last was not new with Polk is proved by the Commodore Jones "affair" under President Tyler in 1842. But Polk placed war last and tried the other means first.

Curiously enough Polk was inaugurated on almost the same day that Governor Micheltorena abdicated and became, thereby, the last Mexican appointed governor of California. Polk came into the presidency on March 5, 1845, and Micheltorena sailed from Monterey with his ragged army of Mexican ex-convicts—the *cholos*—on March 10, 1845. From March 5, 1845, one of the most important influences in California was a man who had never seen it, Gringo President James K. Polk. From that date on, the future of California and the character of life along the Royal Highway was no longer to be determined by Mexico City, but by Washington.

What President Polk understood at once was the fact that, if internal rumblings of independence were going on in California, he needed to know it. To learn such things, he needed a man on the scene who could keep him constantly advised of what was going on and of when to strike. Who was that man?

President Polk found him in the person of a gentleman by the name of Thomas O. Larkin. The man was from Massachusetts. That sounded good to begin with. He had arrived in California in 1832, and this gringo was well liked by Californians and other

Americans as well. He had traveled the length of the Royal Highway and he resided in Monterey. He was a businessman, a merchant, an importer and a respected citizen. In 1843 President Tyler had appointed him United States Consul to California. He is the only man in history who has ever occupied such an office.

The fact that Polk opened discussions with Larkin even while Slidell was still trying to purchase California from the uncertain Mexican government shows plainly that Polk was determined not to stop with Plan One, but to start Plan Two at the same time, and not to stop until he had exhausted Plan Four—namely, war.

On October 17, 1845, Polk's Secretary of State, James Buchanan, appointed Thomas O. Larkin confidential agent for the State Department. Two copies of this appointment, along with instructions, were sent to Larkin—one by sea, which he received in good time, and the other by a personal messenger, in case the ship carrying the orders should be lost. The man sent to deliver this "message to García" was Lieutenant Archibald H. Gillespie. This type of work has been popularized as the "Secret Service" and more recently as the "Office of Strategic Services." Gillespie crossed Mexico disguised as a sufferer from tuberculosis seeking health in California. Not trusting his histrionic ability, and fearing capture by the Mexicans, Gillespie read and committed to memory the instructions to Larkin, and then destroyed the document.

So there was no doubt about Larkin getting his new orders, both written and oral. Larkin, weighing all matters carefully and reading as much as he could between the lines, decided that Secretary of State Buchanan's dispatch meant that he was to exert every effort, pull every wire and grease every palm for the peaceful annexation of California by the United States. Being a businessman he went at it at once in a businesslike way. There were a number of capable Americans in California who lived up and down the Royal Highway from San Diego to San Francisco. They were, of course, Mexican citizens, and a number of them had married the daughters of prominent California families. But they were still gringos and it was to the gringo that Larkin made quiet overtures.

He approached by letter or in person three important men who were widely separated along the Royal Highway. One was John J. Warner who had a huge rancho in the mountains back of San Diego. Another was Abel Stearns of Los Angeles. A third was Jacob Leese who lived in Sonoma, the site of Mission San Francisco Solano, not many miles north of San Francisco Bay and the northern terminus of the Royal Highway. Stearns, an influential character in the southern part of the territory, was secretly appointed a kind of subagent for Larkin. Stearns, be it remembered, had once been "banished" from California by the nincompoop governor, Manuel Victoria, and he had little love for Mexico.

Thus the infiltration of the gringo—or what might be designated in twentieth-century revolutionary terms as the "fifth column"—began its work.

Secretary of State Buchanan's instructions to Larkin were general, even bland, but none the less unmistakable. For one thing, he wanted it made clear that Washington was in no way fomenting a revolution in California. That was farthest from his thought. But just in case the Californians happened to consider the possibility—admittedly vague but not beyond consideration—of separating *themselves* from Mexico, the United States would be interested and might—just *might*—assume the role of adviser or even protector.

Also, if Mexico should be so dastardly as to *sell* California to any foreign powers which might as well remain unmentioned (England and France and Spain and Russia—just to make it plain), the United States would take action to prevent such a transaction and would, if necessary for the protection of the Californians, move in to prevent the territory from suffering such a fate.

Finally, since distance made communication long and arduous and since Thomas O. Larkin was on the scene and conversant with any and all exigencies, the President of the United States

wished him to know that he had that executive's full confidence
and that Thomas O. Larkin's discretion, in the matter of some un-
precedented event, would be trusted by the President should it be
necessary to make some move or express some policy without waiting to communicate with Washington.

In other words, James K. Polk handed Thomas O. Larkin a
signed blank check. All Larkin had to do was write in the words
"for California" and the United States would not only honor it
but fight for it.

There were a number of native Californians who were equally
as dissatisfied with the meaningless Mexican government as were
the territory's outstanding gringos. One of these was Don Mariano
Vallejo of Sonoma, and another was General José Castro of Monterey, who at one time had been acting governor following the
death of the capable Figueroa. Castro was in a mood to welcome a
change, and cautiously Thomas O. Larkin let him put two and
two together. Governor Pío Pico, however, was not tipped off to
the fact that anything subversive might be going on. Pico lived in
Los Angeles, and Larkin figured that Abel Stearns could take care
of that part of the territory.

One of Larkin's problems was to keep Castro's enthusiasm in
check. Castro was all for independence and wrote a prospectus for
a free California. That was all right in theory, but Larkin wanted
more political weight on his side before making any open declaration. Various meetings of leading citizens were held at key points
along the Royal Highway—juntas they were called—in which
many things were discussed from schools to sewerage, with occasionally a word or two on the possible benefits of future independence. The meetings, held at San Diego, Los Angeles, Santa
Barbara and San Jose, were not for the discussion of any one particular subject, said Larkin, but were merely being held to offer an
opportunity for Californians to get together to talk over any and
all pertinent problems. At almost every meeting, however, once
the local business had been settled, the discussion seemed inevitably

to turn to the idea of an independent California. Odd, but that's what happened. Larkin's seeds of propaganda were being sown very well, and unquestionably would have sprouted and even burgeoned had not two unforeseen events happened in that most significant year of 1846.

One was that President Polk found a way to aggravate Mexico into acts of aggressive violence along the Rio Grande, and therefore was able to ask Congress for a declaration of war with a straight face. This would not in itself have upset Larkin's whispering campaign for independence, but would merely have served to speed it up.

What did throw the royal monkey wrench into the works was the shortsighted and not too intelligent ambition of another gringo who had the unfortunate gift of always doing the right thing at precisely the wrong time. Then, when it did dawn on him that he had made a mistake, his method of correcting it was to make another and even greater error. This well-intentioned but politically clumsy dullard insisted on raising the American flag at the wrong time, and wrote like a zealous boy scout to Larkin, "We will fight to extremity and refuse quarter, trusting our country to avenge our death. We will, every man of us, die under the flag of our country."

This twelve-year-old jingoism was exactly the kind of thing that Larkin did not want. Nobody attacked this gringo and when he began to understand that he had not only made a fool of himself but emphasized American seizure at the very moment when it should have been kept quiet, he did the next worst thing. He pulled down the American flag from a peak where he had hoisted it near Monterey, and went to Sonoma and offered his support, military and forensic, to an abortive independence movement that had nothing to do with Larkin or Washington and only served to confuse the entire issue. The name of this bull in a California china shop was John C. Frémont.

"A Bear Always
Stands His Ground" ⎱ 17

BORN in Georgia (two authorities insist it was in South
Carolina) in 1813 of a French father and a Virginia-born mother,
John Charles Frémont might easily have been a President of the
United States. He was nominated for this office by the Republican
Party in 1856 when he was forty-three years old and was defeated
by James Buchanan, the Democrat's candidate, in a race that was
fairly close.

Frémont had a good education, and at the age of twenty-eight,
after serving in the West as a second lieutenant in the explorative
efforts of the United States Topographical Corps, he had the good
luck to marry the daughter of one of the most influential and pro-
expansionism senators, Thomas Hart Benton of Missouri.

Frémont would doubtless have made a better actor than a politician or statesman or soldier, for he dramatized almost everything
he did. He even eloped with Jessie Benton, although there seemed
no need for such a course as there was no strong parental objection
to the marriage.

At any rate, Papa Benton got his son-in-law a good job as leader
of a couple of Western expeditions devoted to scientific interests
on the surface, but secretly intended to open the Far West to
American influence and to find a way, if not too overt, in the seizing of Oregon and California. Thus the lieutenant became a captain and later a colonel and inevitably a general, and finally a
candidate for President.

The first two expeditions can be omitted as they had no relationship to life along the Royal Highway directly, although indirectly

the very presence of an officer of the Army of the United States in Oregon and California would indicate more than mere mild interest on the part of Washington, to say the least.

That at any time John C. Frémont lacked the courage and the stamina to stand by his decisions cannot honestly be said. He was brave and tenacious—courageous sometimes to the point of being foolhardy—and he was at no time a coward. The fact that his emotional nature was stronger than his intellect was not entirely his fault. The blame would have to be placed on genetics or psychiatry or God—or all three.

Frémont has been dubbed the "Pathfinder of the West," although this is not quite true. Wherever he went the trail had been blazed before, and he had the invaluable experience of the mountain men such as Kit Carson, Thomas Fitzpatrick, Joseph Walker and Alexis Godey, who at various times acted as his scouts and guides.

After two scientific and exploratory trips covering much of the West, Frémont made his third journey, starting in 1845, and after many hardships crossed the Sierra Nevada Mountains just hours ahead of being snowbound and facing death by starvation, and arrived at Sutter's Fort at the confluence of the American River with the Sacramento. There the expedition rested at what Sutter called his self-sufficient colony of "New Helvetia." This property of Sutter's was a land grant from the governor in 1841 of 49,000 acres of ground, with the proviso, of course, that Sutter, a Swiss, become a Mexican citizen. So Sutter became a "Mexican" although he considered himself a Californian, and he added to his property by purchasing the defunct Russian colony's leftover assets at Bodega Bay. At this time Sutter at his fort—later the site of the city of Sacramento—and Don Mariano Vallejo who lived at Sonoma were the two richest and most influential citizens north of San Francisco Bay.

Early in 1846 Frémont decided to pay a visit to California's capital, Monterey. The rough and tough mountain men of his expedition were recovering at Sutter's Fort, but they needed to be refitted with new equipment, supplies and horses. Frémont, therefore, called upon Thomas O. Larkin, United States Consul at Monterey. Thus, for the first time, expansionist President Polk's secret agent and expansionist Senator Benton's appraising son-in-law met. But Frémont had no secret orders or credentials to present to Larkin, and Larkin, always astute and considering his progress toward an independent California satisfactory, did not tip his hand. From a Mexican point of view, Frémont had no right to be in California at all. To reverse the figure, if a Mexican so-called "scientific and topographical" party had decided to "explore" Missouri at that time, Senator Benton and President Polk would have ordered them to leave or be driven out.

Governor Pío Pico was in Los Angeles, so Larkin introduced Frémont to General José Castro, military commander of California. Castro was civil and even pleasant, and Frémont was on his best behavior and acting the visiting gentleman. Castro then gave Frémont permission to convene his men at a rancho about a dozen miles south of the town of San Jose. The expedition of mountaineers, trappers, scientists, engineers and some Delaware Indians totaled about sixty persons. Frémont was supposed to stay in this place until his men were ready to march, and then he agreed he would leave California by the southern route, cross Arizona by the Gila River Valley and move on east.

Frémont, given an inch, took a yard and, after assembling his force near San Jose, did not stay there, but moved on south down the Royal Highway to the ranch of William E. P. Hartnell. Also Frémont, unable to control his tongue, openly boasted that his explorations had opened the way for 10,000 American colonists who would flock into Oregon and California within the next six months.

Castro was alarmed. He had great respect for Larkin and he

knew that Larkin, as an agent for Washington, would support a movement for an independent California. That was one thing. But Frémont, an expansionist senator's son-in-law, nosing about and not heeding instructions and bragging of a new and overwhelming American influx—that, to José Castro, was a horse of another color. An independent California was desirable, but a gringo California was not. Castro decided that Frémont was dangerous, that he might incite the gringos to seize power (President Polk's Plan Three), and that California would suddenly become an American territory. He wished for just one thing—for Frémont to pack up and get out.

Instead of that, Frémont with a refreshed and heavily armed band of sixty men was camped within striking distance of Monterey. Then the inevitable trouble began with an altercation over horses. Don Sebastián Peralta complained to Castro that Frémont's men had taken a number of his horses without payment. When he confronted one of Frémont's men about returning the animals, the big burly American spit a stream of tobacco juice and told Don Sebastián where he could go. Don Sebastián was affronted.

On February 20, 1846, the alcalde of Monterey summoned Frémont to court to explain and adjust the Peralta horse-stealing episode. Frémont was insulted. He refused to appear in any contemptible Mexican court, he, a captain in the United States Army! He wrote a curt reply, saying in effect that he was too important to be hailed into court by any California jackanapes, and that the complaints of those who hovered around his camp were the lies of tramps and thieves.

On the fifth of March Castro sent Frémont a final message. It was a peremptory order that he and his men leave California at once. If not, he would be driven out.

This gave Frémont the opportunity for exactly the kind of dramatics that he loved. He marched his forces up to a promontory known as Gavilan Peak (Hawk's Peak), built a crude log fort and raised the American flag over it. It was open defiance, and it dared Castro to attack. From his vantage point Frémont could see up and down the Royal Highway for many miles, and against an attacking force he had a fine impregnable position. So, for the second time, the Stars and Stripes flew over California. Commodore Thomas Ap Catesby Jones had flown his flag over Monterey for two days of international error in 1842. In 1846 Frémont kept his flag up for three days before hauling it down and marching away.

Castro's weak forces were marshaled but had not the strength to dislodge Frémont. They could, however, starve him out, something that did not seem to occur to this brilliant tactician when he made his childish display of temper.

Frémont sent a note to Larkin, part of which was quoted in the preceding chapter, full of saber-rattling and dying-at-his-post nonsense, and Larkin thought Frémont must have lost his senses. Not a shot had been fired. Frémont's actions made him something of an emotional fool. Larkin must indeed have heaved a long sigh to have this blundering idiot alienating the Californians and upsetting all his own good work. He didn't understand that Frémont simply couldn't help playing soldier.

After three days of waiting for the attack that never came, Frémont decided that he couldn't stay camped on Gavilan Peak forever where there was no water and no food. Under cover of darkness he hauled down the American flag and marched his men east, through the coast range and into the San Joaquin Valley. Here he turned north, instead of south toward the trail to Arizona as he had said he was going, and returned to Sutter's Fort.

The whole Hawk's Peak episode was ridiculous and unfortunate. Intelligent Californians and gringos alike were outraged by it. It made bad feeling all around and even started rumors such as the one that all American-born residents, Mexican citizens or not, would have to leave the country.

Having successfully upset Consul Larkin's applecart, Frémont proceeded to ruin all of Larkin's efforts, finally and conclusively, by his next move.

Shortly after the Hawk's Peak incident, Secretary of State Buchanan's special messenger, Lieutenant Archibald H. Gillespie, arrived in Monterey to deliver to Consul Larkin, verbatim, his authorization as secret agent and his instructions pertaining thereto. Larkin had already safely received these orders in writing, and Gillespie had simply been an extra precaution in case the written orders never arrived.

But it so happened that Gillespie had been entrusted with the delivery of other papers pertaining to Larkin's consular service—papers which were of routine business matters and which he had not thought it necessary to take the precaution of memorizing and destroying—and furthermore, he was carrying a packet of letters to be delivered to another party.

"Who?" inquired Larkin.

"A man named Frémont," said Gillespie.

"Good God!" said Larkin. "I thought we'd heard the last of him. Who are the letters from?"

"His father-in-law," explained Gillespie. "Senator Thomas Hart Benton of Missouri."

"Well," said Larkin with a quizzical smile as he stared out the window toward distant Gavilan Peak, "he went that way."

Lieutenant Gillespie was a man who took his duty seriously. After a rest of two days in Monterey, he set out to pursue and find Frémont. It was easy enough to trail Frémont to Sutter's Fort, and there Gillespie learned that Frémont and his party had gone north up the valley of the Sacramento River, ostensibly heading for Oregon instead of Arizona, although nobody was able to say why.

Pushing his pursuit, Gillespie overtook the Frémont party on the eighth of May, 1846, while they were camped on the shores of Klamath Lake just over the northern boundary of California in the territory of Oregon.

Exactly what was in the letters from Senator Benton to son-in-law Frémont has been the subject of many a long discussion. But the contents, declared to be in a "secret code" by Frémont which helped dramatize the whole business, caused the senator's son-in-law to do an about-face. His presence was needed in California. Of that he was now assured. No longer was he merely a leader of a scientific expedition, but he was at the same time the commander of an armed force whose purpose it was to safeguard the lives of Americans anywhere and everywhere. Frémont's explanation of how he felt after perusing and digesting the "secret code" has been quoted many times, but as his words indicate the reason for his subsequent actions, they may be quoted again: "His letters [Benton's] made me know distinctly that at last the time had come when England must not get a foothold; that we *must be first.* I was to *act,* discreetly but positively."

All well and good no doubt, but what Senator Benton seems always to have overlooked was the fact that his son-in-law's abilities to act discreetly were in no way commensurate with his talents to act positively. Frémont's idea of being discreet was to start a revolution. The result was the famous Bear Flag revolt, an incident of trivialities, gaucheries and alcoholism which was of little real significance in the long view, but which was a sensation at the time. It brought into unrecognized existence the stillborn "California Republic," and has its reverberations to this day since every state building is required to fly the singular, but not unattractive, "Bear Flag."

Frémont and his forces, after losing two members when stealthily attacked by Klamath Indians and decimating an Indian village in retaliation, hurriedly marched down the Sacramento Valley, hell-bent for something.

Since he was again back in the California muddle as its avowed and accredited savior, it wasn't long before Frémont saw to it that something violent and dramatic happened. The first incident was bloodless, but it led inevitably to fighting, shooting and the loss of life.

The whole thing was unnecessary, as by this time President Polk had had enough of dillydallying over purchasing California or having the Californians declare their own independence or having the gringos set up a self-protective government; he had utilized his Plan Four, and the war between Mexico and the United States was on. Communication being what it was in 1846, nobody in California knew it yet.

The first clash of Frémont's men and the Californians occurred on June 10.

Ezekiel Merritt, a gawky, ungrammatical extrovert, could see no reason why a Californian ("greaser" to him) should be collecting a band of horses in the Sacramento Valley to be sent to General José Castro at Monterey to enable him to organize a troop of cavalry. The man collecting the horses was Lieutenant Francisco Arce.

In Spanish Arce is pronounced "Arsay" with the emphasis on the first syllable. Ezekiel Merritt thought it would be a great joke to "run his arss [as he pronounced it] into San Francisco Bay." So, with a group of hoodlums, for no legitimate reason whatever, Merritt raided Lieutenant Arce's horse-collecting party, sent the members fleeing southward and having rounded up all the stampeded horses, delivered them to Frémont's camp on the Sacramento River. How was General José Castro going to like that? Well, if he didn't like it, let him come get the horses. He could have them if he was man enough to take them.

Excited and delighted with their show of bravura, and realizing that Castro must do something, the bellicose gringos decided they needed a base of operations and full control of the area north of San Francisco Bay. They asked Frémont what they should do.

Frémont's position was delicate and he was shrewd enough to understand it. First, he believed (he later declared in a court-martial) that England was determined to seize California. Just why he should believe so, apart from Senator Benton's letters which did not say definitely that such was the case (unless he had misread the secret code), and upon what local evidence he could base such a belief, he never succeeded in making clear. But to forestall such a calamity, even though there wasn't a single British soldier or sailor in California, Frémont felt it necessary to encourage the gringo settlers to revolt and set up an independent California. He couldn't be their actual leader as that would involve his own government's open sanctioning of the revolt. But, on the other hand, he felt he could not stand by and see such a revolt fail. The result was that he encouraged the revolt verbally and looked the other way politically, for a few days at least, until the whole thing became so exciting and infectious that he couldn't resist participating in the fun and again playing soldier.

The only town of any consequence in northern California was Sonoma, a mere hamlet at the northern end of the Royal Highway, but the site of a garrison and of the last and twenty-first of the Franciscan Missions, San Francisco Solano de Sonoma. There were no soldiers in the garrison, as General José Castro had mustered all his men at Monterey. In the town of Sonoma lived Don Mariano Vallejo, a gentleman and a man of wealth and position. He and Sutter, as has been mentioned, were the most influential citizens in all of northern California. Vallejo, along with Castro, had received word from Larkin that the government of the United States would not be disinterested should the leading citizens of California decide to separate the territory from Mexico and set up an independent California. Castro was all for this, and so was Vallejo. But that meant a California for Californians to them, and not a California for gringos only, as more or less epitomized by the highhanded actions of John C. Frémont.

Frémont's men, while he himself remained at first in the background, decided to seize the garrison and town of Sonoma and hold it as their base of operations. The sixty men who had affronted José Castro and held Gavilan Peak for three days under the American flag (less two killed by Klamath Indians) now numbered about seventy-five, augmented by gringo settlers of central and northern California.

Four days after the horse-stealing episode, a gang made up of about half of the Frémont contingent marched into Sonoma at dawn. This was June 14, 1846. There was nobody to capture in the garrison, so the attackers surrounded the home of Don Mariano Vallejo simply because he was Castro's adjutant in charge of northern California and had a few antediluvian guns in his house. They demanded his immediate surrender. They also captured Jacob Leese, simply because he did not seem to embrace their efforts when they thought he should. But Leese was in cahoots with Larkin, would have no truck with unofficial hoodlums, and said so. So the hoodlums "arrested" him, on what charge nobody could say.

Don Mariano Vallejo, finding his house surrounded at dawn by a band of armed men, and a mean-looking bunch of plug-uglies at that, called out to them to find out why he was being molested.

The leaders of the force were Ezekiel Merritt, Robert Semple, John Grigsby, William B. Ide, William Knight and William Todd. This last man was a nephew of Mrs. Abraham Lincoln.

They told Vallejo that he was under arrest and that Sonoma was in the possession of the invading gringos—themselves. And they warned Vallejo that he had better surrender peaceably or it would mean his life. Whereupon, Vallejo, far above any of them in manners and morals, exercised an old Spanish custom. Instead of getting excited and bolting the door, thereby giving them a chance to tear down the house or set fire to it, he smilingly said that it was an unusually chilly dawn for June, and wouldn't the leaders like to step inside and discuss the matter with him over a glass of wine or perhaps some brandy?

That sounded good to Messrs. Merritt, Semple and Knight, so those three went inside to receive Vallejo's formal capitulation and surrender of himself and northern California, while the rest of the mob fingered their guns outside.

The three emissaries had to wait while Vallejo dressed. Formality was his middle name, and he carefully put on his uniform, brushed off the dust, combed his side whiskers and buckled on his sword. Meanwhile a sleepy servant brought glasses and a decanter of brandy and several bottles of wine to the waiting belligerents.

They sampled the brandy and then the wine, went back to the brandy, and then opened more wine. Vallejo seemed to be taking an interminable time toward sartorial perfection, but at last he appeared, all smiles, his sword clinking, and apologized for his delay. If only he had known the gentlemen were coming! But at least he hoped the brandy had warmed their hearts. Immediately he called for the servant to bring some more. Hospitality at the last house north on the Royal Highway must not be remiss. Tobacco-juice-spitting Ezekiel Merritt started to speak but belched instead. Sympathetically, Vallejo passed him the decanter of brandy.

Outside there were about thirty-five armed and impatient men. They talked in groups, they glared at the house, they paced back and forth. One solid hour had gone by and the house was silent and there was no sign of the returning emissaries with formal capitulation. Those outside held a conference, and it was decided to send John Grigsby in to see what under the sun was going on. The sun, in fact, was just rising. It had all the indications of being a beautiful California June day.

John Grigsby knocked on the door. After repeated knockings a servant came and let him in. The door closed. The warriors outside sat down or paced back and forth or stared at the house in sullen impatience. Fifteen minutes went by—then twenty—then half an hour. The sun was now well up. Forty-five minutes after Grigsby's disappearance, William B. Ide decided something odd must be going on inside that house. Could Vallejo be secretly slaughtering each entrant and waiting for the next victim? Ide decided to find out.

All the revolutionists gathered round while Ide rapped on the door with the butt of his pistol. This time not even the servant came. Swearing and furious, Ide pushed the door with all his might and almost fell into the house. The door had never been locked at any time. He disappeared inside and the door swung closed after him.

Outside the heroes waited.

Inside, Insurrectionist Ide walked cautiously down a wide hall, saw no sign of life, peeked into a parlor, saw nobody, passed on to a room that was Don Vallejo's office and came upon a strange sight.

Robert Semple, a giant of a man, six feet eight inches tall, was seated at a table talking to himself as he laboriously and painstakingly tried to write the articles of capitulation on a large sheet of paper. He looked up at Ide, bleary and rheumy, and said, "How the hell do you spell indemenity—I mean indemeninenty—indeminity—? Oh, hell! *You* write this." And with a gasp he reached for a dreg of brandy still left in a tumbler. Not being satisfied with the dreg, he poured more from a decanter into the glass.

Ide looked on amazed.

Don Mariano Vallejo was seated, smiling pleasantly, and smoking a cigar. A servant was just removing his breakfast dishes.

Ezekiel Merritt was seated at the table across from Semple. But his head was in his arms on the table and he was asleep. William Knight lay back sprawled in a chair. He opened one eye, looked at Ide, groaned and closed his eye. John Grigsby was lying on the floor. He was snoring peacefully, unaware that he was still holding a smashed wine glass in one hand.

"The victors," explained Vallejo, with Spanish warmth and wit, "are preparing the articles of capitulation for me to sign. Naturally,

I shall be most happy to do so as soon as I read them over. I don't believe we have met. I am Mariano Vallejo. Would you care for a glass of brandy?"

"Jesus," said Ide, "what a war!"

"We are all at peace," said Vallejo. "War is unthinkable."

"No, I don't want no brandy and I better finish this here writin'," said Ide. And he took Semple's place at the diplomatic table. He was able to read the early chapters of Semple's document, but in the later chapters something seemed to have gone wrong with the chirography. Ide made what he could of it, and finished it off in what he considered the best international style, using words such as "abrogate" which he spelled "abbergate," and "ordnance" which was close enough as "ordinanse." Then he handed the document to Vallejo.

Carefully placing his cigar in an ash tray, Vallejo started to read the articles. About halfway through he smiled and said, "I must apologize. I cannot read English. But I am happy to sign this remarkable document none the less. Would you pass me the pen and ink?"

Ide handed him the pen and the bottle of ink and Vallejo signed the paper which made him a prisoner and turned over all military supplies in Sonoma to the Americans. Also the Californians agreed to submit to a new republican government to be formed by the Americans and to take up no arms against it. In return, the document granted protection of their property and the safety of their lives to the Californians.

Grigsby, who had been "out" on the floor, staggered to his feet, reeking of brandy, and said, "Where's Frémont? He's gotta pass on this."

But Frémont, instigator of the whole movement, was not too anxious to be identified with it until he was certain it would be successful. He was camped some miles away, waiting for news of the revolt.

Ide carried the document outside and read it aloud to the revolutionists. While he was doing this Merritt, Knight and Semple, along with Grigsby, managed to stagger out of the house.

When Ide finished reading the capitulation proclamation, he added that California was no longer "greaser" country and a new government had to be formed at once. The fact that this surrender by Vallejo would carry no weight in Monterey or Los Angeles or San Diego, or that it couldn't be official unless Pío Pico, the governor, signed it and abdicated, never seemed to enter the heads of any of them.

General Vallejo, his brother Salvador and Colonel Victor Prudon were sent as prisoners to Frémont's camp. Francisca Vallejo was in tears, for she was afraid her husband's life would be taken by these rough gringos. Jacob Leese, who was one of Larkin's men but not known as such to the revolutionists, and who had been "arrested" for being unsympathetic toward the revolt, was sent along to Frémont with the other three prisoners. His wife was Rosalia Vallejo Leese and she was angry instead of tearful and left no room for doubt about what she thought of these *yanqui cholos*. Years later she wrote a bitter indictment of the episode which presents the details in their true light and quite in contrast with the romantic aura that has grown up around it.

Ide, who had consumed no wine or brandy, had concluded his speech by shouting, "Nothing remains but to see this thing through!" The mob yelled its approval and he became its *ipso facto* leader. Semple, Merritt and Grigsby were none too pleased as each had considered himself the leader. But they left Ide in charge in Sonoma and rode off to deliver the four prisoners to Frémont.

Ide, now drunk with power instead of liquor, made another speech and insisted that the first act of the new government was to raise its flag. Since the revolt had not been an act planned at

Washington, it was a purely local uprising and the new government was not that of the United States, but that of itself. It needed its own flag.

William Todd, nephew of Mrs. Lincoln, was the only artist in the company or perhaps he would be more correctly identified as a painter. At any rate, he was appointed the Betsy Ross of the movement, and he designed and made the flag.

Some stories say he demanded one of Doña Francisca's petticoats, others say he used an old flour sack, and still others hold that he obtained a piece of unbleached cotton cloth, five feet by three. In the upper left corner he painted a five-pointed star in red. Across the bottom of the flag was a band of red. At the top center, and facing the star, Todd painted what he was pleased to call a bear. The Californians all thought it was a pig, but Todd insisted that it was a grizzly. When asked why, Todd explained that the bear was the strongest animal in California, and that "a bear always stands his ground." All this art work was done on the grass before the Vallejo house and as the breeze flapped the cotton about, Todd made several smears and finally had to call upon the aid of a small boy to hold the ends down while he worked. Carefully Todd painted in bold letters under the star and bear the words "California Republic." As he neared the end of the lettering, in his haste to get the job done, he left the *i* out of Republic and had to do the last three letters over again. This confused his spacing somewhat, but still there was no mistaking the intent.

At last the flag was completed. Todd surveyed it with satisfaction. "There we are, son," he said to the boy who had held the cotton from flapping. "You've taken part in one of the greatest events in the history of California. You'll remember it all your life. What's your name, sonny?"

"I am the son of Mariano Vallejo," said the boy with some irony, and went back into his house.

The Mexican flag was hauled down from the small garrison and the Bear Flag went up. The Republic of California was proclaimed. It was about noon on June 14, 1846.

"A bear always stands his ground," reiterated Ide, "and as long as the stars shine we stand for the cause."

The next move was to form a government. Ide was automatically "president" although nothing much could be done except to draw up a broad statement of the policies of the new republic which in good time would be incorporated into a formal constitution.

So far, the whole revolution had been bloodless, but that condition lasted only another twenty-four hours. Native Californians were justly indignant over the California Republic, and when a band of *vaqueros* ran into two gringos (who had nothing to do with the revolt) there was shooting, the Americans were captured and both were shot. Their names were Cowie and Fowler and they have a forgotten place in history as the first casualties of the Bear Flag revolt. That kind of thing led quickly to a reprisal and more bloodshed. "Soldiers" of the Bear Flag captured an old man and his two sons who had rowed across the Golden Gate from the San Francisco side. They seemed to be able to give no quick explanation for their presence, so, with no trial whatever, the Bear Flag men murdered them. That made a total of five deaths of innocent citizens, none of whom had had any participation in the revolt at all.

Frémont, delighted at the success of the revolution, now came forward and assumed military command of the forces of the California Republic. He galloped here and galloped there, and doubtless considered himself the George Washington of northern California. He made a night attack on the presidio at San Francisco only to find it abandoned. The cannon were rusted and useless, but Frémont had them spiked anyway so that their oxidized might would never be turned on the California Republic.

General José Castro sent an expedition to attack and seize Sonoma and bring the Bear-Flaggers to their knees. This expedition crossed the Golden Gate and made contact with the Americans near San Rafael. Frémont's men fired first, killing a Californian (some historians say two), and immediately Castro's force, commanded by Joaquín de la Torre, fled in panic. Frémont's men pursued them to the north shore of the Golden Gate but they escaped across the narrow neck of water to safety. It was another great victory for Frémont. The whole revolution was now his party. He issued a directive declaring all of California independent of Mexico and under martial law with himself as the ultimate authority. Ide became jealous of Frémont, claiming that he, Ide, had pulled the chestnuts out of the fire only to have Frémont munch them. Frémont said Ide was an upstart. Merritt, Semple and Knight were jealous of Ide, as they felt he had usurped power when they were the ones who had captured and forced the surrender of Don Mariano Vallejo. They forgot that it was Don Mariano's wine and brandy that had usurped their senses. Grigsby was at outs with all the others; he felt his efforts had been slighted entirely.

Two weeks went by and then three, and there seemed to be no Thomas Jefferson to emerge in order to write the necessary constitution.

Don Mariano Vallejo and the other prisoners had meanwhile been sent to Sutter's Fort at the orders of Frémont and were to be confined there for the duration of the war, whatever that might be.

Then, on July 9, when the California Republic was twenty-five days old, a messenger reached Frémont at Sonoma—now his "headquarters"—with the news that the United States had been at war with Mexico since May 13 last, and the whole Bear Flag revolt had been unnecessary.

Commodore John D. Sloat, with a strong naval force, had seized and occupied Monterey. General Stephen W. Kearny, in command of the "Army of the West," was marching overland and would take San Diego and then turn north. Frémont was to organize a force to move south and meet Kearny, thereby seizing all of California.

Incidentally, the courier wished to know, what was that curious flag flying over Sonoma? The courier was Lieutenant Joseph Warren Revere of the U.S.S. *Cyane,* and he had orders from Commodore Sloat to raise the American flag over Sonoma. Lieutenant Revere cared not a hoot whether Frémont, now commanding the forces of the California Republic, outranked him or not—get that thing down!

And so, on July 9, 1846, Frémont struck the Bear Flag at Sonoma, the only place it had ever flown, and immediately, on the same staff, Lieutenant Revere raised the Stars and Stripes.

Thus, on the twenty-fifth day of its existence, the California Republic came to an end. The movement has gained color and romantic tradition during the hundred and more years since its brief life. The original Bear Flag was preserved, but unfortunately was taken to San Francisco and was lost in the great fire of 1906. Californians, natives or adopted sons alike, are proud of the Bear Flag; it is the state's official emblem and must be flown over all state institutions. The modern flag is an improvement over William Todd's crude original, the design having been somewhat better balanced and arranged on its white field. But it is substantially the same, and it flies today and will fly as long as California exists —for "a bear always stands his ground."

This Is War

NOTHING succeeds like success may be an old cliché, but it was true of the career of John Charles Frémont in the month of July 1846. He got just about everything he had hoped for, found Americans flocking to him until he had a group of about 260, was promoted from a captain to a major in the United States Army, became the commanding officer of the "California Battalion," sometimes called the "Bear Flag" men, in the war of the United States against Mexico, and rattled the saber up and down the Royal Highway from Sonoma to San Diego and back again. Probably he had more fun than anybody in California at the time; and to cap it all, this was no boyhood game with wooden guns and yells of "Bang! Bang!"—this was a real war in which people were being killed. Wonderful! Who could ask for more?

At first the war seemed to be over with little or no effort at all. The American flag was raised over nonresistant Monterey on July 7, 1846. General José Castro and his forces had retreated south down the Royal Highway to confer with Governor Pío Pico in Los Angeles on a plan of action—if any. So all of northern California was there for the taking.

On July 9, 1846, the Stars and Stripes went up over San Francisco (still called Yerba Buena—"Good Herb"; only the presidio itself was known as San Francisco at that time) at the orders of Captain John B. Montgomery, commanding, under Commodore Sloat, the U.S.S. *Portsmouth*. The name Portsmouth Square, famous in San Francisco through the years for various reasons—notably rows of saloons, the Robert Louis Stevenson monument, the red-light dis-

221

trict and the city morgue—came into being to honor the name of this warship. On the same day the Bear Flag came down and the American flag went up at Sonoma.

Two days later the Stars and Stripes went up again, this time over Sutter's Fort in the Sacramento Valley. And on July 16 the Red, White and Blue supplanted Mexico's red, white and green over San Jose. Virtually all of the settled part of northern California and a goodly portion of the Royal Highway were now under American control. Apart from the Bear Flag revolt, not a shot had been fired.

The fact that General Kearny was marching across Arizona to seize southern California, beginning at San Diego, sounded fine, but since he had to march all the way from Leavenworth, Kansas, nobody in Monterey knew just where Kearny was or when he would arrive at San Diego or if he would meet armed resistance on the way.

The original plan of sending Major Frémont and his California Battalion down the Royal Highway in a kind of pincers movement to meet Kearny, who would presumably be marching north, was quickly altered when on July 23, 1846, Commodore Robert F. Stockton replaced Commodore John D. Sloat as commander in chief of all land and sea operations for the conquest of California. Stockton was unwilling to wait for Kearny. He wanted a strong force in the south at once. For all he knew Kearny might be several months getting across the deserts of the southwest, which was, in truth, the case. So Stockton sent Frémont and his Bear Flag men south to San Diego on the U.S.S. *Cyane.* With Frémont were other American armed forces, totaling 300 men in all, and along with them was Lieutenant Gillespie, who had brought the tidings to Larkin and the packet of letters to Frémont. Stockton had promoted Gillespie to captain. At the same time as Frémont was seizing San Diego, Stockton himself, with 375 men, landed at San Pedro and moved inland to take Los Angeles.

It was all too easy.

Frémont occupied San Diego without any resistance at all. And General Castro and Governor Pío Pico were so discomfited by seeing their California house of cards falling apart that they fled in panic. Castro went east from Mission San Gabriel, over the old Anza Trail and never stopped until he was safe in the Mexican state of Sonora. Pío Pico, apparently terrified, dismissed what was to be the final session of the *diputación* in Los Angeles—the last vestige of Mexican rule—announced his abdication, and hid for a time at one of his ranches near San Bernardino. But he felt so insecure that he finally disguised himself, took a circuitous route and at last crossed the border and hid in the Mexican territory of Baja California.

Frémont, having found nobody who would play war in San Diego, raised the American flag over the town on July 29, and then marched his Bear Flag men north to meet Commodore Stockton in Los Angeles. The American flag went up over the City of the Angels on August 13, 1846, and to all intents and purposes the conquest of California seemed to be over. With both Castro and Pico in ignominious flight, the Californians appeared to have not a leader worthy of the name.

The ease with which the country fell abjectly before the slightest threat of power was deceptive, however, and both Frémont and Stockton were too quick in assuming that they had taken the entire territory without the loss of life or even a hostile shot. In such circumstances it is natural that they made their first mistakes. On September 2 Stockton appointed Frémont military governor of California. Both Stockton and Frémont left Captain Gillespie in charge at Los Angeles with a command of fifty men, and they took the bulk of their forces and sailed from San Pedro back to Monterey to organize a government. They thought the war was over. And they had the laugh on General Kearny, who hadn't even arrived yet.

It is true that the Californians woefully lacked leadership. This was her hour when California needed a Sola, a Figueroa, or even an Echeandía. But as always, times of stress bring out the man. He was a soldier whose name was unknown up to that time, for he had been a minor officer under General Castro. He resented Frémont's appointment as governor. He resented every gringo in Christendom. What is more, he had the courage to say so and to take up arms against them. He "assumed" the governorship of California and he appointed two men to serve as his military leaders. This man, who at least could not "take it lying down," and who brought the California campaign to the status of real war and went down fighting, was José María Flores of Los Angeles.

Flores' two military leaders and counselors were José Carrillo of Santa Barbara and Andres Pico of Los Angeles. Their first objective was, quite obviously, the recapture of Los Angeles and the military defeat of Captain Gillespie and his fifty soldiers. They attacked him on September 23, 1846.

Gillespie, realizing that he was far outnumbered—the forces of José Carrillo and Andres Pico numbered at least 300—took a position on a hill back of the church and overlooking the plaza. This was known by the unimaginative name of Fort Hill, and Hill Street between Temple Street and Sunset Boulevard in Los Angeles today marks the location. Gillespie suddenly found himself an island surrounded by the enemy with the nearest help in Monterey about four hundred miles up the Royal Highway to the north. He was soldier enough to understand that he faced surrender or annihilation—unless, of course, he could get help. A man in his command named John Brown, and known to the Californians as Juan Flaco or Thin John, volunteered to ride to Monterey and solicit aid from Stockton and Frémont, who thought the war was over. Gillespie sent Brown on his mission for help and determined to hold on at Fort Hill as long as possible.

John Brown's ride from Los Angeles to Monterey and on to San

Photo courtesy of the Security-First National Bank of Los Angeles

The Cahuenga Pass in 1899

Photo courtesy of W. W. Robinson and the University of California Press
A Spence Air Photo

Modern Hollywood from the air. The Royal Highway may be seen curving through the Cahuenga Pass with the San Fernando Valley beyond.

Thomas O. Larkin, first and only
United States consul to California

John Charles Frémont

Don Abel Stearns, a prominent citizen and able political leader at the end of the chaotic Mexican period

Francisco, for he found Stockton had gone north, would have been
famous in history and the subject of stories and poems had it occurred on the eastern seaboard in the Revolutionary War or the
War of 1812 or any other war at all. Paul Revere's efforts were puny
by comparison.

John Brown rode five hundred miles, pursued at times by as
many as fifteen Californians, through country that was almost entirely hostile, had one horse shot dead under him, once walked
twenty-seven miles at night, and made the trip from Captain Gillespie in Los Angeles to Commodore Stockton in San Francisco in
less than five days. That's a hundred miles a day. It can't be done?
Try it on horseback even today through friendly country. It would
be almost impossible. But—Brown did it. Someone who likes to
rhyme nonsensical English words with Spanish adjectives has para-
phrased it thus:

> Listen, my children, and you'll get a shocko
> At the marvelous ride of Long John Flaco.

Brown is said to have made the four hundred miles to Monterey
without sleep or even rest. One version has it that he carried Gillespie's message written on cigarette papers, concealed in his hair,
but that is a little hard to take. Gillespie didn't need to send a
written message. All Brown had to do was to tell Stockton that
the Californians had Gillespie besieged and would in time wipe
him out.

At any rate, Brown slipped through the guard at Fort Hill just
after dark on September 24 and rode, hell for leather, for the
Cahuenga Pass. He was spotted and fifteen Californians quickly
mounted their horses and pursued him. Regardless of their shaky
politics and their vacillatory fighting ability, Californians were
expert and superb riders.

But Juan Flaco excelled in this same department. It was a breakneck race through the dark for the Cahuenga Pass. If the Californians could get only one rider there first, he would have a good chance of killing the gringo from ambush.

A rising full moon aided Brown in following the road, but it also aided his pursuers who could get an occasional glimpse of him a few hundred yards in the lead. Moreover, the Californians knew their El Camino Real and all possible short cuts and Brown did not. Still, he managed to stay just ahead of pistol range until he came to a broad ditch, or gulch, or what the Californians called an arroyo.

While he desperately sought some way to cross the gap, the first of the Californians came bearing down in the moonlight and opened fire. Brown spurred his horse, rode full speed straight for the arroyo, and, by inches, the animal managed to leap the gap. Brown raced on and, looking back, could see the Californians urging their mounts to take the leap. But the animals refused, and the pursuers had to follow the arroyo for a mile to the north before they could find a place where they could descend one bank and scramble up the other side. This gave Brown a great advantage, and on he went.

The exact location of this arroyo will never be known. Brown described it as "about two miles" from Fort Hill. That would put it, conceivably, somewhere near the present Sunset Boulevard and the Silver Lake district of modern Los Angeles. But all this was well over a century ago. Arroyos have come and arroyos have gone in the years of erosion and flash floods which so often changed the contour of the California terrain. The exact site of Juan Flaco's leap will always be a matter of speculation.

But Brown's gain was soon offset. Two miles farther his horse dropped dead under him. The single shot fired by the first of the Californians had passed through its body. Up to that moment Brown had not known that it had been struck. There was no sound of the pursuing Californians. Taking his bearings by moonlight and keeping what were someday to be called the Hollywood Mountains on his right, Brown struck out on foot for the Cahuenga Pass. He was easily able to elude pursuing horsemen, simply by hiding a few times in the chaparral. The Californians, not knowing Brown's horse lay dead, were still looking for a mounted gringo. They never found him, and Brown marched all night for a distance of twenty-seven miles. At dawn he came to a rancho, and he inveigled, with some show of force, the unwilling ranchero into giving him a fresh horse.

So on went Juan Flaco up the Royal Highway, leaving all pursuit hopelessly in the rear. Obtaining fresh horses as best he could, chiefly because the hostile rancheros did not know the reason for his journey, he rode almost continuously day and night and arrived in Monterey on September 28 with Gillespie's plea to Stockton for immediate aid, only to find that Stockton was in San Francisco, another hundred miles to the north.

After less than three hours of sleep Brown rode on to San Francisco and reached Commodore Stockton just five full days after leaving besieged Gillespie. For a horseback ride between Los Angeles and San Francisco, this speed record still stands.

Stockton at once ordered the U.S.S. *Savannah* to the port of San Pedro where the ship's force of 350 men would march to Los Angeles to save, if possible, the beleaguered Gillespie and his men.

The *Savannah* became trapped in heavy fog off the Golden Gate and did not match the running time of Juan Flaco. She did not arrive at San Pedro until October 7, 1846.

Meanwhile, what of Gillespie? He had surrendered on terms dictated by "Governor" Flores. Down came the American flag over Los Angeles and up went the Mexican flag again. Flores and his generals, José Carrillo and Andres Pico, had no place for prisoners and yet they dared not execute the entire captured garrison for fear of reprisals. So they made a deal with Gillespie in which he promised to march to San Pedro and put his men on a merchant ship waiting there to embark, and never return.

At last the Californians had won a victory. It gave the whole southern part of the territory a great boost in morale. San Diego was recaptured and everything from Tijuana to Santa Barbara was again under the aegis of the red, white and green. Governor Flores, in opposition to Governor Frémont, was the hero of Los Angeles, which was now, of course, the provisional capital.

As soon as the men on the U.S.S. *Savannah* arrived, Captain Gillespie, still irked over his defeat, forgot his promise to the Flores government, which had spared his life and the lives of his men, and allied his soldiers with the new force to attack Los Angeles. "All's fair in love and war" was Gillespie's attitude; or perhaps because Flores didn't stand him up before a firing squad, Gillespie embraced the policy of the old army game of never giving a sucker an even break.

But the combined attack on Los Angeles turned out to be a sorry affair. The attacking force, nearly 400 strong, never even reached the outskirts of the town. The Californians on horseback, using lances and carbines, made stabs and feints and by guerrilla tactics had the gringos banded together for defense short of their objective. The Californians had one decrepit piece of artillery known as the "old woman's gun." It was a small cannon, technically a four-pounder. The story goes that an old California woman had hidden it in the brush of the Los Angeles river bottom when Frémont and Stockton took the town, and when José Castro and Pío Pico so ignominiously fled. Now the Flores' forces had resurrected it. While it killed nobody, it was a positive menace, and if you happened to be struck by a ball from that four-pounder your interest in war would suddenly and surely cease. The piece was mounted on a crude caisson made of an axle and two wagon wheels. The Californians would haul it up to firing range, send a shot into the gringo ranks by touching the cannon off with a cigarette, run for cover themselves to avoid the recoil, and then lasso the old woman's gun and haul it away before any American squad could rush up and seize it. If wars can be funny at all, California has its claim.

But there was nothing funny about it to the half-dozen Americans and two or three Californians who were killed in this fight—sometimes called the Battle of Dominguez Rancho, as that particular ranch house near what is now the intersection of Manchester Avenue and South Figueroa Street was as close to the town as Gillespie's forces could get. After two days of a losing battle Gillespie decided to fall back to San Pedro and the protection of the *Savannah*. All the way back his flanks were harried and an occasional cannon ball from the old woman's gun kept everyone scurrying this way and that. The Americans buried their dead on a small sandy island off San Pedro, later called Dead Man's Island in honor of the first American soldiers to fall in the conquest of California. The island has long since been washed away by the changing tides of the harbor district.

Victories in the south encouraged the Californians of the north to rise again, and under Joaquín de la Torre, who had been routed once before by Frémont, the Californians clashed with Americans near Mission San Juan Bautista not very far from where Frémont had raised the American flag some months before on Gavilan Peak. This fight—or skirmish—sometimes dignified by the name of the Battle of Natividad, cost the lives of half a dozen Californians and four Americans and ended in a draw. With that, the northern Californians went back into military retirement and there was no more fighting along that section of the Royal Highway.

But things were still pretty well botched in the south and it was up to Frémont and Stockton to make good.

The long-coming General Stephen W. Kearny and his "Army of the West" had now entered the desert region west of the Colorado River and they were having a hard time of it crossing that difficult area which years later was to burgeon as California's famous Imperial Valley. But what Frémont and Stockton did not know was the fact that the Army of the West, sounding rather glorious, numbered only 100 men and two howitzers. The reason for this was simple. When Frémont and Stockton first took San Diego and Los Angeles without a single casualty or so much as a shot, Stockton had sent the famous Western scout, Kit Carson, east, overland, to Washington to report that all of California had fallen, that Castro and Pico had fled and that it was all over. Kit Carson met General Kearny in New Mexico and gave him this news. So Kearny believing everything under control on the west coast, left most of the Army of the West to hold New Mexico and himself led only a token force on as his belated effort to enter the now closed (in his mind) California campaign.

Since Gillespie had been twice defeated, Stockton and Frémont had to start all over again. Stockton sailed for San Diego and successfully recaptured the town. He sent Frémont down the Royal Highway from Monterey to mop up the middle of the territory and to close in on Flores and Los Angeles from the north while he moved up from the south in a major pincers movement to put an end to this recalcitrant town.

Frémont found the midriff of California a military nonentity until he neared Santa Barbara. When he was still some miles north, an American rancher named Benjamin Foxen warned Frémont that the Californians were lying in wait for him in the narrow defile known as the Gaviota Pass. It is a matter of debate whether Frémont, had he been surprised at the Gaviota, would have been destroyed or would have driven the Californians from the pass. Posterity will never know, for Frémont, while always saber rattling, had no desire to be trapped in the dangerous pass, and he took another route, pointed out to him by Benjamin Foxen, and avoided the Gaviota entirely.

This road was a more difficult route over the now well-known and scenically beautiful San Marcos Pass. Foxen, it is said, led Frémont to the summit, pointed out Santa Barbara below and returned to his ranch. Frémont's exhausted men, not at all anxious for a fight, came into Santa Barbara on a Sunday morning while most of the citizens were at Mass in the mission. A few American residents turned out to welcome the soldiers, and somebody sent a messenger north to the Californians lurking in the Gaviota ambush to tell them they could forget the whole thing and come home because Frémont was already in town and Santa Barbara had capitulated.

General Stephen W. Kearny, however, ran into quite a different situation, and he never forgave Frémont and Stockton for giving him a bad steer by telling him, through Kit Carson, that the California campaign was over when it hadn't yet begun.

Kearny, unsuspecting, ran head on, with only 100 sorely tried and tired men, into the bloodiest engagement in the entire war. It was Flores' general, Andres Pico, who opposed Kearny, and the Americans were badly defeated. Had the Californians had any real talent for militarism, they might have wiped out Kearny's force to the last man. Fortunately for Kearny, and in the end for the Californians, no such tragedy occurred.

The engagement is known as the Battle of San Pascual, and it took place on December 6, 1846, not on the Royal Highway, but in the rolling country just east of it, about halfway between J. J. Warner's ranch and San Diego. Near by was an Indian village called San Pascual. Today a monument marks the site.

General Andres Pico with about 100 mounted men moved his forces between Kearny's position and San Diego. The American troops, also mounted (mostly on mules), but badly enervated from the grueling desert march from New Mexico, down the valley of the Gila River in Arizona and across the burning sands of southeastern California (country later used by Hollywood studios as "location" for Sahara Desert scenes), were in no shape to fight. Yet fight they did, and it was Kearny who attacked—not Andres Pico—as soon as contact was made.

At the first volley the Californians fled and the weary Americans pursued them. This resulted in a long-strung-out line of Americans with no protection on their flanks, and their two howitzers far in the rear.

Suddenly the Californians wheeled their horses and charged the extended American line, rolling it up and cutting it to pieces. While the Californians had some carbines and a few pistols, their chief weapon was the long lance. Crude as it was, even medieval, this lance made of an eight-foot-long willow pole tipped with a sharp metal barb was a nasty weapon when handled by a charging and expert horseman. Captain Benjamin Moore was virtually decapitated. Captain Johnston got a lance through his chest and died immediately. General Kearny received two vicious wounds. No two historians agree, but it is generally assumed that Kearny lost 20 of his men in Andres Pico's counterattack, and that at least 20 more were seriously or mortally wounded. That, if true, would mean 40 casualties out of 100 men, and no combat group, even if fresh and ready for battle, can take a 40 percent loss in half an hour and still be a functioning unit.

The Americans were routed and, for a while, almost helpless. For some reason Andres Pico and his men did not follow up this advantage, but withdrew from the field, leaving it to the stunned, the shocked, the dead and the dying. It is said that there were no losses among the Californians, but this would seem unlikely in what amounted to an hour of combat, the first half of which was pursuit, and the second half all vicious fighting at close quarters.

Considering all conditions, General Stephen W. Kearny should not have attacked; but it must be remembered that he arrived in California with only a part of his Army of the West, believing that the war was long since over. The results of San Pascual did not endear Stockton and Frémont to Kearny.

And in Los Angeles?

Again there was reason for jubilance, and again the government of José Flores, with the aid of its brilliant general, Andres Pico, had won a victory.

It was, of course, the end for the Flores government, but in the elation of the moment in Los Angeles nobody could see the longer perspective. Stockton held San Diego; Kearny's beaten men survived until Stockton could send them reinforcements and lead them safely into San Diego; Frémont had taken Santa Barbara and was moving down on Los Angeles from the north. When Frémont reached the San Fernando Valley, and Stockton and Kearny moved north from San Diego to a location near what is today the town of Whittier, all of California was under American domination except for an area approximating Los Angeles County today.

José Flores and his loyal supporters and never-say-die generals, José Carrillo and Andres Pico, put up a last-ditch fight. But it was no more than that. After a few skirmishes in which lives were lost on both sides, the pincers movement was too much for José Flores. The Californians had no navy to bring relief by sea; Frémont was advancing from the north to the Cahuenga Pass, Stockton and what remained of Kearny were pressing up from the south to the edge of the pueblo of Los Angeles. In a day or two there would be nothing left of California for the Californians except the little plaza in Los Angeles itself.

José María Flores, with tears running down his cheeks, had to admit that the gringos had taken California. He appointed Andres Pico arbiter to surrender to the conquerors. Flores had tried, and tried hard, to save California for the Californians. This last of the native governors counted himself a failure. Fearing execution at the hands of the Americans, he fled to Mission San Gabriel, and then south and east over the Anza Trail to Arizona and finally to Sonora in Mexico. From there on history loses him. He represented Spain's and Mexico's dying gasp. His courage and integrity deserve a salute.

Andres Pico surrendered to the great conqueror, John Charles Frémont, on January 13, 1847, and the fighting in California was ended. This "California Appomattox," as one respected historian inadvisedly puts it (the real Appomattox was still eighteen years in the future) took place at the old Cahuenga ranch house at the north end of the Cahuenga Pass.

Captain Archibald H. Gillespie had the dubious honor of raising the American flag over Los Angeles for the second time, having lost it there once and having been unable to retake it later, and his ego must have felt a lot better for it.

A new day, a new order, a new culture—all were about to take over California. The Americans had it. The war was over.

Gold? That's Different! { 19

BETWEEN the Bear Flag revolt in 1846 and the first constitutional convention at Monterey in 1849, three brief and hectic years in view of California's long history, a number of events, some surprising, some amazing, some significant and some ridiculous, all took place along the Royal Highway.

John Charles Frémont, who had been a captain when he stood behind the curtain of the Bear Flag, advanced to major, then colonel, and finally governor of California, an appointment made by Commodore Stockton. General Kearny differed with Stockton on who was running this California show. Kearny felt, with some reason, that the Stockton-Frémont combine had badly botched the seizure of the territory by their stating once that they had subdued all resistance only to find that they had to do it all over again. With the added proof of two Californian lance wounds in his body, suffered at the fiasco of San Pascual, Kearny's frame of mind was quite understandable.

When Stockton returned to Washington, Frémont lasted just forty days as governor. Then Kearny deposed him and assumed the office himself as a military governor under American occupation. After serving for three months, he, too, left for Washington, and appointed Colonel Richard B. Mason in his stead. Kearny then had Frémont placed under arrest at Fort Leavenworth, Kansas, on charges of insubordination. Frémont's court-martial lasted four months in Washington. He was found guilty and sentenced to dishonorable discharge from the army. Papa-in-law Senator Thomas Hart Benton was highly incensed at President Polk for permitting

235

his son-in-law to stand trial. Polk, however, approved the court's decision but suspended the sentence, thereby permitting Frémont to hold his rank (and salary) in the army. Frémont, in a huff, refused this clemency and resigned. The army accepted his resignation. Senator Benton and President Polk were no longer of one mind and relations were strained, to say the least.

Frémont's trial ended in January 1848, and shortly thereafter, on February 2, 1848, representatives of the governments of the United States and Mexico signed the Treaty of Guadalupe Hidalgo, which formally ended the war between the two nations. Mexico lost everything, of course, the United States grabbing all of New Mexico, part of Colorado, most of Arizona, and all of Utah, Nevada and California. The border was definitely set from the Rio Grande River at a point near El Paso, Texas, west to the Pacific Ocean at a point south of San Diego, and revised later by the addition of the Gadsden Purchase in 1853. Mexico got the sum of $15,000,000 as balm. Just who got away with that consolation prize, history doesn't say. But it certainly never trickled down to the laborer, the peon or the Indian. California was now a part of the United States, although the Californians had had nothing to say about it except for José María Flores' courageous but hopeless military resistance.

Along El Camino Real itself, which could now be given, legitimately, its English translation of the Royal Highway, several significant events took place in this period of adjustment.

Traveling time between Los Angeles and San Francisco, which had been weeks apart had been reduced to five days by Juan Flaco's famous ride. Nobody could duplicate it, to be sure, but it indicated that if the road were improved so that it became practical for wagons and stagecoaches instead of horsemen and *carretas* (oxcarts), the running time between the various California cities and towns could be shortened and the road might serve as an artery of trade as well as communication. Formerly all long-distance trading of goods had to be done by sea.

Also, during this period, California's first newspaper came into existence. Volume one, number one, appeared on August 15, 1846. It was called, rather obviously, the *Californian,* and its owners and publishers were Walter Colton and Robert Semple. The presswork was done at Monterey and the paper was a weekly. Robert Semple was one of the Bear Flag leaders and was usually called Dr. Semple. His medical degree may be a matter of debate, but his tremendous size and booming voice impressed everyone, and he seemed to demand some kind of title. "Doctor" filled the want.

Walter Colton had been a navy chaplain on the U.S.S. *Congress,* and because of his education, sympathetic nature and logical mind, Commodore Stockton had made him alcalde of Monterey. The word alcalde could be translated as judge, or justice of the peace. But the job itself included everything from magistrate to father-confessor to the people of Monterey. Whatever their problems from a missing hen to marital infidelity, they brought them to Reverend Colton and humbly accepted this alcalde's decisions.

Colton kept a diary which was published in 1850 by A. S. Barnes and Company of New York, under the title *Three Years in California.* It has been long out of print but makes charming reading, even today, as its firsthand accounts of daily events along the Royal Highway more than a century ago are the observations of a man of taste and wisdom and humor.

In his diary Colton described the first California newspaper and its birth. Since his own words cannot be excelled, a quotation is in order.

Saturday, Aug. 15. Today the first newspaper ever published in California made its appearance. The honor, if such it be, in writting its Prospectus, fell to me. It is to be issued on every Saturday, and is published by Semple and Colton. Little did I think when relinquishing the editorship of the North American in Philadelphia, that my next feat in this line would be off here in California. My partner is an emigrant from Kentucky, who stands six feet eight in his stockings. He is in a buckskin dress, a foxskin cap; is true with his rifle, ready with his pen, and quick at the type-case.

He created the materials of our office out of the chaos of a small concern, which had been used by a Roman Catholic monk in printing a few sectarian tracts.

This was the old wreck of a press that had arrived from Boston in 1834 at the request of California's first printer, Agustín Zamorano. After Zamorano's departure from California the press had little use. Finally Mariano Vallejo had it transported to Sonoma, the northern limit of the Royal Highway, where a few avisos and one or two official, or semiofficial, documents were printed. For some reason Vallejo had the press and its battered type returned to Monterey where it was used once or twice and finally relegated to an old adobe storeroom and forgotten. Here Walter Colton found it in 1846. It must have been at least seventy-five years old at the time. In his diary Colton describes it.

The press was old enough to be preserved as a curiosity; the mice had burrowed in the balls; there were no rules, no leads, and the types were rusty and all in pi. It was only by scouring that the letters could be made to show their faces. A sheet or two of tin were procured, and these, with a jack-knife, were cut into rules and leads. Luckily we found, with the press, the greater part of a keg of ink; and now came the main scratch for paper. None could be found, except what is used to envelop the tobacco of the cigar smoked here by the natives. A coaster had a small supply of this on board, which we procured. It is in sheets a little larger than the common-sized foolscap. And this is the size of our first paper, which we have christened the Californian.

Though small in dimensions, our first number is as full of news as a black-walnut is of meat. We have received by couriers, during the week, intelligence from all important military posts through the territory. Very little of this has transpired; it reaches the public for the first time through our sheet. We have, also, the declaration of war between the United States and Mexico, with an abstract of the debate in the senate. A crowd was waiting when the first sheet was thrown from the press. It produced quite a little sensation. Never was a bank run upon harder; not, however, by people with paper to get specie, but exactly the reverse. One-half of the paper is in English, the other in Spanish. The subscription for a year is five dollars; the price of a single sheet is twelve and a half cents; and is considered cheap at that.

There is pardonable pride in Colton's words. That he was pleased to be the editor and staff of California's first paper is obvious. He wrote just about the whole paper himself and the type-setting and presswork were Semple's department. In his diary a week later Colton cannot resist recording the issuance of volume one, number two.

Saturday, Aug. 22. Our little paper, the Californian, made its appearance again today. Many subscribers have sent in their names since our last, and have paid in advance. It is not larger than a sheet of foolscap; but this foolscap parallel stops, I hope, with the shape. Be this as it may, its appearance is looked for with as much interest as was the arrival of the mail.

Among other "firsts" for California during this period were the first American public school, the first United States post office and the first bank. All three institutions were opened in 1848 in San Francisco, which suddenly became a rapidly growing town.

The public school was located on Portsmouth Square and its principal was Thomas Douglas, a graduate of Yale. When the hopeless crudity of the Mexican school system is recalled, a system which had barely existed for the last fifty years, the importance of this first American school cannot be overestimated. From it gradually grew the entire public-school system of California. Education in California eventually became an institution to which the state could point with pride.

The first American post office was soon followed by similar

offices in Monterey, San Diego, Los Angeles and Santa Barbara.

The first bank, located on Kearny Street in San Francisco by two reputable men, Naglee and Sinton, was originally called an "exchange and deposits office" before it assumed the dignity of the single word "bank."

Then, on September 1, 1849, came the first constitutional convention, made up mostly of Americans, a few Californians and a few European-born citizens. The giant, "Dr." Robert Semple, presided and did a far better job than he had done during his temporary leadership of the Bear Flag revolt. There were forty-eight delegates, and it was a "young" convention in more ways than one, for the majority of the men were well under the age of forty. Elam Brown of San Jose, at fifty-two, was the oldest American there, and José Carrillo, at fifty-three, was the oldest Californian. J. M. Jones and J. M. H. Hollingsworth, ranchers from the San Joaquin Valley, were the youngest representatives, each being twenty-five. The average age of the convention was thirty-six. Among the well-known names in the group were Johann Sutter, Thomas O. Larkin, Mariano Vallejo, Abel Stearns, Pablo de la Guerra and Antonio Pico, all of whom had been more or less prominent in California history before. But it was predominantly an American-controlled convention. Only six of the forty-eight members had been born in California. Sutter had been born in Switzerland, and other foreign-born delegates were natives of France, Spain and Scotland. But the majority were Americans hailing from fifteen different Eastern states most of which were north of the Mason-Dixon line.

The convention sat for six weeks, and during that time it provided for the rights of the individual, his life, liberty and property, fixed the boundaries of the state as they exist today, provided for state officers and a state legislature, set up a constitution adapted from the plans of the states of New York and Iowa and forever outlawed slavery. All forty-eight delegates signed the constitution on October 13, 1849. It was then presented to the people of the

Photo courtesy of the Security-First National Bank of Los Angeles

San Pedro, port of Los Angeles, in 1873. Deadman's Island, in the background, has since washed away.

An architectural monstrosity of the elegant eighties

Typical ranch of the Royal Highway

Lettuce ranch in the Salinas Valley

territory for a vote of approval or disapproval. A favorable majority would, of course, mean public ratification of the document. This vote was held just one month later, November 13, 1849. It had been a wet fall and there had been three days of heavy (and welcome) rain before election day. The soaked and bogged condition of the Royal Highway kept many voters away from the polls. Also, apathy on the part of the native Californians helped keep the total vote down. But regardless of rainy weather or lack of interest, the citizens of California swept the constitution into a working reality by a vote of 12,064 to 811. Gone forever were Spain, Mexico and martial law under the American Army; and Peter H. Burnett became the first constitutional governor of California. At last California had a reliable government which, from 1849, has continued to function up to the present moment and certainly shows no signs of the plague of revolution in years to come.

But important as were all these events to California—newspaper, post office, bank, school, Juan Flaco's ride and the constitutional convention—something else had happened.

It was an event so momentous that at first most Californians couldn't believe it; an event that was to affect in some manner every living soul in the state; an event that whisked the new government from its infancy to its adolescence, completely skipping its childhood; an event that was heard around the world and brought men and women from every walk of life and every quarter of the globe; an event that quadrupled the population in one year. Today everyone knows the story: there was plenty of free gold in California and all you had to do was to go there and pick it up.

James W. Marshall discovered gold in the tailrace of a sawmill while shutting off the water on January 24, 1848, on the property of Johann Sutter, called New Helvetia, a good many miles from the Royal Highway. For a while the news was doubted, and when it was finally verified by indisputable tests to both Sutter and Marshall, they tried to keep it a secret. But an event of this significance, even if only gossip, could not be held down to the cognizance of a few men. Soon the news was abroad, and quite naturally, the first newspaper in the territory, Colton's and Semple's *Californian,* reported it.

Ironically enough, gold had been discovered in California some years before. It had been found in Los Angeles County (or what later became Los Angeles County) at a point about eight miles east of what is today the small town of Newhall. A canyon, sometimes called Feliciana but more popularly known as Placerita Canyon, runs easterly from the present Newhall, and in this canyon a man named Francisco Lopez, a jack-of-all-trades employed by the Mission San Gabriel Arcángel, dug up some wild onions and with them dug up some gold. The date was March 9, 1842. Not much was made of it, but it did cause a slight ripple of interest. In November of 1842 Abel Stearns, of Los Angeles, sent twenty ounces of this California "stuff" to the U. S. Mint in Philadelphia. The mint reported that the "stuff" was gold indeed. But the yield was so slight, and the wild onions were in such greater abundance, that this first gold strike never caught on in the public imagination.

Marshall's discovery was another story. Again irony, fate, destiny—or what you will—entered the scene.

If there was any one objective that the Spanish *conquistadores* sought, it was gold. The one primal cause for the opening of Mexico and the American Southwest and California goes back to the insatiable desire for gold on the part of the men of Spain. Even the name California as early as 1510 had been identified with gold in the clumsy prose of Ordóñez de Montalvo when he wrote that California (to him an island) was abundant with gold, and the weapons of the women—no men were permitted to live on the island—"were all made of gold." Montalvo continued with the statement, "The island everywhere abounds with gold . . . and upon it no other metal was found."

For three and a half centuries the Spaniards had searched for gold in the Americas, North, South and Central, and had found a goodly share of it. But California, throughout the heyday of the Spanish Empire and well into the period of its decadence, had been of little interest. California was one of the lesser acquisitions of Spain, had been a mere northern outpost to Mexico, and at last Mexico had lost it to the more powerful United States. Incredible as it may be, almost simultaneous with the loss, came first the rumor and then the gossip and at last the authentication, that there was gold, and an incredible amount of it, in California.

The news came down from the foothills of the Sierras to Sutter's Fort—and soon it was told in Sonoma and San Francisco and San Jose and Monterey. In another week it had reached San Luis Obispo, then Santa Barbara, and at last Los Angeles and San Diego. At first nobody believed it. It was too fantastic. Gold? Sure, I've got a crop of it, too. Know any more good jokes?

But somebody must be taking it seriously, for Johann Sutter sent a representative to the capital, Monterey, to obtain an exclusive grant to all the mineral rights on his property. The voice of the fourth estate, Colton's and Semple's *Californian,* decided against further printing of such false rumors as might unnecessarily excite its readers. Walter Colton, however, did record in his diary for May 29, 1848: "Our town was startled out of its quiet dreams today, by the announcement that gold had been discovered on the American Fork. The men wondered and talked, and the women, too; but neither believed."

Perhaps nobody believed. It was all too good to be true. But as the rumors and gossip and stories persisted, one or two people began to accept them; and finally the very thought of gold in the earth, waiting for somebody—anybody—you!—to come pick it up, caught on like an infectious disease. Still, Walter Colton was skeptical. For June 5, 1848, he recorded in his diary:

Another report reached us this morning from the American Fork. The rumor ran, that several workmen, while excavating for a millrace, had thrown up little shining scales of yellow ore, that proved to be gold; that an old Sonorian, who had spent his life in gold mines, pronounced it the genuine thing. Still the public incredulity remained, save here and there a glimmer of faith, like the flash of a fire-fly at night. One good old lady, however, declared that she had been dreaming of gold every night for several weeks, and that it had so frustrated her simple household economy, that she had relieved her conscience, by confessing to her priest!

But while he slept on it during the night of June 5, incredulity reached the breaking point for Walter Colton, and he decided to do something about it. His entry in his diary for June 6 shows a different attitude entirely. No longer is it a question of shrugging this news off. Overnight it became a matter worthy of serious investigation.

Tuesday, June 6. Being troubled with the golden dream almost as much as the good lady, I determined to put an end to the suspense, and dispatched a messenger this morning to the American Fork. He will have to ride, going and returning, some four hundred miles, but his report will be reliable. We shall then know whether this gold is fact or fiction—a tangible reality on the earth, or a fanciful treasure at the base of some rainbow, retreating over hill and waterfall, to lure pursuit and disappoint hope.

The period of suspense while Colton's messenger rode to the mines and returned was punctuated by a single entry in the diary for June 12—just six days after the messenger had been sent.

Monday, June 12. A straggler came in today from the American Fork, bringing a piece of yellow ore weighing an ounce. The young dashed the dirt from their eyes, and the old from their spectacles. One brought a spyglass, another an iron ladle; some wanted to melt it, others to hammer it, and a few were satisfied with smelling it. All were full of tests; and many, who could not be gratified in making their experiments, declared it humbug. One lady sent me a huge gold ring, in the hope of reaching the truth by comparison; while a gentleman placed the specimen on the top of his gold-headed cane and held it up, challenging the sharpest eyes to detect a difference. But doubts still hovered on the minds of the great mass. They could not conceive that such a treasure could have lain there so long undiscovered. The idea seemed to convict them of stupidity. There is nothing of which a man is so tenacious than his claims to sagacity. He sticks to them like an old bachelor to the idea of his personal attractions, or a toper to the strength of his temperance ability, whenever he shall wish to call it into play.

For the next eight days life went on as usual at Monterey and all along the Royal Highway. Alcalde Colton had nothing more serious to cope with than jealous lovers, a quarreling couple, a horse which had been lost, strayed or stolen, a complaint about dogs, and an Indian buck who appeared before him and asked to be locked in jail for a month. When Colton inquired of the reason for this unusual request, it turned out that this Indian wished to marry an Indian girl. But since he was a notorious drunkard, the girl refused to accept him unless he stayed cold sober for a month. He had vowed to do it, and had been "on the wagon" for three days. It had been three days of torture and temptation and he knew he couldn't resist alcohol much longer. So would the kind alcalde please lock him up where he would be unable to get anything to drink except water. Obligingly Colton sentenced the Indian to a month in jail, and the buck went to his incarceration a happy man.

Such was life in California's capital city up to June 20, 1848. On that day Colton's investigator of this gold rumor got back from the American Fork. Colton describes the scene in his diary.

Tuesday, June 20. My messenger sent to the mines, has returned with specimens of the gold; he dismounted in a sea of upturned faces. As he drew forth the yellow lumps from his pockets, and passed them around among the eager crowd, the doubts which had lingered till now, fled. All admitted they were gold, except one old man, who still persisted they were some Yankee invention, got up to reconcile the people to the change of flag. The excitement produced was intense; and many were soon busy in their hasty preparations for a departure to the mines. The family who had kept house for me caught the moving infection. Husband and wife were both packing up; the blacksmith dropped his hammer, the carpenter his plane, the mason his trowel, the farmer his sickle, the baker his loaf, and the tapster his bottle. All were off for the mines, some on horses, some on carts, and some on crutches, and one went in a litter. An American woman, who had recently established a boarding house here, pulled up stakes, and was off before her lodgers had even time to pay their bills. Debtors ran, of course. I have only a community of women left, and a gang of prisoners, with here and there a soldier, who will give his captain the slip at the first chance. I don't blame the fellow a whit; seven dollars a month, while others are making two or three hundred a day! That is too much for human nature to stand.

There is not another entry in the diary until July 15, almost a month later. By that time the flow of population to the mines was being seriously felt.

Saturday, July 15. The gold fever has reached every servant in Monterey; none are to be trusted in their engagement beyond a week, and as for compulsion, it is like attempting to drive fish into a net with the ocean before them. Gen. Mason, Lieut. Lanman, and myself, form a mess; we have a house and all the table furniture and culinary apparatus requisite; but our servants have run, one after another, till we are almost in despair: even Sambo, who we thought would stick by from laziness, if no other cause, ran last night; and this morning, for the fortieth time, we had to take to the kitchen, and cook our own breakfast. A general of the United States Army, a commander of a man-of-war, and the Alcalde of Monterey, in a smoking kitchen, grinding coffee, toasting a herring, and pealing onions! These gold mines are going to upset all the domestic arrangements of society, turning the head to the tail, and the tail to the head.

But the worst was yet to come.

Tuesday, July 18. Another bag of gold from the mines, and another spasm in the community. It was brought down by a sailor from Yuba River, and contains a hundred and thirty-six ounces. It is the most beautiful gold that has appeared in the market. . . . My carpenters, at work on the school-house, on seeing it, threw down their saws and planes, shouldered their picks, and are off for the Yuba. Three seamen ran from the *Warren,* forfeiting their four years' pay; and a whole platoon of soldiers from the fort left only their colors behind. One old woman declared she would never again break an egg or kill a chicken, without examining yolk and gizzard.

What was going on in Monterey was typical of every town along the Royal Highway from San Diego to Sonoma. Two former ranchers, William Daylor and Perry McCoon, who had abandoned their crops and their stock, made $17,000 in one week in the month of July 1848. And from then on the rush, the stampede, the hysteria, spread from California to the Eastern states, and throughout the world.

Sailors jumped their ships as soon as the vessels dropped anchor in San Francisco Bay. Dozens of ships, and then several hundred, were abandoned. Not only did the entire Monterey garrison desert, but in many instances officers rushed to the diggings along with their men. Neither threats nor punishments nor rewards could control the hunger for gold. Save for the throngs moving northward, who made few purchases in their haste, business along the Royal Highway came to a standstill. The population of the towns was depleted, until there was none left but the lame, the halt and the blind, and even they made their efforts to get to the great source of immediate wealth that lay there in California's Sierra Nevada Mountains for the taking.

Colton and Semple's newspaper, the *Californian,* was compelled to suspend publication. There were no subscribers or no advertisers left. That the gold fever attacked every living soul in California, in some form or another, was evident. It was a happy fever. Once a man had contracted the disease he was eager, vital, active and armed with that perennial intangible—hope.

One of the holdouts, one of the last on the local scene to succumb to the germ, was Reverend and Alcalde Walter Colton himself. But at last it was too much, even for him. He convinced himself that there was nothing left for him to do in Monterey, and that it was his duty to look this new field over. On September 9, 1848, he wrote in his diary: "The only capital required is muscle and honest purpose." And a week later he broke into effusive and periphrastic prose as follows:

I met a man today from the mines in patched buckskins, rough as a badger from his hole, who had fifteen thousand dollars in yellow dust, swung at his back. Talk to him of brooches, gold-headed canes, and Carpenter's coats! Why he can unpack a lump of gold that would throw all Chestnut-street [Colton is thinking of Philadelphia] into spasms. And there is more where this came from. *His* rights in the great domain are equal to yours, and his prospects of getting it out vastly better. With these advantages he bends the knee to no man, but strides along in his buckskins, a lord of earth by a higher prescriptive privilege than what emanates from the partiality of kings. His patent is medallioned with rivers which roll over golden sands, and embossed with mountains that have lifted for ages their golden coronets to heaven. Clear out of the way with your crests, and crowns, and pedigree trees, and let this democrat pass. Every drop of blood in his veins tells that it flows from a great heart, which God has made and which man shall never enslave. Such are the genuine sons of California; such may they live and die.

There were no two ways about it. Walter Colton had caught the gold fever. His was a late case and he came down with it royally. On September 20, 1848, he set out for the mines. He had procured a good horse for this journey, and the night before he left some other gold seeker stole it. The good alcalde was fit to be tied. He offered as much as $200 for another horse. To run down the thief and bring him to justice no longer meant anything to him. He wrote: "There was no time now for ferreting out thieves or hunting stolen animals." But horses were at a premium and not to be had without paying an exorbitant price. This no longer mattered to Walter Colton. "My only resource now was with Mr. T——," he wrote, "who had three horses in his corral." Purchasing one of the last animals in Monterey, the late alcalde states, "I struck a bargain . . . and throwing on my saddle, was under way in a few minutes."

Gold? It made a difference.

Devil Take the Hindmost

{20}

By June 1, 1848, 2,000 men were digging for gold. By July first there were 4,000. By December of 1848 the number was anybody's guess, and the value of the gold taken from the earth was estimated at $4,000,000. This was merely the beginning.

The population of California before the gold rush, in 1848, was somewhere between 20,000 and 25,000 (excluding Indians). Almost all of these people lived either on the Royal Highway or in towns or on ranches adjacent to it. Not more than 2,000 of them were Americans.

By the end of 1849 the population of California was estimated at 100,000, with 53,000—or more than half—Americans, and with the vast majority of this populace somewhere between the mushrooming city of Sacramento and the various diggings. The people who lived along the Royal Highway had been reduced to less than half of the general estimate of 20,000 to 25,000 for 1848. Towns such as Santa Barbara and San Luis Obispo were depleted of most of their male population. Along with San Jose and San Diego and San Buenaventura, they dozed peacefully, the places where the only excitement was occasioned by a stolen rooster, a wandering and decrepit horse or a cockfight. Their populace, made up of friends and relatives of those who had gone to the mines, patiently awaited news of sudden riches.

Most of the mission buildings, now in a state of complete desuetude, were gradually collapsing. The mission lands, however, were all put to profitable use by their purchasers or leaseholders. Owls might live in the belfry of San Carlos Borroméo, and the buttresses

250

and arches of San Juan Capistrano could collapse, for the value was not so much in the buildings but in the rich lands surrounding them. Very few Indians owned any of this secularized property by 1849. They had sold it, or traded it, or gambled it away, or been cheated out of it in one way or another without even knowing it. This was the very thing that Governor José Figueroa had foreseen and had striven to prevent.

The Indian population was rapidly decreasing. Disease and a high rate of infant mortality were still taking their toll. Some Indians went to the more remote mountain and desert areas as yet untouched by the white race. A few were able to find jobs as domestics. Some became virtual serfs on the ranchos they might have owned, working for a standard of living far below that of the poorest white man, exactly as they had during the mission days. Some gravitated to the cities and towns, living in brush shelters in the river bottoms and the dumping grounds. Some worked in the vineyards and the distilleries, harvesting the grapes or tramping them all day long to produce the valuable juice that would soon become wine. Often they were paid in wine, or *aguardiente,* a raw brandy. On this they got dead-drunk over the week ends, only to go back to work on Monday to earn more *aguardiente* for the next week end. If the Indians got drunk in the towns—Los Angeles was a case in point—they were arrested and jailed for the week end. The city then punished them for their misdemeanor by renting them to farmers or vintners at $1.00 to $3.00 for a week's labor. If the Indian was to be paid $3.00, the city took two of it, and at the end of the week the miscreant received $1.00. This would be on a Saturday. But the week's earnings would not be paid in cash; instead the Indian was given a jug of *aguardiente.* On this he proceeded to get drunk and was therefore jailed again, allowed to sober up over Sunday, and was again rented out as a convict laborer for the ensuing week. This went on as long as the Indian lived.

It was a sorry sequel to Padre Serra's dream.

As for the missions themselves, eventually the Supreme Court decided that the buildings, ruins or not, belonged to the church. And with the buildings went one or two adjacent or surrounding acres. Thus the plundered wreck of the mission system, stripped of all its real assets, was finally given over to the control of the Archbishop of California.

So the Franciscans were gone, the Spaniards were gone, the Mexicans were gone, the Indians were slowly dying off and the Californians were now American citizens. The gold rush brought in a flux of crooks and pimps and whores and army deserters and escaped felons; and along with the riffraff, a good number of honest men from piano tuners to barbers, from printers to corset salesmen—all looking for quick wealth.

It was a new California and it was devil take the hindmost. The state was not a state. It was certainly not the now defunct California Republic of the Bear Flag. But it was not officially a territory of the United States. Just what was it? The chaotic days from the signing of the Treaty of Guadalupe Hidalgo that ended the Mexican War in 1848 up to September 9, 1850, when President Millard Fillmore signed the bill passed by both House and Senate, admitting California to the Union as the thirty-first state, has sometimes been called the "No-Government Period."

Mexican law applied in the more remote areas. Some interpretation of American law applied in Monterey under Alcalde Walter Colton. Theoretically the whole area was under martial law administered by the series of military governors following the kicking out of Frémont by General Kearny. Three months later, when he left for Washington, Kearny appointed Colonel Richard B. Mason military governor. He was followed by General Persifor F. Smith, who, in turn, was succeeded by General Bennett Riley. General Riley, presumably, ran the country until the constitutional convention of 1849 elected Peter H. Burnett, a Democrat, the first civil and American governor of California. Burnett held the office of chief executive of an area that was not an independent nation, nor yet a state, nor yet a territory—but was simply a geographical designation called California—until President Millard Fillmore's strokes of the pen created the state of California. After that, Burnett remained in office as the state's first governor.

The reason for all this confusion was not gold, but a much greater and more acute national issue—namely, slavery. Once the Federal government had wrested California from Mexico, a problem had to be faced which was not only California's but was the nation's. Was the state to enter the Union as slave or free? There were hardly any Negroes in the area, yet almost all of it, and certainly all the settled part of it, was well below the Mason-Dixon line. Geographically it was certainly a Southern state. Politically it was dominated by newly arrived Americans, most of whom came from Northern or free states. The constitutional convention prohibited slavery once and for all. Yet the Wilmot Proviso, which had tried to exclude slavery from all the land taken from Mexico, was voted down by the United States Senate.

Henry Clay, the great mediator, had proposed his compromise plan, one of the provisions of which included the admission of California into the Union as a free state. Dominating the Senate were Webster and Calhoun, as well as Clay. The issue was debated to death. While the Senate harangued month after month, California waited. A few of the framers of the state's constitution became impatient and suggested an independent republic to include Oregon as well as California and to seize Baja California at the same time. Nothing came of it, fortunately or unfortunately. For highhanded as the seizing of Baja California from Mexico would have been—international robbery could be the only description—in the long view it would have had its advantages. Anyone who has traveled the full length of the Royal Highway from Loreto in Baja California to Sonoma, north of the Golden Gate, or anyone who has traveled only a hundred miles below the present international border and taken a good look at Baja California, must realize that the future of the Mexican territory is hopeless. Mexico has done nothing to improve or develop it since the days of José de Gálvez, Gaspar de Portolá and Padre Serra. It is true that the area is largely desert and mountains and lacks water. But the natural resources have barely been touched. The few sun-baked towns—Loreto is one—are "out of this world," and life goes on today much as it did in the nineteenth century or even the eighteenth. Had the Americans grabbed it in 1849—stolen it would be the correct phrase—Baja California would now be a land of mines, ranches, vineyards, clean and thriving small cities, popular resorts, good highways and safe airports. Instead, most of it looks exactly the same today as it did when Portolá and Serra blazed the trail that was to become El Camino Real.

But in 1849 the California that we know today was in such a period of transition that Baja California was of little interest. The gold rush had brought some amazing changes. Life in California had been synonymous with life along the Royal Highway. Now the emphasis was suddenly altered, and life in California meant life in the mountain area, the High Sierra country. Towns and camps sprang up overnight, and gone was the Spanish heritage, for these towns had names such as Red Dog, Poker Flat, Rough and Ready, You Bet, Skunk Gulch, Angel's Camp and Hell's Delight. The population of San Diego could not equal that of Chinese Camp which had ambition to become the state capital. The population of Los Angeles was less than that of Hangtown, once called Old Dry Diggings, but later changed to Hangtown because the story got about that it was a place where criminals were hanged first and tried later. It is the pleasant community of Placerville today.

Every town and hamlet along the Royal Highway was affected by the rush to the mines. Monterey even lost its stature as the capital, and the constitutional convention selected San Jose for that honor. San Jose didn't keep it long. The only town that was not depleted, but grew furiously instead, was Yerba Buena, which gradually assumed the name San Francisco.

Travel from San Diego to San Francisco was still best done on horseback. There were no wagons up until 1849, and no stage-coaches until 1858. The Spanish *carreta* was always used for journeys between towns, but was too slow and cumbersome for prolonged travel. The solid wheels of this vehicle were cut transversely from the trunk of a tree, usually being about three feet in diameter, sometimes greater, with holes through the center to accommodate a thick wooden axle. Slow and creaking as they were, however, the *carretas* were put to good use, and in view of the length of the Royal Highway they often covered a considerable distance. In his diary Walter Colton describes travel in 1849:

It is singular how the Californians reckon distances. They will speak of a place as only a short gallop off, when it is fifty or a hundred miles distant. They think nothing of riding a hundred and forty miles in a day, and breaking down three horses in doing it, and following this up by the week. They subsist almost exclusively on meat, and when travelling, sleep under the open sky. They drive their ox-carts, loaded with lumber or provisions, two hundred miles to market. Their conceptions seem to annihilate space.

If most communities along the Royal Highway north from San Diego suffered a temporary setback because of the gold rush, San Francisco was the exception that proved the rule. From a population estimated at 850 at the time Marshall discovered gold, the town grew to 35,000 by the end of 1849, a period of less than two years, and had reached 42,000 by the end of 1852. There was never anything like it before or since in the history of California. San Francisco offered the main avenue to the mines that lay inland,

and those mines produced $10,000,000 in gold in 1849, $41,000,000 in 1850 and $76,000,000 in 1851. These figures are only approximations, but they are the estimate of the California State Mining Bureau and are inclined to be on the conservative side. The Bay of San Francisco was a veritable forest made up of the masts of ships abandoned by officers and crews alike. By the time the city had reached a population of 50,000 in 1853, there were another 50,000 men searching for gold in the Sierra country, and most of them had passed through San Francisco on their way to the mines.

At that same time, 1850, Los Angeles had a population of 1,610, according to the first U. S. Census. Santa Barbara was slightly larger with an estimated 1,800, and San Diego had about 1,400 people. All these figures are exclusive of Indians. San Francisco, obviously, was the only real city on the Royal Highway, and the community continued to grow in leaps and bounds. Into this melting pot by the Golden Gate poured 36,000 people, by sea alone, in 1850, and they came from almost everywhere on earth—all European countries, Australia, Armenia, Africa, China, Japan and Siam. The cosmopolitan aura that has always been inherent in San Francisco brought a dynamism and a color and a vitality that contrasted entirely with the easygoing days of the Mexican rancho and made San Francisco the most distinctive community on the Royal Highway.

With all of this international polyglot the town became tough and dirty and lawless. Rains made the streets a sea of mud. An entire carriage would sink into a quagmire. At Clay and Kearny streets a man drowned in a huge mud puddle. Nobody missed him, or found him, for days.

The demand for food and drink and lodging so far exceeded supply that prices soared to fantastic levels. Half the town was a tent city. Various sections developed as units somewhat exclusive unto themselves. "Little Chile" and "Happy Valley" were a contrast to the tougher area below Telegraph Hill. And "Sydney

Town" was one of the roughest sections, unsafe for a solitary stranger whose wallet might be fair game for the ex-convicts and hoodlums from Australia known as "Sydney Ducks." Another gang of thieves and mobsters was known as the "Hounds," which flaunted its power, had a tent as its headquarters near Portsmouth Square which it called "Tammany Hall," and devoted its time to the "protection of society" by beating up defenseless *Chilenos* or Chinese or anybody who could be attacked without danger of retaliation. A series of disastrous fires wiped out the city again and again, only to have it rise from its own ashes, a little rougher and tougher than before.

A common laborer could earn from $8.00 to $10 a day. A two-story frame house rented for $1,000 a month. A tent was $15 to $20 a week. A room at the new St. Francis Hotel cost $250 a month or $90 by the week. The cheapest meal cost $1.00, and to get one for that price it was necessary to patronize a Chinese "eating house" and not give too much thought to what was in the steaming concoction. New and "luxurious" American restaurants such as Delmonico's charged $5.00 for a meal.

For a report on California's first city, there was a book published in 1855 that gave a first-person account by the author, among other things Californian, of what he saw during his stay in San Francisco in 1852. The book was called *The Land of Gold* and was written by a twenty-five-year-old North Carolinian, later to become famous for his *Impending Crisis in the South.* His name was Hinton R. Helper. That his observations may seem a bit unfair, and inclined somewhat vicariously to the emphasizing of the unpleasant, in no way detracts from his picture of some aspects of San Francisco during the chaotic days of the gold rush. Helper's book was long out of print, but has recently been reissued by Bobbs-Merrill in an edition edited by Lucius Beebe and Charles M. Clegg, who have taken the liberty of changing the title to *Dreadful California.* In his book Helper wrote:

Owing to its advantageous geographical position, and the facilities and accommodation offered for shipping, I think it may be safely said that San Francisco will be a great city, although California can never become a great State. . . .

Degradation, profligacy and vice confront us at every step. Men are passing to and fro with haggard visages and heads declined, muttering to themselves and looking as hungry and ferocious as the prowling beasts of an Asiatic jungle. Before us on either side we see a group of boys clad in slouched hats, dirty shirts, ragged pants, and shabby shoes without socks, who have no regular business. . . .

Not unfrequently these vicious youths repeat their potations so often that they become thoroughly inebriated and may be seen quarreling, fighting, and lying about the streets like hardened and inveterate topers. . . .

It may be remarked that San Francisco is no longer dependent upon the State for her support. San Francisco can now claim to be as much the city of the world as of California. . . .

Returning to our subject, we find ourselves as far advanced on our way as Montgomery street. The course of this street lies north and south through the middle of the most beautiful and wealthy part of the city. It is, therefore, both the Broadway and the Wall street of San Francisco. Every phase and trait of life and character is cognizable here. The dramatist who would study human nature here would have an opportunity of striking out something new, instead of repeating the old creations of his predecessors, for surely never was there so varied a page spread out before the eyes of man. . . .

The grog-shops or tippling-houses constitute the last but not the least prominent feature of Montgomery street that we will notice at the present time. The devil has certainly met with more than usual success in establishing so many of these, his recruiting officers, in this region. We cannot visit any part of the state or city without finding them always at our elbow. San Francisco might allot one to every street corner in the city, or in other words, four to every intersection of the streets, and still her number would not be exhausted. It is astonishing what an amount of time, labor and money is misspent in this nefarious traffic. Out of the two hundred and fifty thousand inhabitants in California, from twelve to fifteen thousand are exclusively engaged in this diabolical but lucrative business.

And what is worse, nearly one-fourth of the bars are attended by young females of the most dissolute and abandoned character, who use every device to entice and mislead the youthful and unsuspecting. Women being somewhat of a novelty here, their saloons are always thronged with customers, many being induced to patronize them merely for the sake of looking at them. What a base prostitution of their destiny and mission! Woman has come here not only to pander to man's vitiated appetites but also to create and foster in him unholier desires. . . .

Were we to remain an hour or two in this vicinity, we should probably see a police officer rolling a lady in a wheelbarrow. Intoxication is quite common among the ladies of this section of San Francisco, and the wheelbarrow or some other vehicle must be employed to convey them to the station-house on account of the total failure of their natural organs of locomotion. . . .

I may not be a competent judge, but this much I will say, that I have seen purer liquors, better segars, finer tobacco, truer guns and pistols, larger dirks and bowie knives, and prettier courtezans here, than in any other place I have ever visited; and it is my unbiased opinion that California can and does furnish the best bad things that are obtainable in America. . . .

The gambling-houses cannot be overlooked in a true sketch of life in San Francisco. One of the largest and most frequented of these, called the Diana, stands a few doors above us. The building extends through the entire block from Clay to Commercial street and has a front proportionate to its depth. The doors which lead into it from either street are kept wide open from nine in the morning and the hall or saloon is generally filled to overflowing with lazy men of little principle, whose chief employment consists in devising some sinister plans of procuring a livelihood without work. . . .

While a careful reading suggests that Hinton Helper enjoyed seeing as well as reporting all this sin without, perhaps, admitting it even to himself, it was one aspect of San Francisco and there was no denying it.

Quite apart from evil, which for some reason always seems to be more compelling than good, there were constructive elements at work along the Royal Highway at this time, and even in San Francisco itself. Looking beyond the saloons, brothels and gambling houses, and that area in general known as the Barbary Coast, it was San Francisco which took the lead in the gold-rush period in schools, churches, theaters, hospitals, libraries, newspapers and magazines. While the city administration was corrupt on the one hand, and graft and boondoggling ran rampant, relief committees and charitable institutions invariably had their financial appeals oversubscribed. The town may have been no paragon of virtue, but it was none the less growing into a great city through its husky, lusty and boisterous adolescence.

Other "cities" came into formal existence with the incorporation in 1850 of Sacramento, San Diego, San Jose, Benicia (planned to be the capital, which, indeed, it was for a brief time) and Los Angeles.

The first California legislature as provided for by the constitutional convention met in the new and temporary capital of San Jose. It was made up of sixteen senators and thirty-six assemblymen, and was dubbed the "Legislature of a Thousand Drinks." The members were not as addicted to alcohol as this sobriquet might indicate. It came, instead, from Senator Thomas J. Green, who, whenever a problem seemed particularly vexatious, suggested "adjourn and take a thousand drinks and there won't be any problem." It was this assembly that elected California's first two United States senators even while the area was still waiting for statehood. One was William M. Gwin, a more-than-competent politician from Tennessee (some historians go so far as to call him a statesman), and the other, incredible as it may seem, was none other than John Charles Frémont. Now no longer a military man due to his court-martial and decision to resign from the army, Frémont returned to California, and again exhibited that luck which he invariably had of somehow landing on his feet. Along with Gwin, California sent him to Washington. He was now Senator Frémont.

This first legislature also created California's first twenty-seven counties. Steadily and efficiently the state was beginning to take shape.

Then, on September 9, 1850, came its formal admittance to the Union. This news did not reach San Francisco until October 18, arriving by the mail steamer *Oregon*. There was a wild celebration that lasted for several days, and a new star was added to the thirty that formed the field of the American flag which flew over Portsmouth Square.

As the news came down the Royal Highway it was received with jubilance by the Americans, with a certain amount of enthusiasm by those Californians who had favored a break with Mexico, and with resignation or apathy or indifference on the part of those who could not learn to like the gringo. There were celebrations—though not so prolonged or so noisy as San Francisco's —in Monterey, Santa Barbara, Los Angeles and San Diego. The gold rush had changed the character of the state. Everything alive, progressive and dominant in it was all *yanqui*. In theory at least, the transitional period, the scramble for power, the era of devil-take-the-hindmost, was over. But that was in theory; unfortunately, in more ways than one, it had only begun.

PART 5

THE THIRTY-FIRST
STATE OF THE UNION

1850 *to* ...

Your Money or
Your Life

21

THERE is no such truism, but there might well be one: if you have a highway, you'll have highwaymen. There were three who operated along the Royal Highway in the period following the gold rush. All three were Mexicans, and there is a significance to this. In a sense they were the antisocial recalcitrants who epitomized the resentment of all native Californians to the invasion and assumption of the gringo. All three bandits hated Americans and said so. All three were precipitated into a life of banditry because of Americans and said so. After their separate careers in crimes ranging through robbery, rape and murder had sufficiently terrorized people from San Diego to Sonoma, American justice, of some form, finally caught up with all three. Two were publicly hanged; a third was shot to death in a running gun fight, then had his head cut off, pickled in alcohol, and exhibited in San Francisco for an entrance fee of $1.00. Juan Flores (not to be identified with the José María Flores who defended California and Los Angeles to the end against Stockton, Kearny and Frémont —although it is most likely that the two were related), unquestionably a homicidal maniac, was one of the bandits, and history has almost forgotten him. Tiburcio Vásquez was another, and his name is still known to Californians. But the most famous of the three, the man whose name has become synonymous with derring-do, cool politeness and sudden death, the man whose villainous exploits have been softened by romantic writing, the man whose name struck terror in the hearts of people up and down the Royal Highway—was Joaquin Murrieta.

The legends and stories about Murrieta are rife. None of them is the whole truth, and yet all of them doubtless have elements of truth in them. The real story of Murrieta runs from melodramatic dime-novel thrills to the psychoanalysis of a mind warped, if not unhinged, by suffering the cruelty of man to man.

Keeping the lurid details down to a minimum, all stories seemingly agree that Joaquin Murrieta was born in Mexico and came, as a young man with an especially attractive young wife called Carmen, to California in the year 1849. An older brother had come to California earlier and had written Joaquin of the discovery of gold. Within one year Joaquin found his brother, saw him lynched on a false charge of horse stealing, was viciously beaten while his wife Carmen was criminally attacked and then murdered by three hoodlum gringo miners, and finally Joaquin was tied to a tree and horsewhipped by Americans for no other reason than the fact that he was a Mexican and not wanted in the gold diggings.

If all, or only part of this, was true, it was enough for Joaquin Murrieta. For a short time he disappeared, only to emerge as a highwayman and murderer. His depredations were not exclusively aimed at Americans, but were carried out against any race, Mexican, Chinese or Indian, which would seem to indicate that he had gone mentally berserk, although he affirmed his murderous intentions toward all Americans at all times.

Murrieta was not a big man, was on the slender side, had black hair and black eyes which came to have a permanent look of the madness of one hunted and defiant, was an excellent shot with rifle or pistol, was skillful with a lariat, was a superb knife thrower and a horseman supreme. These assets, along with a sense of the dramatic, a devilishly cool manner and a histrionic ability to disguise himself as an ignorant laborer, a priest, anybody's cowhand or even a woman, made him exceedingly dangerous and difficult to apprehend.

At first he operated alone, and his technique was to wait in ambush for a solitary traveler, lasso him and yank him from his horse, cut his throat and ride away with whatever wealth the victim had happened to have on his person. In time he fell in with other outlaws and inevitably became their leader. His forays ranged throughout the gold towns in the High Sierras and up and down the Royal Highway, and nobody could be sure just where he was, what he was planning or where he would strike next.

Murrieta's gang was as evil a bunch of tough *hombres* as any in criminal history. Their number varied from time to time from half a dozen to twenty or more desperadoes. Among those who achieved infamy along with their leader was Joaquin Valenzuela, tall, dark and saturnine, and because of his given name, often mistaken for the real Joaquin. Robbery was his chief interest and occupation.

Another was Luís Vulvia. While robbery was the immediate motive for his career in crime, he apparently was a sex maniac as well, and his basic satisfaction was derived from leaving his victims in a condition similar to those of Jack the Ripper.

Pedro Gonzalez was the horse-thief specialist of the gang, and Murrieta depended on him to keep his merry men well supplied with good fast animals. Gonzalez stole horses from ranchos as widely separated as San Diego and the Oregon border. Often, when Murrieta led an attack on a cache of gold in the High Sierra country, Gonzalez and a few others would be sent to steal horses from ranchos as much as two or three hundred miles away. Then they would assemble for a rendezvous at some previously appointed site and prepare for their next atrocity. Murrieta, of course, would be blamed for the gold theft in the mountains and the horse theft in the valley, and nobody could say for sure just when he had been where. All this, coupled with the fact that many "greasers" looked more or less alike to Americans, made Murrieta just that much more elusive and difficult to identify.

Another member of the gang was a young bandit named Claudio. History is not certain of his last name. Some people think he was Claudio Murrieta, a brother of Joaquin. He is said to have been a handsome Latin type, and served as a kind of lieutenant or adjutant to the chief. He was a born gambler, and no desperate odds were too great for him to take, whether the stakes were in cards or in lives.

But the pillar of this criminal society was a stocky, gorilla-shaped murderer who was Murrieta's most dependable killer. He was obviously a sadist, preferred to torture his victims to death by slow and ingenious methods, and is said to have remarked, "Brandy makes some men drunk, but give me blood." Unlike the others, who were of light, lithe, athletic build, this lumbering beast was beetle-browed, pock-marked and had had part of his right hand shot off, leaving it with three fingers. This earned him the nickname Three-fingered Jack, although it is believed that his real name was Juan García and that he was a half-breed. He particularly detested Chinamen, and his pet sport was to capture six or eight Orientals, bind their hands, tie their queues together so that none could escape, and then slowly and gleefully slit the throat of each one.

Then there were a number of others who have become mere names in history—Manuel Sevalio, Fernando Fuentes, Florencio Cruz, Rafael Quintano, José Ochovo; and still others lost to the record—all villains of some kind, all gringo haters, and all with their hands stained with somebody's blood.

So it is plain to see that it was not exactly a bunch of gay and jolly fellows who haunted the Royal Highway, and as the viciousness and fiendishness of their deeds got abroad, the words "It's Murrieta!" caused people to tremble in their boots.

Romantic tradition has grown up around these murderers, and Murrieta himself has been the hero of at least one motion picture and one radio serial. The reasons for this are obvious, for the man had unquestionable daring and courage and would play three-card monte for hours in a public saloon, defying the danger of recognition. If and when his name happened to be mentioned in any scurrilous or derogatory way he would upset the table, scatter the cards, draw a gun and say, "Be more careful of your words, señores, for I am Joaquin Murrieta." Then, as tradition would have it, he'd calmly light a cigarette and walk out the door. His horse was never tethered, but had long been taught to stand with its reins over its head and neck, in the best cow-horse style. Possibly punctuating his exit by putting a few shots into the open door of the saloon, Murrieta would leap onto his waiting horse and rapidly ride away. Or he would turn up at a fandango with some of his cutthroats, enter into the spirit of the party, dance merrily with all the lovely girls, and ride off into the night without harming a hair of their pretty heads. Tradition likes to accept this embroidery, and it is easy to see that for movies and radio and television Murrieta has become the Robin Hood of California.

But the real man could not have been the hero-bandit that it would be pleasant to believe. After the murder of an officer of the law in Santa Clara, Murrieta, alone this time and wounded, fled south and took refuge at the Mission San Carlos Borroméo del Rio Carmelo. Here, at the very grave of the great Padre Junípero Serra, this murderer sought refuge and found it. Mission San Carlos was one of the last to suffer decay and collapse after secularization, and there was still a priest officiating there in 1853. While he was recovering in this sanctuary, Murrieta permitted the priest to paint his portrait. This oil painting was sent to Los Angeles by the priest in 1855, after Murrieta's death, to a woman, unidentified, who was supposed to turn it over to the surviving relatives. Unable to find any living relatives, she kept the portrait in an attic for years, and it was finally discovered after her death by Major Horace Bell of Los Angeles who was the administrator of the estate. He had the few damaged spots retouched and this one painting of California's most notorious bandit was preserved for posterity. That the artist caught the real man, the half-mad, defiant killer, instead of the romantic gentleman-bandit, there is no doubt.

After a few more deeds of horror ranging from rape through arson and robbery to murder, especially around Los Angeles, Governor John Bigler offered a reward of $5,000 for Joaquin Murrieta, dead or alive, and lesser amounts for various members of his gang with Three-fingered Jack second on the list. The state legislature (the capital was now the town of Benicia, and in another year would be removed for the last time to Sacramento) passed a bill in May 1853 authorizing the creation of a company of armed and mounted men, a kind of state militia, for the sole purpose of ridding California of its bandits. The leader had the innocuous name of Harry Love. But Harry Love was a man of mettle and he dedicated himself to the success of this venture. He selected twenty recruits, to be known as the "California Rangers." The men enlisted for a period of ninety days and were paid $150 per month. These state troopers, who might well have been called the California Mounted Police, had to be expert horsemen, superb marksmen and perfectly capable of handling themselves in any terrain, be it the coastal valleys, the dry deserts or the High Sierras. It took Love a month to select the men he wanted. He had the title of captain and his twenty men were "rangers." By the first of June the twenty-one were in the field, and what in today's language would be called "Operation Murrieta" got under way.

Murrieta knew of this at once. While his gang now numbered about twenty men, he had innumerable friends and confederates up and down the Royal Highway. And there were many Mexican-born or California-born citizens who were not only afraid of him, but because of latent anti-gringo feelings, admired him. The story is told, and quite possibly could be true, that Murrieta rode into Monterey, saw a poster offering $5,000 for his capture dead or alive, wrote on it, *I'll pay $10,000 to the man who can do it—*

Joaquin Murrieta, and rode off leaving this thrasonical brag for Love and his men to think about.

Whether he sensed that the game was up, and planned to ride to Mexico leaving a final trail of gringo blood behind him, as some of his biographers think likely, or whether he simply continued to rob and burn and loot with no direction in mind like a dog run mad, is still conjecture. But he did steer clear of Captain Harry Love and his rangers by rounding up his desperadoes and riding south, down the Royal Highway, leaving scenes of horrors as he went. This ride of rapine began in San Jose just before Harry Love and his men went into the field.

The bandit gang hid by day and rode by night, and God himself was no help to the lone traveler or small ranch owner they happened to meet. When they left the Salinas Valley and crossed the mountains to San Luis Obispo they left two corpses and one burned ranch house behind them. They went through San Luis Obispo in a body at midnight and were seen and identified, but nobody dared attack them. Several days went by and no more was heard of them. Then an entire family was found hideously murdered near Santa Ynez. The bandits were still riding south.

They passed through Santa Barbara at night, and the populace stayed indoors in fear and trembling unequaled by any such condition since the days of Bouchard the pirate.

Sheriffs and deputies in Los Angeles and San Diego were alert and waiting. The gang seemed to fan out in order to sift through the Los Angeles area, for Joaquin Murrieta was seen at Mission San Gabriel, and somebody else saw Three-fingered Jack at the port of San Pedro some miles to the south. These reports may have been the results of hysteria, but there was no doubt about the death of a ranchero's wife near San Juan Capistrano, for the manner of killing bore all the indications of having been done by Luís Vulvia, the sex maniac.

It appeared that Murrieta was definitely headed for Baja California, possibly intending to follow the Royal Highway all the way to its lower end at Loreto and then escape by boat across the Gulf of California to the Mexican mainland. Not far below San Juan Capistrano the bodies of two Chinamen were found, their queues tied together and their throats slit. Everybody said, "Three-fingered Jack!"

But if escape to Mexico was his plan, something caused Murrieta to change his mind. For no accountable reason he doubled back on his tracks, stole a choice assortment of fresh horses from the ranch of Andres Pico near Los Angeles and headed north again, this time following the trail from Mission San Fernando by way of Castaic Creek and the Tejon Pass to the upper end of the San Joaquin Valley, or what is the route of U.S. Highway 99 today. While he couldn't foresee it, this turnabout led him straight to his Waterloo.

Captain Harry Love and his rangers, days behind on a cold trail, were only as far south as San Juan Bautista, not far from Monterey, when a messenger sent by Andres Pico reported that the bandits had doubled back on their tracks and were heading north in the San Joaquin Valley.

Making a guess as to just about where they ought to be in view of this news and the time that it took to reach him, Captain Love decided to ride east from the Royal Highway, through the Coast Range and try to intercept the bandit gang as it moved north. Knowing that Murrieta had many friends, tipsters and spies, Love made ostentatious preparations for a long ride south to Los Angeles, but at nightfall swung easterly through a part of California that is very lightly traveled even today. Just below the present community of King City on U.S. Highway 101, there is a pass through the mountains by way of Priest Valley that leads on to the broad plains of the San Joaquin. Harry Love chose this pass, and after an all-night ride the rangers reached the end of the mountain area and looked out at dawn over the broad San Joaquin Valley.

A few miles away a column of blue smoke was rising. It was somebody's campfire. With all of California, an area as big as England, in which to search, Love and his men couldn't believe that this one column of smoke indicated the camping place of the very men they were seeking. That the rangers were somewhere within several hundred miles of the bandit gang was a certainty, but that in one night's ride easterly from the Royal Highway they had come straight to their quarry seemed impossible to suppose. Love and all his men took it for granted that the smoke was coming from the breakfast fire of some *vaqueros* rounding up cattle or wild horses. But just to ask for information they decided to ride over to that camp, and being good rangers they followed an arroyo, simply as a routine precaution, which was deep enough to give them concealment. They were not in fighting formation, and the twenty-one riders were strung out over a half mile or more with Love in the lead.

Only one member of the twenty-one had even seen Murrieta. He was William Byrnes, who had known him in the gold-rush country and would be able to recognize him immediately. Byrnes, however, rode seventh in the file of riders, none of whom was anticipating any immediate hostile action.

The number of men with Murrieta in that morning camp has been disputed. Some say there were only seven, others give the number as fifteen. Regardless of that, Captain Love rode up out of the arroyo within thirty yards of the camp and was followed by ranger after ranger. The bandits were completely surprised. Some were still sleeping on the ground, wrapped in their blankets, and one slim chap was saddling his horse. A stocky burly fellow was cooking beans and bacon over the fire that had indicated their campsite.

Harry Love, still thinking he had come upon a *vaquero* camp, called out a cheerful "Good morning!"

Immediately these *vaqueros* sprang into action: those who had been asleep jumped up from their blankets; those who were already up reached for their guns; the slim chap saddling his horse called, "Who are you and what do you want?", and the cook, a beetle-browed, simianlike creature, turned to stare, a coffeepot in his hand. And that hand, clasping the utensil, had only three fingers.

The slim chap reached for a gun.

"Drop it!" commanded Love, pointing his gun at the man.

Ranger W. S. Henderson was directly behind Captain Love. The others were emerging in file from the arroyo—the third, the fourth and the fifth—Rangers George Evans, John Nuttall and Robert Masters.

"Cover that man," commanded Love.

Henderson, not knowing it, casually aimed his six-shooter at Murrieta. At the same time Love took a good look at the scowling cook and was shocked when he saw three fingers only on that cook's right hand. At once Love realized that these must be the men he wanted. And at the very same instant the sixth ranger, Lafayette Black, followed by the seventh, rode up out of the arroyo and into the camp. The seventh ranger, William Byrnes, gasped.

"That's Murrieta!" he yelled, pointing at the slim chap who had been saddling a horse.

In the next few seconds history cannot record exactly what happened. Too many shots were fired too fast for any accurate summary.

But it is known that Murrieta fired three quick shots at Henderson and Henderson returned the fire. In the explosive excitement of the moment as each group was faced with the sudden realization of the identity of the other, bullets flew indiscriminately and inaccurately. Three-fingered Jack blazed away at Captain Love with a bullet that parted the captain's hair. Murrieta, with no time left to finish the saddling of his horse, threw the saddle aside, leaped on the animal bareback and was off at full speed. Hender-

son, being nearest to Murrieta, went after him. Murrieta, clinging
to his mount by his knees and one arm, fired back at Henderson.

When he saw Henderson pursue Murrieta, followed by Byrnes
and Black, Love turned his attention to Three-fingered Jack.
The half-breed, unable to get near any of the gang's horses, plunged
into the chaparral on foot with Love, Evans and Nuttall after him.
The remainder of the bandits and the rest of the file of rangers,
who had heard the shooting and were coming on at full gallop
with their guns ready, engaged in a general melee that soon over-
came the bandits. Those who were not killed surrendered. There
seems to be no agreement on the number, but it is known for a
certainty that two of the bandits, Florencio Cruz and José Ochovo,
were taken alive. It is believed that Luís Vulvia hid in the underbrush and somehow managed to crawl far enough away to escape
detection. For all anybody knows he may have been wounded and
died in the underbrush. The bodies of Pedro Gonzalez and Rafael
Quintano were identified by Ochovo later. The confusion of details is due to the fact that neither Love nor any of his rangers
could say for sure just how many men were in the bandit camp
when they so unexpectedly came upon it.

But there is no doubt about what happened to Three-fingered
Jack and Joaquin Murrieta. Captain Love and several others pursued Jack through the chaparral and across arroyos for almost half
a mile. Occasionally the desperate half-breed would stop for breath
and fire at the oncoming rangers. In spite of the fact that they
were mounted and he was not, he was as difficult as a jack rabbit
to trap. Crawling through brush that horsemen had to detour
around, dodging and darting and stopping, he made a difficult
target, while Love and his men stood out sharply in the line of fire.
Two of the pursuers had their horses shot dead from under them,
but at last a bullet from Love got Three-fingered Jack through the
body. Badly wounded, he could not flee with his former agility,
and at last Love bore down upon him, calling on him to surrender.

Three-fingered Jack's answer was his last bullet, for Love's next shot tore the top of his head off.

Murrieta, by this time, was a good mile or more in the opposite direction. Henderson, Byrnes and Black were gaining on him, but to do so were courting death, for Joaquin would suddenly wheel his horse and fire, clinging to the far side of the animal like an Indian. Then he would be off again in another direction.

Ranger Black's horse was shot dead, and Black was out of the fight. But a bullet from Henderson got Murrieta's horse. Thrown clear as his horse stumbled and died, Murrieta rose for his last stand. He and Henderson fired simultaneously at each other. Shaken by the fall, Murrieta's aim was bad. Henderson's was not. He put three bullets through the outlaw's body, Byrnes added two more, and the Mexican staggered, collapsed and died. It is believed that at the time of his death he was twenty-five years old.

When the toll was finally taken it was found that four of the bandits were dead and two were prisoners; how many escaped wounded to die later, or escaped scot-free, will never be known.

Several rangers were wounded but none seriously. Five of their horses had been killed.

Love and his men were not a squeamish lot; they breakfasted at what had been the outlaws' camp, using the same fire that had sent up the curl of smoke that touched off the battle. Elated with their victory, they discussed the reward and how it should be divided. Then somebody suggested that there might not be any reward. It was all well and good to ride home and declare that they had killed Murrieta and Three-fingered Jack, but what actual and valid proof did they have? Suppose some other bandit, out of sheer vanity, turned up sometime and boasted that *he* was Murrieta. The rumor would be believed. Everybody would say that Murrieta had outwitted them, and that they were liars. Proof, and no doubt about it, was required.

"Well, if we should cut his head off and take it to the governor's office in a sack, I guess that would be proof enough," said Harry Love.

Everybody agreed there would be no disputing that evidence.

So the gruesome job was done. Joaquin Murrieta's head was hacked off and his body left for the coyotes and the vultures. In the case of Three-fingered Jack, the head was in such bad condition due to Love's last shot that it was impossible to make use of it. But Jack had another feature that offered even more positive identification—his three-fingered hand. The rangers chopped it off at the wrist. Now, with these two trophies, let any man say they hadn't done their job!

Love sent Rangers Byrnes (who had known Murrieta) and Black with the evidence to the nearest army post, some ninety miles away in the San Joaquin Valley, and there the surgeon preserved the head and the hand in alcohol.

So famous was Murrieta at the time that even his head had a value for the curious and the morbid. The head, along with the hand of Three-fingered Jack, was exhibited in San Francisco in August 1853, and later the exhibition went on tour to many California towns. A typical handbill read:

JOAQUIN'S HEAD
is to be seen
AT KING'S
Corner Halleck and Sansome Streets
Opposite the American Theatre
Admission $1.00   Aug. 18th

This unpleasant show went on for years, and eventually somebody stole both the head and Three-fingered Jack's hand, which always was exhibited at the same time. After that theft the last corporeal vestiges of the two murderers disappeared forever.

The annihilation of Joaquin Murrieta and his gang did not end crime along the Royal Highway. A few years later a lone bandit named Tiburcio Vásquez plagued the road, was guilty of a number of murders and was finally caught and hanged at San Jose in 1874. Schools were closed on the day of his execution so that children might see the evildoer and learn thereby that a life of crime would someday lead to the gallows. While his name is still recalled today, Vásquez never achieved the terrible fame of Murrieta. Lesser highwaymen have come and gone, but none of them ever measured up to Joaquin. By 1875 the era of the highwayman had passed into history.

Robbery in California, however, was still going on. There were more ways than one to demand your money or your life. It was only the simple and direct and single-purposed outlaw who used a gun and held up the weary traveler or the unguarded stagecoach. There were far more subtle and legal means of stealing in this thirty-first state of the Union. To these pilferers, the bandit was a crude amateur. They were not interested in the contents of a wallet or the gold in a strongbox. They stole whole ranchos, forty, fifty or sixty thousand acres at a time.

President Polk himself, at the time of the Treaty of Guadalupe Hidalgo which formally ended the Mexican War, had insisted that within the terms must be a clause for the protection of the Californians, which would recognize and guarantee all legitimate titles to all property, personal and real, existing in the territory. In other words, a conquered people were not to be robbed and dispossessed; instead, their rights to their land were to be inviolably respected.

But a little more than a year after "achieving" statehood, Californians found that President Polk was gone, the Treaty of Guadalupe Hidalgo was a scrap of paper to be forgotten, and the Congress of the United States had passed a bill on March 3, 1851, establishing a land commission. If you were a Californian you had to submit to this commission, made up of only three men, all your claims to the land you owned, no matter if it had been granted to you by the King of Spain, the Republic of Mexico or God himself. If you couldn't prove it was yours, no matter if you and your family had lived on it and developed it for three or four generations, it would become public domain and you could just pack up your things and go elsewhere. Should you ignore the requirements of submitting your title to the new land commission for as much as two full years—or by March 3, 1853—you forfeited all title whether legitimate or not.

Compared to the highwaymen who usually wanted only the cash you carried on your person, this Land Act could take every bit of your property down to your last acre and your last cow. The highwaymen were rank amateurs; the government at Washington had found a way to rob you legally and professionally. Many a native Californian with a large rancho along the Royal Highway rued the day the gringo came. The bandit wanted your money or your life. The gringo took both. What a privilege to live in this thirty-first state of his Union!

Title, Title, Who's Got a Title?

22

SUPPOSE your name was Valdez or Dominguez and you owned 40,000 or 60,000 acres which had been in your family since 1797 (it is now 1853), and this property was known as Rancho de las Virgenes, or Rancho de las Aguas or any other name, and it comprised an area equal to all of Beverly Hills, Westwood, Sawtelle, Brentwood and most of Santa Monica, and the fact that it was a grant to your grandfather from Governor Diego de Borica had been understood for the last half century and more, but you had no documents to authenticate it, ransack old trunks as you might—what could you do to prove your title?

Nothing.

And at the end of two years, simply because you had no piece of old and crumbling paper or parchment (or even if you had it might be found out of order), how would you like to be told that your title was a figment of your imagination and that the 40,000 acres called Rancho de las Virgenes, or any other name, was public domain and any number of gringo squatters had a right to settle on it, file on it and in good time get title to various choice sections of it, and eventually all of it?

You wouldn't like it.

So you would appeal to the land commission, and that body would shrug it off and say that if you hadn't a valid title, and they would be the judges of its validity even if you had one, the land never was yours in the first place.

Desperate over losing all your land and the houses, stock and grain thereon, you would appeal to the senior senator from California to Washington and ask his aid in preserving to you and yours what had been your family's land for over fifty years. His name was John C. Frémont.

Then you'd discover that the first land-title claim to be investigated by the land commission—and approved by that body—was a claim on Rancho de las Mariposas, a valuable property indeed, worth as much as your own, and the claim was filed by none other than John C. Frémont. So he had his, without doubt. But when you wrote to this man, your senator, he didn't take the trouble to reply.

Again you wouldn't like it, and by this time that would be an understatement. Also, by this time you'd be told to get out by the squatters who were settling on your rancho and they would leave no doubt in your mind about it, for they would tell you that you were a dirty blankety-blank greaser and you'd better get the hell off *their* land or they'd run you off with a shotgun.

By this time you would discover that the man who had instigated the Land Act, and thereby knew all about it from the start, and had it confirm his own claim first, was also John C. Frémont.

Something would certainly seem to you to be rotten in the State of California. But it did you no good to think it or to say it, for you were suddenly impoverished and helpless. If you didn't like it here, did you know what you could do? Go back to Mexico where your ancestors came from—and *stay* there.

All that was one side of the picture.

But, as always, it takes two sides to make an argument. Piratical, unjust, double-crossing of a pledged trust as the Land Act of 1851 may appear to be, and granting all the misery and heartbreak that it caused, some system of clarification of title had to be put into operation. In many cases Don Pedro Valdez or Don Sebastián Dominguez was unable to say exactly what land he owned with any more accuracy than from a certain hill to a distant mountain, or as far as he could see from such-and-such a peak, or up to a certain arroyo which, it turned out, had been re-formed or recut by rains and flash floods and was nowhere near where he thought it was, or perhaps was even nonexistent.

All these general and even vague estimates of who owned what along the Royal Highway might have been adjusted without injury to anyone had it not been for the gold rush and all the social and economic confusion that followed in its wake. But when it is noted that the population of California quadrupled itself in one year, and then quadrupled itself again in another two, it is easy to see that a Congress in distant Washington could not comprehend the local problem when it changed rapidly month by month and when information took months to reach the Atlantic seaboard.

With 250,000 people in a state that only a few years before had less than 30,000, and most of these people newly arrived Americans with others still pouring into this state that had lately been a territory of another nation, the social adjustment could not be a fair and leisurely process. Things happened fast. Moreover, the American tempo was not that of the native Californian. The result was that the Californian got hurt in this new scramble for power and property. He was not deliberately cheated by the invader; he was cheated by destiny.

In turn, some of the Californians' claims were spurious or even fraudulent. Many land grants had been made in the last months and weeks before American invasion. Some of these were ridiculous. Apart from vague boundaries, some claimants to land had no more right to it than squatter rights; but they pretended, or even convinced themselves, that father or grandfather did have a deed somewhere from a Mexican governor or a Spanish king. Nobody seemed to question the right of a king in Madrid to grant land he had never seen and didn't own; and nobody seemed to consider that in the final analysis the Indians had at least priority on their side, and the king did not. But regardless of the social ethics of the situation, it was a surety that somebody was going to own California and find some self-justified means of doing so. Washington tried to make a fair allotment, but the complexities of the problem caused it to get somewhat out of hand.

Henry W. Halleck came to California in 1848 for the purpose of preparing a report on land grants prior to American annexation. Immediately he was beset by the problems of ill-defined Mexican boundaries, sound claims, vague claims, irregular claims and fraudulent claims. His report served to convince Washington that California needed a land commission.

Halleck was followed in 1849 by William Carey Jones, who made sincere efforts to segregate the just claims from the unjust. He arrived at Monterey and traveled south down the Royal Highway to San Diego and back again. He developed a high degree of respect for many California claims and titles, but again, his report convinced Congress that an on-the-scene commission to settle legitimate ownership was the only answer.

It was Senator Frémont and Senator Gwin (with a little impetus from Senator Thomas Hart Benton who still felt that past President Polk had wronged his dear son-in-law) who managed to put the bill through Congress. It provided for the appointment of the three land commissioners. It was a little highhanded, but, it did settle the matter.

The board, appointed by President Fillmore, was made up of Harry Thornton, James Wilson and Hiland Hall. Their names scarcely ring a bell in California history today, but they were faced with one of the most important jobs in the history of the state. It was up to them to decide who owned what.

The fact that they decided immediately that John C. Frémont owned Rancho de las Mariposas, and decided, in time, that the Dominguez family did not own Rancho de las Virgenes simply because the Dominguez family did not take the trouble to submit its perfectly valid title for their consideration, gave the board a bad name among the native Californians. Frémont's title was assured. The Dominguez family lost its land which became public domain. What kind of commission was this?

Unsavory as these examples may be, the board tried to be fair, patient and honest. The original personnel was changed in 1853, and President Pierce appointed three new commissioners. During the five years of its existence the board passed on more than 800 cases involving more than 12,000,000 acres of California real estate. About 520 claims were authenticated and approximately 275 were rejected. This meant that 520 Californians (or Frémont-Californians) were protected in title by the United States. And it meant that 275 native Californians lost their ranchos, some unjustly, some through negligence and some because their claims were fraudulent from the start. It was not a happy picture, but it was the only one that could be painted.

The worst features of the whole situation were, first, the moneylenders who reaped a rich harvest; and, second, the interminable time it took to clear and substantiate a title. Incredible as it may seem, the average case took seventeen years! And there are cases on record of native Californians who carried on the fight for their land as long as thirty-five years and finally won. In that time a generation had come and another one had gone.

The moneylenders offered to finance, for the rancho claimant, the cost of pressing his claims before the land commission. Sometimes these moneylenders were also attorneys. The ranchero was not an American; the attorneys were. For an interest in the deal the American attorney would plead the cause of the native Californian before the American board of commissioners. All the attorney wanted for his fee was a mortgage on the Californian's land.

Or perhaps the Californian had made no contact with any attorneys simply because he could not afford legal counsel. In view of the fact that the average ranchero—or don or *caballero*—was considered a wealthy man, one might wonder why he could not afford a lawyer. The answer is simple: the wealth of the native Californian was not in liquid capital, but in his land and cattle. Land and cattle cannot pay bills; cash can. Therefore a loan from a moneylender would ease the situation and enable Don So-and-So to acquire the cash to offer a lawyer a fee to defend his title before the land commission. All Don So-and-So had to do was to sign a piece of paper stating that he promised to pay to the moneylender the sum of $1,000 or $5,000 or whatever it might be that he needed at the time. There was a little matter of interest on the money borrowed, but this was a trivial item to Don So-and-So. What did a small percentage matter? He had never borrowed money before, and the moneylender and his pound of flesh had been unknown in any community along the Royal Highway prior to 1851. So Don So-and-So signed the little paper and forgot it. For generations the word of the patriarch of his family had been as good as a bond. Now he, as patriarch, would naturally repay the loan. The fact that the rate of interest was 5 percent or even 10 percent per *month,* compounded monthly, meant little. All Don So-and-So knew was that he had borrowed a rather piffling sum of money in view of his assets, and that in good time he would repay it. There was no doubt about his repaying it, for, if he didn't, there was a clause in the little piece of paper saying that the moneylender could take his rancho. So indubitably Don So-and-So would repay the loan in a year or two or three or more. He had not even stopped to figure up what the sum would be at 5 percent per month (or more) compounded monthly, over a few years. The end result was, of course, that the moneylender got a 20,000 to 40,000-acre ranch for a cash loan of $5,000 which could never be redeemed. Slowly the Californians, and it must be said with tragic tardiness, learned the word usury.

On the other hand, all was not graft on the part of the American opportunists and naïveté on the part of the Californians. The land commission was completely taken in by a Frenchman who had become a Mexican citizen. His name was José Y. Limantour. He presented a claim for a mere 600,000 acres. Included in this were all the islands in San Francisco Bay, the Farallon Islands off the coast, and the heart of downtown San Francisco. He had received this grant from Governor Micheltorena and apparently everything was in order and he had the papers to prove it. The land commission okayed it. Then a hue and cry was raised by the Americans when they learned that their own commission had, figuratively, dispossessed them, and had given title to Limantour of the ground on which stood the presidio, the customhouse, the U. S. Mint and just about all of downtown San Francisco.

Limantour was very nice about it and understood that the city of San Francisco could not be moved elsewhere. He was willing to make a compromise with the American squatters by giving them quitclaim deeds for a fee. In a panic to preserve their business investments, many Americans paid Limantour for titles. In all, he is believed to have collected about $300,000.

Meanwhile, a further investigation by the United States District Court revealed that Limantour's papers were palpable forgeries. There wasn't an iota of truth in any of his claims. Limantour was arrested and immediately posted bond of $30,000. This set him free, whereupon he packed up and went back to Mexico, having salvaged well over $250,000. The climate of Mexico seemed to agree with him, for he was never interested in returning to California again. And more than one Californian must have laughed up his sleeve.

So the pot could not call the kettle black; and while the Land Act of 1851 injured a number of innocent persons, ruined good citizens, increased confusion instead of rectifying it, made graft and usury a business and violated an international agreement, it also protected more just claims than it ruined, ferreted out many frauds, gave the incoming settlers assurance of title and on the whole changed the emphasis in real estate from the Mexican way to the American way.

One claim that should be mentioned has no direct bearing on the Land Act but has more than a modicum of poetic justice. It was filed by Mariano G. Vallejo and was for personal damages, theft of cattle and unjust imprisonment by the Bear Flag men and John C. Frémont. Vallejo's itemized bill to Uncle Sam amounted to $117,875. The government took this under consideration and chopped off items here and there, admitted that the Vallejo family had suffered certain invasion of privacy, and finally paid the good don the sum of $48,700. Vallejo smilingly accepted. So that sum, plus the expenses involved in order to arrive at it, is what it cost the United States to pay for the raising of the Bear Flag. Senator Frémont made no comment.

During the post-gold-rush period up to 1870, and even during the gold rush, there were certain events of especial significance that happened along the Royal Highway.

For the first time southern California had a publication. It was the *Los Angeles Star* founded on May 17, 1851. The Spanish version of the paper predominated. It was called *La Estrella de Los Angeles,* was printed half in Spanish and half in English, and had of necessity, two editors: one was Manuel Rojo and the other was John A. Lewis. The *Star* fared better than Colton and Semple's short-lived *Californian* at Monterey and lasted until October 1, 1864. Biased, opinionated, daring and vigorous, it was for a number of years the most self-sufficient newspaper along the Royal Highway.

Also during this period of chaos and adjustment the first Vigilance Committee was formed in San Francisco. The gang of bullies known as "the Hounds" had designated itself an organization for the public good, but it had turned out to be a group of jingoes and thugs who were far more of a menace to society than the innocent citizens it selected to beat to a pulp. Out of this lawless mess came a public effort to make San Francisco a safe place in which to live. At its best the first Vigilance Committee may be called a kind of socialized police force. At least the impulse back of it was dedicated to the public's welfare. And it worked reasonably well. Its job was to mete out justice as expressed by public opinion. Four thieves or murderers were hanged and a number of others were deported.

Another new experience for the people of the Royal Highway occurred in 1855 when the state had its first financial panic. On February 22 the bank of Page, Bacon and Company, in San Francisco, failed to open its doors. The bank was not observing Washington's birthday, but was closed simply because it did not have the liquid cash to meet its obligations.

This financial failure marked the end of the boom years and flush times. Adams and Company were forced to close their chain of banks a few days later. Hundreds of small businessmen failed, losses were estimated in millions, and most people couldn't comprehend it because there was still plenty of gold in "them thar hills."

In 1856 the first sensational murder took place between men in reasonably high, and certainly public, positions. James King of William (as he always called himself to distinguish his identity from other James Kings), the editor of the *San Francisco Bulletin,* was assassinated by James Casey, a politician. Casey was assisted in the slaying by one of his gangster hired hands named Charles Cora, who had previously murdered a man named Willam Richardson, a United States marshal. Public opinion was strongly in favor of the slain editor who had been leading a crusade against crime in his newspaper. That crusade had stepped sharply on Casey's toes. So James King of William was shot. The wheels within wheels of the political ramifications belong to a story of San Francisco itself rather than to the story of the Royal Highway. From the long perspective of a California event rather than a municipal tragedy, the most important result of this slaying was the reorganization of the Vigilance Committee, which, again acting as the spokesman of public opinion, hanged Casey and Cora

"Street of Spain" in modern Santa Barbara

Señora Clotilda de la Guerra Sepulveda. The style of dress is characteristic of the Mexican period.

Photo by Edward Weston

In the vineyard country north of San Francisco Bay

Photo courtesy of the Security-First National Bank of Los Angeles

Main street in Los Angeles in 1878

on Sacramento Street on the very day of James King of William's funeral. Justice in California could not, and would not, wait for the law's delays and evasions.

With all this emphasis on San Francisco, things were happening of some importance at the far end of the Royal Highway, and one of these was the "Jackass Mail" at San Diego.

The first attempt at an overland mail service between California and the East was initiated in 1851 between Hangtown in the gold-rush area and Salt Lake City. This long, desolate and dangerous section was no more than a mule trail and was first identified as the Jackass Mail. It functioned, with irregular service, until superseded by the more famous Pony Express. From the Mormon capital there was occasional and unscheduled stagecoach service to Council Bluffs or Kansas City, and points east.

In 1857 another Jackass Mail was put into service between San Antonio, Texas, and San Diego on the Royal Highway. The carriers went through twice a month, and the journey took twenty-one days or more. Part of this route followed the old Anza Trail. It was the route used from the Rio Grande Valley by General Stephen W. Kearny until he ran into trouble and lances not far from San Diego at the Battle of San Pascual. This southern Jackass Mail was a precursor of the more famous Butterfield Stage Service which was begun in 1858.

Prior to the opening of the Butterfield line, which by-passed sleepy and sunny San Diego entirely and had as its termini St. Louis and San Francisco, there was another and extremely colorful and probably odoriferous attempt at overland communication by the use of camels. These desert beasts were brought from Africa at the suggestion of Lieutenant Edward F. Beale to Jefferson Davis, then Secretary of War. The theory was simple: if camel caravans were practical in the Sahara they would be practical also in the deserts of the American Southwest. The first camel corps came from the Rio Grande Valley, across Arizona and the desert area of southeastern California, and into Los Angeles on January 8, 1858, where the outfit must have afforded the citizens of the City of the Angels an odd sight. Fourteen camels "parked" in the plaza caused everyone to turn out for a good look. The project was not successful, although its failure was not exclusively the fault of the camels. The patient beasts plodded over mountains and across deserts, outstripping the horse and the mule in their stoical endurance. The big drawback was the fact that they required fully experienced camel drivers in order to give their best efforts. One or two drivers had been brought from Africa, notably Hadji Ali whose Arabic name soon became "Hi Jolly" to American ears and tongues. But most of the drivers were newly recruited Americans, and the peculiar rolling gait of the camels made their amateur drivers seasick. Another unfortunate factor was their incongruity. For some reason the camels scared man and beast alike. Some men, upon seeing a procession of fourteen or more of these African beasts, swore that they must be suffering from delirium tremens; and as for horses, mules and cattle, the very sight and smell of the camels caused neighing, bucking, panic and stampedes. So, after a few unsatisfactory trips, the caravans were abandoned as a plan of conquering desert communication, and the camels were turned loose to survive as best they could. They ran wild, usually in bands, multiplied and continued to be seen in the remote areas of the desert country for many years.

Later in the same year that the camel experiment was begun, 1858, the Butterfield Overland Mail offered its service to the public, with a twenty-three-day schedule between St. Louis and San Francisco. This stage service was the first government-subsidized public carrier to serve California and had a congressional appropriation of $600,000 annually. It touched the Royal Highway in a few points, but for the most part its California route remained farther inland than the coastal slope. Swinging in a great oxbow from St. Louis across the Southwest—Oklahoma, Texas, New Mexico and Arizona—the Butterfield line skipped San Diego. It touched at J. J. Warner's ranch and then went north and west to Los Angeles where the coaches hauled up at the Bella Union Hotel. From there it followed the Royal Highway as far as Mission San Fernando. Then it went inland, following the general route of what is now U.S. Highway 99, via Fort Tejon and the San Joaquin Valley. Farther north it crossed the coast range of mountains through the Pacheco Pass into the town of Gilroy. This put the stagecoaches back again on the Royal Highway, and they followed the road on through San Jose to San Francisco. It was a rough and uncomfortable trip, but if you were in St. Louis and had business in San Francisco, the Butterfield line would get you to that Far Western terminus in twenty-three days. This was considered rapid transit indeed.

The line functioned for a little less than three years. In 1861, due to the outbreak of the Civil War, the government no longer wanted its one life line to the Far West, which was pro-Union, to swing through the South. The route was abandoned, and its founder, John Butterfield, was given a new contract to open a stage service from St. Louis to California by way of the Overland Trail on a seventeen-day schedule. This removed the Butterfield stagecoaches from any further contact with the Royal Highway.

The Civil War itself had only slight reverberations along El Camino Real. The city of San Francisco was predominantly for the Union; the American population of the city of Los Angeles was inclined to favor the Confederacy. But to the native Californians the distant conflict meant little. Let the gringos fight among themselves, and the more that got killed the better.

During this period stagecoach service between local points increased. One stage ran three times a week between San Francisco and San Jose. The distance was approximately fifty miles, the trip either way took nine hours, the coaches held eight passengers (or in a pinch, ten), and the fare per person was $32 or two ounces of gold. In wet weather the journey consumed as much as sixteen hours and the passengers often had to get out in mud axle-deep and help push. Later the exorbitant price was reduced to $16 and finally to $10. This was the best transportation along the Royal Highway in the 1850s, and while it was not an experience to delight the soul, it was transportation of a kind and it did move faster than the old Spanish *carreta*.

The condition of the road itself in 1850, and on up to 1900, would be described, in comparison to the present-day highway, as deplorable. There were no bridges. Rivers had to be forded, and, if the water was high, there was nothing to do but wait for the river to fall. Along the Rincon hills between Santa Barbara and Ventura there was no road at all. These hills, or mountains, come down to the sea, leaving a scant beach and, in many places, no beach whatever. Here the Royal Highway simply went out into the ocean, and a stagecoach and four had to move slowly through the surf. Between San Diego and San Francisco there were numerous cliffs and passes that were entirely ungraded, narrow and dangerous. Often the passengers got out and walked as the cumbersome stagecoach moved between a steep cliff on one side and a precipitous drop on the other. Such famous and colorful scenes were notably the Torrey Pines Grade near San Diego, the Conejo Grade in Ventura County, the Gaviota Pass, and the Cuesta Grade north of San Luis Obispo. The Royal Highway all through the last half of the nineteenth century was up and down and twist and turn quite in contrast to the present high-gear streamlined road.

Since the influx of gold-rush population was in central and northern California, the southern part of the state lagged behind in adequate transportation. But in time the stagecoach began to appear. Actually the Butterfield line connected Los Angeles and San Francisco by stage in 1858. But this was primarily a transcontinental service and was little used by the Californians. By 1860 a local service was instituted, and eventually the stagecoach reached Santa Barbara from Los Angeles. The journey could be made only at low tide between Ventura and Santa Barbara as the stagecoach had to be pulled through a foot or two of surf. In the 1860s a bimonthly service was finally opened over the Royal Highway between Los Angeles and San Francisco, and in 1867 Phineas Banning opened a stage line between Los Angeles and the port of San Pedro. To be exact, Banning's line ran to the town of Wilmington, adjacent to San Pedro, but for all intents and purposes it was a shuttle service between lethargic Los Angeles (population still less than 5,000 persons while San Francisco had reached 135,000) and the harbor district.

Stagecoach drivers were colorful men, and the fame of many of them has persisted through the years. Three of these "knights of the rein" who handled four or six horses at breakneck speed from the box of a careening top-heavy vehicle over mountains and across deserts and calmly chewed tobacco and told stories at the same time were "Hank" Monk, "Baldy" Hamilton and "Uncle" Billy Mayhew. These men were employed mostly by Wells, Fargo and Company and their exploits were largely in the High Sierra region. But the Royal Highway had a stage driver to rank with any of them, who, like any specialist in any field, considered his employment, not a job, but a fine art. His name was Charley Parkhurst.

There are accounts in print that call this driver "Cockeyed" Charley and insist that he wore a black patch over his bad eye. Some say the eye was missing entirely. Regardless of his ocular limitations, Charley Parkhurst was admittedly the finest and fastest stagecoach driver along the Royal Highway. His section of the road was the Salinas Valley and the area as far north of the valley as Santa Cruz on the Bay of Monterey and San Jose farther inland. Still, unquestionably at times he must have visited San Francisco and probably Los Angeles.

Besides the characteristic of the faulty or missing eye, Charley was known for his unceasing stream of profanity and a similar, but periodic, stream of tobacco juice. He could put away quantities of whisky with the heaviest of the drinkers, and apart from admitting that he had come to California from the East in 1848, he refused to talk of his past.

Finally Charley slowed down, not only in his stagecoach pace but in his reactions and reflexes. He retired from driving and opened a little bar and halfway house where he could watch other drivers come and go. In 1879 Charley went to bed one night and never woke up. And only then, after his death, was it discovered that Charley was a woman! She was born Charlotte Parkhurst, probably about 1810, in New Hampshire, and as "Charley" she had voted in an election in Santa Cruz in 1866—being the first female to cast a ballot along the Royal Highway some fifty years before woman suffrage went into effect. There are a lot of people in Santa Cruz who do not know of this claim to distinction on the part of their city.

On March 23, 1868, two years after Charley—or Charlotte— voted, and while he, or she, was still very much alive regardless of her title as male or female and hence her right to cast a ballot, an event took place that was of inestimable influence on the future of life in California. The state legislature passed a bill creating the University of California, dedicated to the promotion of "literature, the arts and the sciences" and "entirely free of all political and sectarian influence" and open to both sexes and all races, creeds and colors. Again the matter of title was important, for what was to become the state's great institution of higher learning, and one of the outstanding universities in the world, was partly financed by a land grant, the sale of tidewater lands around San Francisco Bay and, of course, appropriations from the legislature and gifts from individuals.

The history of the University of California from the signing of the bill creating it by Governor Henry H. Haight, through the opening of its doors in Oakland in 1869, its first graduating class of twelve students in 1873, its move to Berkeley and on up to date through its state-wide expansion, notably the evolution of the University of California at Los Angeles—all is a book in itself. But it makes one wish, with pardonable sentimentality, that such far-sighted pioneers in the plea for education as Diego de Borica or José Figueroa could take a look at the campus at Berkeley or the campus at Los Angeles today.

All during these years, from the Land Act of 1851 up to 1870, new residents kept pouring into California. While the big rush due to gold was over, the incoming stream of immigration never stopped, and the state continued its growth not only in and around San Francisco, but all along the Royal Highway. The squatter continued to be a problem well into the seventies; as for the great and baronial landowners, their estates, even if validated unto themselves, were gradually being broken up because of the increase in value of small tracts of land. Even if he owned 40,000 acres, it became good business sense on the part of Don So-and-So, who was obviously rich in land and poor in dollars, to sell 2,000 or 4,000 acres and reimburse himself thereby for part of the expenses he had incurred in order to prove his legitimate right to a title.

Thus it is plain that the twenty years between 1850 and 1870 brought more changes to California than any other similar period in its history. The state changed not only its flag and its government, but its social and cultural ideas.

The meeting of the Central Pacific in 1869 with the Union Pacific at Promontory Point, Utah, meant that a railroad connected the East Coast with the West. California, formerly weeks or months removed from New York, Philadelphia and Washington, was now only days away. The day of the bandit, the stagecoach, the great rancho or hacienda, the Mexican concept of life—all were gone. The Spanish background was rapidly becoming a heritage. It was a new California and its title was irrevocably American.

Sunny Seventies Make Elegant Eighties

23

THE twenty years beginning in 1870 and ending in 1890 saw many developments along the Royal Highway, and no two were more contrasting than the first big event and the last. The period began with the looting, murdering and hanging by a lawless mob of 500 men of twenty or more defenseless Chinese in Los Angeles; and ended on New Year's Day, 1890, with the first Tournament of Roses, including parades, races and a football game in Pasadena.

In a general sense the two events—the one vicious and inimical and the other gay and public-spirited—are symbolic of the changes along the Royal Highway during those twenty years.

The Chinese problem began unostentatiously and was not properly recognized as a problem until conditions took a turn toward violence. In 1850 there were only a few thousand Chinese in California and they were mostly in San Francisco. By 1870 it is estimated that there were 100,000 Chinese scattered throughout the state from San Diego to the Oregon line. Some of these were capable merchants and cultured Orientals, but the vast majority were the lowest order of coolies from the coastal ports of China and their women were mainly prostitutes.

Two years before, in 1868, China and the United States had signed the Burlingame Treaty, which, among its various provisos, agreed to accept Chinese on an equality with the people of any nation, and granted John Chinaman all the privileges of becoming an American citizen with the exception of the right to vote.

The plan was not feasible. The Chinese made no efforts to comprehend the American culture, and clannishly kept to themselves. To the American, John Chinaman became a pest. His standard of living was unspeakably filthy, he bred diseases, such as leprosy and syphilis, he thrived on opium and other strange vices, he ignored American laws, he worked all day on Sundays, he bought and sold his women, he ate revolting concoctions, he engaged in private tong wars and, worst of all, he was a source of cheap labor that kept white men out of potential jobs. If it took the Irish to build the Union Pacific, it was John Chinaman's cheap labor that built the Central Pacific and enabled the two roads to meet and provide the nation with its first transcontinental railroad.

Fanning out over the state, the Chinese took over the laundry business, became domestic servants and ranch-house cooks, opened their own restaurants (everybody believed they ate rats), and began to start small farms on which they raised vegetables with an ingenuity and with unhygienic methods that the white man couldn't and wouldn't match.

Not only was the Chinaman a nuisance, but more of his kind were constantly arriving. It seemed that every coolie in China hoped to come to California—and China had a population of 400,000,000. Something had to be done about it.

Since legislation did not lead the way, irked, annoyed and finally irate individuals did.

The first riot occurred in calm and sunny San Diego in 1868. Previously Chinese had been persecuted and beaten and robbed and booted out of mining areas, but these were sporadic occurrences and to some extent had happened to Mexicans, Indians and other minority groups in the gold-rush scramble. But when the normally peaceful citizens of San Diego rose in wrath and destroyed laundries and restaurants, it indicated that a real race problem had developed. The Chinese of San Diego fled north over the Royal Highway to Los Angeles, and even to this day San Diego has never had a proportionately large "Chinatown."

Then, in 1871, came the worst riot of all, something that might properly be called a massacre. Nobody seems able to get to the bottom of it. Very likely the violence had been smoldering for a long time before it burst into flame. The Chinese in Los Angeles had been quarreling among themselves and a tong war had broken out. This seemed the last straw, and two police officers went down into Chinatown to break it up. The incensed and hysterical Chinese were milling about in a slum district, the main thoroughfare of which was called Nigger Alley. One end of this narrow street, Calle de los Negros, touched the plaza and the Royal Highway, and the other end disappeared into a labyrinth of shacks and mud in the direction of the river bottom. Just what happened when the two officers attempted to quell the tong-warring Chinese is not clear, but all accounts agree that both were knifed and seriously wounded. Some historians say a third member of the police force was present and was killed. Regardless of further details, two white officers of the law were stabbed and bleeding, and the Chinese were responsible.

In no time at all 500 armed citizens of Los Angeles descended on Chinatown and virtually wiped it out. Innocent Chinese were dragged screaming from their shanties and hovels and beaten and then hanged. All shops and laundries and restaurants were demolished and some were burned. The police force made no effort to stop the carnage and doubtless some of the bitterest members of the attacking group were police-force friends of the two Americans who had been stabbed.

Then the thing got farther out of hand and became a Roman holiday. Not content with smashing everything, theft and looting went on by hoodlums who had no interest except to take advantage of the moment. Most of the terrified Chinese who met death were dragged from Nigger Alley to Commercial Street and New High Street, the main business area of Los Angeles at that time, and hanged on improvised gallows. The rioting, which began about five o'clock in the afternoon, lasted well into the night.

Exactly how many Chinese were killed will never be known. Major Horace Bell, in his book *On the Old West Coast,* gives a detailed account of the massacre, but the veracity of his story has been seriously questioned. At any rate, it must have been quite a surprise to the out-of-town visitor to Los Angeles who arrived on the morning of October 25, 1871, to see the bodies of twenty or more Chinese hanging by their necks in the business district of the city. There had been great enthusiasm in hanging them, but nobody wanted to take the trouble to cut them down. In fact, that next morning, nobody even knew who did it—"Must have been somebody who didn't like Chinamen"—and nobody was ever brought to trial. This event was the outstanding "incident" along the Royal Highway at the dawn of the sunny seventies.

And while other and more important and certainly more pleasant events occurred during the sunny seventies, life was not quite so sunny and so cheerful as the words imply. Among the events of some importance can be cited the beginning of the first cable railway in California. This was entirely a local transit problem in the city of San Francisco. The Clay Street line was the first in operation, and in spite of efforts to get rid of them, the cable cars are still serving San Franciscans at the present writing, or nearly eighty years after that first distinctive and unmistakable *clang-clang-clang.*

In 1872 José Lobero opened the first community theater in California at Santa Barbara. Lobero had come to Santa Barbara in 1859 and had made some money by running a saloon (proper Santa Barbarans prefer to call it a tavern). But his real love was music, and as soon as he could afford it, he built a theater and wrote, directed and produced an opera. The Lobero Theater was the center of social and cultural life in Santa Barbara for many years. Lobero himself eventually lost both the theater, which was an indulgence, and his saloon, which made the money to finance the indulgence. In both failing health and failing financial circumstances, Lobero heard the muse no more; he committed suicide in the late 1880s. But his theater, now completely rebuilt, still functions, still bears his name, is one of the cultural attractions of modern Santa Barbara and is architecturally the most beautiful playhouse on the Royal Highway.

In 1876 the first railroad connection between San Francisco and Los Angeles was established. This was of tremendous importance in cementing trade between the two metropolitan areas—if Los Angeles could be dignified by the word metropolitan at that time.

And in 1879 the University of Southern California was founded in Los Angeles through the beneficence (and real-estate acumen) of J. G. Downey (a former governor), O. W. Childs and I. W. Hellman. For some reason, which seems unaccountable, this privately endowed institution, later famous for its football prowess, has never achieved the scholastic status of the University of California.

The year 1879 seemed determined to send the seventies into history with a glorious finish, for a young Scot arrived in California and spent three months in Monterey.

Monterey, now no longer the capital as that honor had finally been bestowed on Sacramento, and no longer the chief port as it had been surpassed by San Francisco, San Pedro and San Diego, was a sleepy little town with not very much future except to go on being Monterey. But it charmed the young Scot and he wrote beautifully about it. Since it would be impossible to find a better description of the Monterey peninsula, one hundred and ten years after Portolá and his men first saw it, than in the words of this twenty-nine-year-old author, a few quotations follow.

The Bay of Monterey has been compared . . . to a bent fishinghook. . . . Santa Cruz sits exposed at the shank; the mouth of the Salinas river is at the middle of the bend; and Monterey itself is cosily ensconced beside the barb. . . . The waves which lap so quietly about the jetties of Monterey grow louder and larger in the distance . . . and from all round, even in quiet weather, the low distant, thrilling roar of the Pacific hangs over the coast and the adjacent country like smoke above a battle. . . .

Crowds of ducks and sea-gulls hover over the sea. Sandpipers trot in and out by troops after the retiring waves, trilling together in a chorus of infinitesimal song. Strange sea-tangles, new to the European eye, the bones of whales, or sometimes a whole whale's carcase, white with carrion-gulls and poisoning the wind, lie scattered here and there along the sands. . . .

The one common note of all this country is the haunting presence of the ocean . . . go where you will, you have but to pause and listen to hear the voice of the Pacific.

This, of course, is the unmistakable, balanced and limpid prose of Robert Louis Stevenson. He was especially impressed with what he called the "vast, wet, melancholy fogs" that floated in from the sea.

. . . they crawl in scarves among the sandhills; they float, a little higher, in clouds of a gigantic size and often of a wild configuration; to the south, where they have struck the seaward shoulder of the mountains of Santa Lucia, they double back and spire up skyward like smoke. . . . It takes but a little while till the invasion is complete. The sea . . . has submerged the earth. Monterey is curtained in for the night in thick, wet, salt, and frigid clouds, so to remain till day returns; and before the sun's rays they slowly disperse and retreat in broken squadrons to the bosom of the sea.

The character of the town of Monterey itself charmed Stevenson, and he summed up its peculiar atmosphere, mood and spirit by declaring:

. . . a perpetual surprise to find, in that world of absolutely mannerless Americans, a people full of deportment, solemnly courteous, and doing all things with grace and decorum . . . a strange thing to lie awake in nineteenth-century America, and hear the guitar accompany, and one of these old heart-breaking Spanish love songs mount into the night air, perhaps in a deep baritone, perhaps in that high-pitched, pathetic, womanish alto which is so common among Mexican men, and which strikes on the unaccustomed ear as something not entirely human but altogether sad.

It is still possible to see the house where Stevenson lived in Monterey. During his three-month stay he was working on *The Amateur Emigrant* and occasionally made contributions to the local newspaper. He seems to have had a happy time and to have got acquainted with almost everybody in the town. In a letter to a friend he wrote:

I will send you herewith a Monterey paper where works of R. L. S. appear. . . . I lodge with Dr. Heintz; take my meals with Simoneau; have been only two days ago shaved by the tonsorial artist Michaels; drink daily at the Bohemia saloon; get my daily paper from Hadsell's . . . in short, there is scarce a person advertised in that paper but I know him, and I may add scarce a person in Monterey but is there advertised. . . . Monterey is a place where there is no summer or winter . . . and pines and sand and distant hills and a bay all filled with real water from the Pacific. . . .

While Robert Louis Stevenson was writing in Monterey another author was at work in San Francisco. As an author he is less well known than Stevenson, for authorship was merely his means toward the end of expressing his own economic theory. But his one outstanding book has sold over 5,000,000 copies since its first printing in San Francisco in 1879, and that, quite likely, is more than the sum total of all of Stevenson's work. The book was *Progress and Poverty* and its author was a San Francisco printer named Henry George.

Properly speaking, Henry George was a student of economics rather than literature. The land question in California, the struggle for title, the inherent richness of the resources of the world and the appalling poverty of the masses of people, set him off on a thesis to which he dedicated the rest of his life. While no match for Stevenson in the beauty of his prose, the portents of his ideas caused a furor. Henry George wanted to abolish individual owner-ship of land. From what he had seen in California he was certain that want and distress would increase even while the nation, at large, was adding to its land holdings.

In brief, Henry George insisted that landlords are nonproducers and that their return—rent—on socially valuable land was an un-earned increment. Land, he declared, was essential to laborers, but since it belonged to private owners, increases in its production only served to increase its rent. Rent, to Henry George, was an evil force, or device, that labor had to pay for the opportunity of functioning. Labor was the real initiating force, and without the production resulting from labor, there would be no capital. So both labor and capital should be freed from the shackles of private ownership of land, and all land should have placed on it a "single tax" amounting to the whole of what was now paid in rent. Henry George believed that this would be the panacea that would abolish all other forms and complications of taxes, and leave labor and capital unpenalized and free to express themselves in individual effort. There would be no mass poverty and there would be no pools of individual wealth.

It is doubtless unfair to Henry George's concept to paraphrase it so baldly when it took him almost 600 pages to make his argu-ment detailed and clear.

His book, often lampooned and ridiculed (he had to pay for the manufacturing cost of the first edition for no publisher would risk it), became the first best seller to come from the Royal High-way. Thus the new and land-rich area of California while coming more and more under private ownership as the state developed and population increased during the sunny seventies, caused one radical freethinker to express himself in a voice so strong that his book is still in print today.

And just what was the economic status of life along the Royal Highway as the period went into the category of history? It is easy to visualize the quiet, peaceful, Spanish and Mexican nostalgia of Monterey that Stevenson so accurately caught. But the changing economic scene is less tangible and more difficult to analyze. On the whole, the seventies must be appraised as a discontented period. Nobody was getting exactly what he wanted or had anticipated.

Economically, life along the Royal Highway was still in a period of adjustment. Neither the industry nor the agriculture of the state was sufficient to satisfy the needs of the greatly increased population. Liquid capital was scarce, wages were low and unemployment was rife in the cities. There might be a year of good crops followed by a drought and a year of poor harvest, and the individual farmer or rancher had no reserve, or cushion of capital, to ease the shock. A crop loss often meant a loss of land to a mortgage holder. Only a few of the products of the soil for which modern California is famous were raised on a large commercial scale. The cattle industry was the only "big business" in the state. Even with the opening of the first transcontinental railroad, business was slow to react. The nation itself was going through a chaotic period of graft and boondoggling, with the Grant administration in Washington, eight years long, generally known as the "nadir of national disgrace." Such frauds as the Credit Mobilier and the Tweed Ring in the East had their minor counterparts in Sacramento politics, the collapse of the Bank of California and the subsequent suicide of its speculator president William C. Ralston. Throughout the seventies life in California stumbled on, economically aimless and politically second-rate, until a series of events changed the whole picture to one of sudden boom, prosperity and elegance.

Reproduction of a water color by an unknown artist showing the plaza at Sonoma, northernmost town on the Royal Highway. Here the Bear Flag was raised on June 14, 1846. The building in the background with the tower was the home of Mariano Vallejo.

The original "Bear Flag" as painted by William Todd and flown over Sonoma for twenty-five days. Native Californians thought the bear was a pig.

There were healthy straws in the wind in the seventies, but it was not until the eighties that every town along the Royal Highway responded to flush times.

One of the earliest of the good indications was the Anaheim experiment. This began as early as 1857 and prospered from the start. The plan began as a co-operative on the part of fifty Germans from San Francisco who called themselves the "Los Angeles Vineyard Society" and who purchased 1,265 acres of the old Rancho San Juan Cajon de Santa Ana on the Royal Highway about thirty miles southeast of Los Angeles. The fifty Germans were an odd assortment to enter a collective farming scheme, some of them having been carpenters, watchmakers, blacksmiths, shoemakers, bookbinders, hatters, brewers and musicians—anything but farmers.

But the scheme worked, and the ground was divided into fifty twenty-acre farms, all surrounding a central section of 200 acres which was reserved for a town. The land cost the Germans $2.00 an acre and was well watered from the adjacent Santa Ana River. They called their town Anaheim, an arbitrarily made-up word from Ana for the original rancho and *heim* meaning home in German. The colony got through the shaky seventies with no trouble at all and became the first successful fruit-growing co-operative in the state.

By 1880 the population of California was about 517,000. Most of these people lived along the coastal slope and adjacent valleys and followed the route of the Royal Highway from San Diego to San Francisco. The metropolitan area about San Francisco had the bulk of urban population, but the southern cities were beginning to move forward, and the flux of men to the mines was now negligible. In the next decade, or through the elegant eighties up to 1890, the population more than doubled, reaching an estimated 1,200,000 by the dawn of the so-called gay nineties.

During the eighties a number of events contributed to one of the greatest booms ever seen in America. The Chinese Exclusion Act was signed by President Chester A. Arthur in 1882. It effectually amended the old Burlingame Treaty of 1868, and denied admission to the United States to all Chinese for the next ten years. In 1892 the act was amended but kept in force, and has been kept in force ever since. Thus the Chinese problem with its cheap competitive labor for white citizens was solved once and for all.

Just before this, in 1881, the second transcontinental railroad reached California, the Southern Pacific, connecting Los Angeles with the Deep South. And in 1885 the Atchison, Topeka and Santa Fe completed its line, a third transcontinental route, making it possible to travel from Los Angeles to Chicago without, ironically enough, ever passing through Atchison or Topeka or Santa Fe. The opening of this line touched off the fireworks. The Southern Pacific had a competitor.

The men of the Southern Pacific knew how to deal with that problem. They promptly slashed their railroad fares in half. Let the so-called Atchison, Topeka and Santa Fe match that!

At this time, to travel from New Orleans or Kansas City to California cost about $125. By the end of 1886 the price war between the two railroads had brought the cost of a ticket down to $25. Each line refused to be undersold. The Santa Fe advertised its new fares: "Kansas City to Los Angeles, $12.00!" Within a day the Southern Pacific published *its* new fares: "Any Mississippi Valley point to Los Angeles, $8.00!" And so the war went on. In March 1887 the Santa Fe hurled its final challenge. "Kansas City to Los Angeles—*One Dollar!*" The Southern Pacific promptly matched it, and for a time that was the rate the public paid.

This fantastic state of affairs meant a wonderful opportunity to get to California for a pittance. As soon as the price war began, both railroads were beseiged with passengers clamoring for tickets. As the price went down the number of persons who decided to go to California went up. In the winter of 1887 both railroads were bringing four and five trains a day into Los Angeles.

These hundreds, and then thousands, of people were not vagrants or tramps or down-and-outers, but were people of means who wanted to see California and perhaps settle there. They brought capital with them. Some were from the urban centers of the East, but the majority were physiocratic, solid, substantial, American stock from every state in the Union. As somebody once put it, every other farmer in America came to California. The population of Los Angeles increased at a rate of 1,200 a month. Every town along the Royal Highway felt the wave of humanity as it washed over the state. San Diego, for example, went from 8,700 to 50,000 population in seven years.

The reason for this great influx was not entirely the price-warring railroads, although they certainly were the adjacent cause. Other reasons were that people were curious about California. Its reputation of cheap, fertile land, and lots of it, had been told throughout the East. There were rumors that anything would grow there. And land values were constantly rising. If you didn't care to farm your land or build a store on a city lot, simply hold them a month or two and you'd be able to sell them at a handsome profit. There was money in oranges. California's citrus fruits had taken first prizes at the New Orleans International Exposition of 1885. Why not buy yourself a little orange grove and sit back and make money by watching your oranges grow? There was nothing to it. And as for the *climate!* It was God's country. How about it? The railroad fare was only one dollar!

The result was the great boom of the eighties that started off soundly and healthily enough, only to reach absurd proportions and finally collapse under its own weight. The first rush of people were good American farmers and shopkeepers, homeseekers and investors, and it was not until the prices began to skyrocket that the crooks and fakers and charlatans and quacks of all kinds began to pour in.

Real estate received the first reaction.

Thousands upon thousands of new citizens needed room in which to live. Demand raised prices. New towns sprang up over night. A choice acre on the Royal Highway exorbitantly priced at $100 in 1885 was worth $1,500 in 1887, and $3,000 in 1888. It might turn out, too, that this very acre would be on the main street of a brand-new town, and the owner, who it would seem was stuck with it by purchasing it at the peak, found he could break it up into six city lots worth $2,500 each! There was no end to the possibilities.

This kind of a thing caused a phrenetic scramble for land—not so much to possess it permanently, but to gamble on its short-term future. In 1887, in Los Angeles County alone, there were more than $100,000,000 worth of recorded transactions, and nobody can estimate how many more that were not recorded.

Los Angeles began to expand in all directions as the supply of city lots could not meet the demand. New suburbs were opened for sale by speculators and promoters who were now flocking to California, and mostly to southern California. These subdivisions, as they were called, were marked out with flags and signs, and seemed to sell equally well if they were in dry sandy river bottoms or pitched on the sides of mountains. So great was the demand at the peak of the boom that people actually stood in line waiting for the moment when a new subdivision would be placed on the market. Not only that, those in line would even sell their places, if they were well up toward the front, to late-comers for as much as $1,000.

The people who had been citizens of Los Angeles up to the beginning of the boom couldn't believe their eyes when they saw land that they wouldn't buy for $5.00 an acre in 1880 being sold to the highest bidder by a smooth-tongued auctioneer who wore a cutaway coat, striped trousers, a bright red vest, and abetted his gesticulations with a gold-headed cane, for $1,000 or even $3,000 for a quarter of an acre. So infectious was the land fever that even the former residents caught it and bought and sold with the avidity of the new arrivals.

The craze reached absurd proportions. One speculator sold 3,000 lots in the Mojave Desert for $250 each. His outlay for this worthless desert acreage made the lots cost him about 15 cents each. His percentage of profit was astronomical. Even worse cases were recorded of plain crookedness. One shyster, for example, explained to his victims that the orange—"that great and glorious golden fruit"—was really native to California after all, in spite of the fact that it had presumably been brought in by the Franciscan fathers. And *he,* mind you, had the only native orange trees in the state. The area was for sale, of course, but naturally the price for such a citrus gold mine was not cheap. He didn't want to sell it, but he was returning to the East and had to dispose of it. Therefore, the price would be neither high nor low, but fair and reasonable. Interested?

Many people were, and incredible as it may seem, they really went out onto the Mojave Desert with this charlatan, looked at the weird desert Joshua trees on which he had tied oranges, and without further investigation purchased this bargain land containing the only native California "orange trees" for $500 an acre. When they finally discovered that they had been duped, they discovered also that the salesman was a man of his word. He had indeed "gone back East"—address unknown.

Apart from the by-product of tricksters and crooks, the boom remained essentially healthy for a good two years. The economy of the state was not changed so much as it was blown up beyond all expectations. Between San Diego and San Luis Obispo, along the Royal Highway, at least forty-five new towns were surveyed, laid out into lots, the ground sold, and building construction begun within eighteen months.

The city of Santa Ana in Orange County, sitting directly across the Royal Highway, a respectable, attractive and rather typical southern California community of the present day, with a population of perhaps 40,000, began with a handbill passed around at Los Angeles railroad stations to incoming Easterners, which invited them, in the following terms, to invest:

PURE GOLD!   PURE GOLD!
Come Get It!
SANTA ANA
The Metropolis of Southern California's Fairest Valley!
QUEEN OF THEM ALL
lovely
LOVELY
LOVELY
Beautiful! Busy! Bustling! Bountiful! Booming!
CAN'T BEAT IT!
It's a big, big BOOM! It's a big, big BOOM!
A GREAT BIG BOOM!
And you?
CAN ACCUMULATE DUCATS BY INVESTING!
Come to Glorious Santa Ana
(free lunch)   (free music)
SEE IT! SEE IT! SEE IT!

The hysteria and the excitement of the gold rush surely had their counterpart in the southern California land rush. So fast did some "towns" spring up that they were never towns at all, but merely a surveyed portion of an old rancho that never did become a community and collapsed when the boom finally burst. One of these was called Richburg, in Los Angeles County, and it never became rich or even a "burg." It was advertised as having all the negative assets, rather than the positive, showing, no doubt, that the stream of sales imagination was beginning to run shallow. Richburg, now nonexistent (the site was near the present Los Angeles suburb of Bellflower) was announced as having "no fog, no frost; no snow, no slush; no touts, no tramps; no alkali; no alcohol; no chumps, no Chinks. What more do you want?" Somebody eventually wrote on one of its long discarded signs, "No people, no nothing. Keep it yourself."

With all of its three-ring-circus characteristics, plus innumerable sideshows, the great boom of the eighties, even when the bubble burst, never quite subsided. It left a mark on the southern section of the Royal Highway, mostly in the area between Los Angeles and its environs and the Mexican border, which lasted for years and may be seen even today. The loudmouthed boasting Californian comes from that area. He is not taken too seriously, and possibly even now he is growing up. Locally he was known as a "booster."

The most important factor of the boom was not its hearty ebullience, or its tawdry shoddiness, or its extraordinary gaucheries, but was simply the fact that in ten years the state had come of certain age—perhaps fourteen would be the proper estimate of its age. Now it was ready to mature. Agriculture, the chief industry, led the way. None of the industries that marked the twentieth century had yet amounted to much, and some hadn't even been thought of—industries such as oil, motion pictures, radio, aviation, food canning and packing, were either nonexistent or experimental—and California along its Royal Highway was primarily a land of agriculture. Cattle and gold, the first two products to catch on in the public mind, were soon outstripped by the collective value of grapes, olives, prunes, plums, persimmons, apricots, pears, figs, cherries, berries, apples, peaches, lemons, grapefruit, oranges; and at a somewhat later date, walnuts, almonds, avocados, lettuce, beets, tomatoes, dates and cotton.

But the one outstanding product of the Royal Highway to the non-Californian seems to have been the orange. William Wolfskill was one of the chief pioneers in the citrus industry. Although the orange was brought to California as early as 1770, it was not raised on a commercial scale until 1841. Wolfskill, a Kentuckian of German ancestry, and one of the "undesirable mountain men" who caused such hell in Los Angeles that the alcalde fled in terror at the mention of their coming, turned out to be a good citizen after all.

From the seedlings of Wolfskill and other pioneers in the citrus industry, notably Matthew Keller, the orange crop slowly increased. At first it gave no indications of becoming a big business. In 1873, however, a pioneer grower at Riverside planted two so-called seedless Washington navel trees. These had been sent from Brazil and used as an experiment by the United States Department of Agriculture. The fruit was definitely superior to the oranges of the Franciscan padres, not only in size and color, but in juice and taste. The trees, sometimes known as the "Bahia orange," thrived in California soil, and in a few years there were many hundreds of acres set out in this new fruit.

Then, in 1881, came the opening of the Southern Pacific Railroad, and in 1885 the Santa Fe. Thus it was possible to ship oranges to eastern markets on a large scale. With the Washington navel orange, complemented by the Valencia, imported in 1876, the fruit could be shipped virtually the year round, for the seedless navels were a winter-ripening fruit and the Valencias a summer-ripening variety. Orange groves developed at a furious rate, and land prices again went up.

The first single carload of oranges was sent east from Los Angeles in 1877. In 1886 the first solid trainload of oranges went to Eastern markets and a giant industry was born. As grove after grove developed, the very appearance of the land was changed. The orange tree is highly decorative as well as productive and the groves greatly enhanced the beauty of the area. The chief citrus-growing region is the coastal slope and the adjacent valleys north from the Mexican border, paralleling the Royal Highway to a point well above Santa Barbara. With the success of the orange, the growing of lemons and grapefruit soon followed.

By the end of the elegant eighties there were approximately 1,000,000 Washington navel trees producing their golden fruit, and the expansion continued throughout the nineties and into the twentieth century.

By 1890, then, after a decade of sunny seventies followed by a decade of elegant eighties, it was again a new California. Even the face of the earth had changed from what had been largely range land to groves, orchards, farms, new and clean little towns, a cosmopolitan San Francisco, and booming, sprawling, expanding Los Angeles. More, perhaps, than even the turn of the century ten years later, the year 1890 marked a milestone in the character of life along the Royal Highway. From a crude statehood in 1850, through banditry, land grabbing, the stagecoach, the railroad, Chinese massacres, boom hysteria, a state university, agriculture, the citrus industry, there finally came some degree of maturity, an expression of conscious pride, and local pomp and circumstance, in what Charles Frederick Holder conceived of and launched as the first "Tournament of Roses" on New Year's Day at Pasadena in 1890. More than 2,000 persons attended this spectacle, and they far outnumbered the guess of the most optimistic predictor. Some of the audience came on foot, some on horseback, some in wagons and a few on bicycles. Five "knights of the rose" jousted for honors and plaudits. Everyone had a grand time. It was even more fun for this generation than had been the hanging of Chinamen by the previous generation twenty years before. And it all ended with the first of what are today known as the annual "Rose Bowl" football games. California had only just grown up.

The Great God Progress

24

THE year was 1900. Incredible as it may seem, only fifty years ago—and that is a short span indeed in view of California's four hundred and more years of history—the first automobile had yet to cross the continent on its own power; there wasn't a taxicab in Los Angeles; the first airplane had yet to try it wings; telephones were a luxury, radio was inconceivable and television was a madman's dream; not a silent movie had been made and talking pictures were an impossibility; C. C. Julian, E. G. Lewis and Aimee Semple McPherson, promoters of petroleum, real estate and religion along the Royal Highway, were unknown; the oil industry was a bad risk because nobody wanted oil; subatomic energy, electric iceboxes and penicillin were unheard of; Franklin Delano Roosevelt was eighteen years old, and Adolph Hitler was eleven; and the Royal Highway was still a road of dust or mud, depending on the weather.

During the decade known as the gay nineties there were some improvements in the road: arroyos were by-passed, a few bridges were built, and a modern highway improvement program was instigated by Governor James H. Budd.

In 1891 the third outstanding educational institution was founded, complementing the University of California and the University of Southern California. At Palo Alto, on the Royal Highway, Mr. and Mrs. Leland Stanford founded Leland Stanford Junior University as a memorial to their son who had died in 1884. Sometimes known as the "Yale of the West," and popularly called simply Stanford, the university has had a distinguished record. David Starr Jordan was its first president.

314

Throughout the nineties agriculture continued to be the leading industry, and the orange growers led the way in co-operative organization. But oranges are not simple to raise and the individual grower often had a harvest of troubles instead of money at the end of the season. The event that saved the growers was the fact that they were, collectively, men of sufficient intelligence to see that they were not competing among themselves to make a profit on their fruit, but that they had far greater external problems to solve.

For example, packing houses and commission merchants charged exorbitant fees for their services, and, on top of that, the freight rates of the railroads were as high as the executives of those roads could safely place them. It took seven, or even eight years for an orange crop to reach maturity. After that period of applied time and invested capital, the grower, more often than not, found that he had a glorious harvest of oranges. But instead of making any money, he also found that it cost him more to pick, pack, haul and ship the fruit than the fruit itself would bring. Ironically enough, if a grower had only fifty acres of oranges, he was better off than a grower who had 450, simply because the smaller of the two lost less money.

It was an untenable situation and the growers met it. The first efforts toward this end were abortive but led to better efforts. In 1885 the Orange Growers' Protective Union was set up. It was primarily a plan for co-operative marketing, and while it did not correct all the evils that the growers faced, it did alleviate some of them, and led directly to the organization of the California Fruit Growers' Exchange. This is the largest and perhaps the most efficient co-operative organization in the world.

The exchange was made up of a number of small organizations which pooled their efforts for the sake of streamlining, avoiding duplication and asserting a unified power and front. In 1893 the first major organization began to function and was called the Southern California Fruit Exchange. With its success and with its expansion, the name was amended in 1905 to its present title—the California Fruit Growers' Exchange. This is the institution that has made the trade name "Sunkist" a household word, and it has, for years, handled 75 percent or more of California's citrus produce. The exchange functions on a co-operative, nonprofit basis, performs its services at cost to its thousands of members, and after handling and selling charges are deducted, pays to the individual grower the cash return for his fruit.

Also, the exchange regulates the grading and packing of oranges, and thereby sets a standard of size and quality. In a Sunkist packing house, the oranges are graded, stamped, wrapped in tissue paper and packed in crates. There are ten sizes of oranges, ranging from 100s which means that number to a box, to 344s, or the smallest oranges of all, running 344 to the box. The crates are cooled before they are shipped in freight cars that are iced in summer months and heated in winter months. Fruit that is below the standard of merchandising value, called "culls" in the industry, is used for by-product distribution such as canned orange juice, marmalade and various citrus oils. The laboratories of the exchange are always experimenting with further uses and methods of treating the crop. The exchange, besides a traffic department and a products department, has also a subsidiary known as the Fruit Growers' Supply Company which either owns or controls nearly 100,000 acres of timber north of the Royal Highway and produces the wood that is made into crates. This same subsidiary also supplies for the growers the nails, tissue wrappers, box labels, fertilizer and orchard heating equipment. Probably to the stranger to the citrus industry, however, the exchange is best known by its advertising department which is responsible for the national magazine ads in striking color layouts that keep the name Sunkist forever before the public. The exchange is really a matter of big business, operating on a co-operative scale for the interest and protection of its members. You can grow oranges in California without being a member, but to do so is almost like refusing to help yourself, or insisting on keeping your money under the mattress instead of in a Federal Reserve bank.

When the big boom of the eighties brought countless thousands to California the "tourist business" or "tourism" became another major industry. Throughout the first half of the nineteenth century there wasn't an inn or tavern or hotel anywhere along the Royal Highway. With the tourist influx and the promotion of California as a kind of national playground a number of hotels began to appear from San Diego to San Francisco. These were not small commercial hotels or inns, but were palaces rivaling any hostelries in the world.

The tourist hotel on a grand scale soon became an institution along the Royal Highway. Usually it was built at some relatively small community, contrasting sharply with the local atmosphere, and bringing the urbanity, culture and sophistication of a world far removed from what was sunny Santa Barbara or dozing Monterey.

One of the first of these great hostelries was the Arlington at Santa Barbara, opened as early as 1876. It astounded the local people with its ninety rooms (a fireplace in each one of them), running water, gas illumination and, a marvel of marvels, a speaking tube in every suite that permitted the occupant to make anything he desired directly known to the main office. Guests were not left to themselves and to their own devices, but were entertained as if they were at some private club, and were taken on beach picnics, tallyho rides, hunting expeditions, sailing trips and bathing parties.

Surpassing Santa Barbara's Arlington, Hotel Del Monte, self-styled the finest hotel in the world, overlooking the Bay of Monterey, was opened in 1880. For luxurious appointments certainly nobody in Monterey had ever seen anything like it. The financing was done by the "Big Four"—Charles Crocker, Leland Stanford,

Mark Hopkins and Collis Huntington—who had been the men back of the Central Pacific. To sleepy Monterey the thing was a white elephant from the start and was dubbed "Crocker's Folly." But the Montereyans were shortsighted, and Hotel Del Monte was an immediate success. People came from all over the world to enjoy life at this beautiful spot containing 126 acres of landscaped park, a private race track, several swimming pools, gorgeous flower gardens and a huge rambling hotel replete with grand halls, full-length mirrors, hot and cold water and that newfangled instrument, the telephone.

With the patent success of the grand hotel, California-style, other interests and communities began to realize the value. In a short time more lavish and sumptuous institutions were built and a host of lesser hotels on a somewhat less showy scale.

Of the first sort, the "largest, biggest, best" or with some other extravagant claim, there followed the Raymond in Pasadena in 1886 and the Hotel del Coronado on the strand across the bay from San Diego in 1888. These were substantially the same type as the Arlington and the Del Monte, offering every conceivable attraction to the wealthy guests, from Shetland ponies for the children to a stockbroker's office to keep the tired businessman *au courant* with the latest quotation on the New York Stock Exchange.

And then there were such well-known hotels, soon built, as the Mission Inn at Riverside, the Maryland and the Green in Pasadena, and the Casa Loma at Redlands. Santa Barbara had the Potter House, and later the Miramar, El Encanto, the Samarkand and the Biltmore. Also at Santa Barbara, or more correctly in its suburb of Montecito, is San Ysidro Ranch, a definite evolution from the grandiose to the more intimate type of cottage hotel.

Numerous taverns and inns were built at various sites along the Royal Highway, and one, which is by-passed by the modern road, was justly famous for years—Mattei's Tavern—a wayside inn and stagecoach station, opened in 1888. This famous tavern is still functioning at the hamlet of Los Olivos in the Santa Ynez Valley. For decades it was famous for its superb food and its Chinese chef. Meat, vegetables, fruits, fowl and trout all came from the ranch of Felix Mattei, and a dinner at the tavern was not a meal but an event.

As you go on up the road from Santa Ynez, the Santa Maria Inn is another famous landmark that cannot be overlooked. Indeed, there are a number of others, but it would take a special book to mention them all. Incidentally, it is curious to note that none of the grand hotels of tourism was built in Los Angeles or San Francisco. The reason for this is twofold: first, the concept was to offer a hostelry that was sufficiently rustic so that the outdoor attributes of California might be utilized; beaches, gardens, parks, trails, polo fields and golf courses; and second, the hotels were planned on such a large scale that they were virtually small cities in themselves and could function as a community apart from the location, be it Monterey, Pasadena, San Diego or Santa Barbara.

The large hostelries of the cities—Los Angeles' Biltmore, Town House and Ambassador, and San Francisco's internationally known Palace (opened as early as 1875), St. Francis, Mark Hopkins and Fairmont—were not and could not be imitation country estates, but were essentially metropolitan hotels.

As the twentieth century began to move around the clock, the great god Progress had evolved a Royal Highway and a civilization that would be well-nigh incomprehensible to the Little Goat— Cabrillo—or to Portolá or Serra or others of the pioneers. And with the twentieth century came an invention that changed the face of the highway just as strongly as the existence of the highway had changed the face of the land. It was the automobile.

Twentieth Century { 25

As YET, the Royal Highway, which Portolá so painfully blazed from Loreto to San Francisco Bay, is not a four-lane or six-lane strip of concrete. South of the Mexican border the road is passable for about a hundred and fifty miles. From that point on it is possible to get over some of it by jeep. But to get all the way to its lower end, Loreto, or on down to the tip of Baja California at Cape San Lucas, would require for practical purposes a light tank.

The road from San Diego to San Francisco is a modern, high-speed highway, with many overpasses and underpasses, and stream-lined freeways that avoid the traffic-congested centers of most of the cities and towns and fans out at San Francisco over two magnificent bridges, the Bay Bridge to Oakland and the Golden Gate Bridge to Marin County. But even all of this is not yet a four-lane highway. The day will come, during this century's next fifty years, when it will be so. In fact, when California's population reaches 20,000,000, which it is certain to do before the year 2000, a four-lane highway between San Diego and San Francisco will be inadequate and sorely overtaxed.

In 1900 there wasn't an inch of hard-surface road along the Royal Highway. The advent of the automobile changed all that. The automobile was well suited to Californians. It increased the speed of communication between towns widely separated, it was well adapted to California's generally equable climate by not catching on fire in the summer or freezing in the winter, and for commercial purposes, in the form of trucks, it became a boon to the

320

transportation of California's agricultural products. California has always been a great automobile state. The Automobile Club of Southern California was founded as early as 1900, at a time when such states as Idaho or Texas or Montana or Mississippi had seen but few cars and had no roads even for the few to run on.

Nevertheless the development of roads suited to the automobile was slow in California. Up to 1909 the Royal Highway was mostly a dirt road, with some stretches of gravel and one or two feeble miles of macadam. The early cars themselves did not serve to improve road conditions, for they were noisy, smelly, undependable and had not "come to stay," but instead inspired the familiar and derisive epithet, "Get a horse!" No motorcar could possibly equal Juan Flaco's famous ride from Los Angeles to San Francisco in four days: an early Oldsmobile or a Haynes or a Pope-Toledo might do it in a week, but that was "going some."

But the indications of things to come were present, and in 1903 the first motorcar crossed the continent under its own power. It was a Packard touring car and it was driven from San Francisco to New York City in fifty-two days. This was something astounding, and again the thing that was still called a "horseless carriage" made headlines.

In 1895 there were four passenger cars in the entire United States —none in California. In 1896 there were sixteen, and in 1897 there were ninety. Fifty years later, in 1947, there were 32,000,000 motor vehicles registered. California had about 2,000,000 of them.

Between 1895 and 1912 approximately 1,000,000 cars were manufactured and sold. Californians bought more than their share of them in view of the national population. But a motorcar without a good road was as impractical as a ship without a navigable waterway. The cars had come; good roads had to follow.

In 1909 Governor James N. Gillett and the state legislature approved and set up a new organization called the California Highway Commission. This was a revitalization of the original organization of 1895 which had considered California's highways as wagon roads and had attempted to improve them accordingly. The new commission was granted an $18,000,000 bond issue to build a state highway system. The Royal Highway was inevitably one of the chief avenues of communication and commerce in the state, and was one of the first roads to be "motorized." The governor and the legislature agreed that "this system of highways is to be constructed and maintained at the expense of the state, except that each county must pay into the Treasury 4 percent per annum upon the sum of money expended in such county in the construction of said state highways, less such proportion of the amount expended as the bonds matured shall bear to the total number of bonds outstanding." When placed before the people for a vote of "yes" or "no" the answer was enthusiastically yes.

Where the mules of Portolá had trodden and where the sandaled feet of the Franciscans had marched, there gradually developed a hard-surfaced, all-weather highway. There were several methods attempted such as oiled macadam depending on saturation for durability, or a layer of concrete which all too often cracked and became hazardous, or the last and finally practical method of a combination of concrete base with an asphaltic top of a thickness depending on the use of the particular road.

Thus, beginning in 1909, the Royal Highway became literally a highway. In 1911 Hiram Johnson became governor of California, and the commissioners that he appointed laid out two main arteries of traffic from the Mexican border to the Oregon line. These are today U.S. 101 and U.S. 99, with 101 being, in many instances, the path blazed by Portolá in 1769. To increase the improvement of the highways, and to add connecting links, a second bond issue for $15,000,000 was approved in 1916, and still another for $40,000,-000 in 1919. The people who were served by the Royal Highway were quick to appreciate the improvement in the road and its value to the state. Good roads, in California, came to be taken for granted. Today, forty years later, along former El Camino Real, widening, bridging, streamlining, multiple-laning, by-passing, overpassing and underpassing are still going on. What the highway will look like in 1999 can be pretty well foreseen. All major cities will be by-passed, or there will be some form of freeway, the four, six, or even eight main lanes will be graded for speeds of slow-moving vehicles as well as vehicles moving at seventy miles or more an hour, and it should be possible to drive from San Diego to San Francisco in eight to ten hours without breaking either the law or your neck.

During this first slow and then rapid modernization of the road, a number of events took place that contributed to Royal Highway history, or at the very least bore on it indirectly.

One was trucking. Many thousands of trucks from Ford "pick-ups" to huge moving vans ply the highway day and night. So-called "truck routes" permit them to pass many cities without entering the business area. The trucking business is both a blessing and a curse. For cheap transportation of produce it cannot be matched. To the more nimble motorist, the truck is a nuisance and sometimes a menace. Furthermore, the heavier trucks are hard on the road and often cause more damage than a hundred passenger cars. But regardless of these commentaries, any Royal Highway traveler is sure to meet many of them on the road today. They move along, ponderous, impersonal, never slow, never fast, almost irrefragable Juggernauts, loaded to the maximum with oranges or lemons or lettuce or grapefruit or cotton or cantaloupes or the perennial bales of alfalfa. Some are huge tank trucks with equally huge trailers dragging a clanking chain. Get behind one of them on an upgrade with oncoming traffic to prevent you from risking a passing spurt, be it day or night, and you will be one of those citizens who will vote yes on the next bond issue to make the whole of the Royal Highway at least a four-lane road.

In 1903 somebody decided the state should have a flower. There were plenty of native poppies and lupin carpeting the valleys, and at some times of the year the poppies grow like weeds along the Royal Highway. So a bill was put through the legislature to create a state flower, and to the consternation of many it turned out to be a plant called eschscholtzia. But it turned out all right after all when the legislature explained that this tongue twister was merely the botanical name of the golden poppy. Still, few Californians driving along their various highways are heard to exclaim, "Look at the eschscholtzias in bloom!"

By 1906—a year never to be forgotten because of the devastating San Francisco earthquake and fire which killed more than 250 people, injured thousands and caused a property damage in excess of $300,000,000—a steadily growing California-consciousness began to manifest itself. History began to be something more than dull facts in an equally dull textbook. An innate state pride was developing. Nostalgia, of a kind, became popular. One of the first examples of this having-reached-maturity-we-are-now-looking-back-at-our-glorious-past attitude was expressed by the move to mark the route of El Camino Real with a series of mission bells. This was begun in July of 1906 with the first highway bell being erected and dedicated at the church opposite the plaza in downtown Los Angeles. This church was never a mission in its own right but was an outpost, or *asistencia,* of Mission San Gabriel Arcángel. Los Angeles County supervisors instigated the move to erect the commemorative bells, and the Automobile Club of Southern California carried it out.

Five years later another looking-backward movement was made a subject of legislation. The Bear Flag, raised by the Americans at Sonoma on June 14, 1846, which the Californians of the day thought was a pig on a white field, and which first read "California Republc" until designer William Todd noted his error and respelled republic, was officially made the state flag. It has been required, from that day on, to fly the Bear Flag on all state buildings (or on one building at an institution comprising many buildings). The contemporary flag, substantially the same as the original but better balanced in its design, is an unusual and attractive standard.

A year later, in 1912, the first of the annual series known as *The Mission Play* was produced at San Gabriel. The author was John Steven McGroarty. This play, or more properly pageant, told the story of the Franciscans in California with such historical figures as Padre Serra, Gaspar de Portolá, Padre Crespi, Padre Palou, Padre Lasuén, Padre Dumetz and others as characters. Just how close to the actual facts this dramatization adhered is debatable, but it certainly served to explain the mission culture to the Californian-newly-arrived-from-Iowa, and it surely awakened an interest in the past of the Royal Highway in all members of the audience. Again California was looking backward as well as forward.

But the forward look, since 1900, has so far outweighed the backward that there can be no comparison. So much has happened in and to California in the first fifty years of the twentieth century that the events equal, if not surpass, the sum total of all that took place between 1540 and 1900. Robert Glass Cleland has written an admirable book called *From Wilderness to Empire, A History of California, 1542-1900.* It takes him 372 pages to tell this flow of history. Dr. Cleland has also written a companion volume called *California in Our Time, 1900-1940,* and it takes him 320 pages to report the events of only those forty years. If the book were to include the decade up to 1950, it would be a longer volume than *From Wilderness to Empire.* Someday some scholar will write *California's Twentieth Century,* and when he does, he will have a difficult time compressing the material down to one fat volume.

Living as we are today in the maelstrom of global history, we find it futile, sometimes dangerous, to strive for a long perspective on the ultimate meaning of current events. The changes and developments that have taken place along the Royal Highway since 1900, and are still taking place, cannot be properly measured or evaluated simply because, to use an old bromide, "we can't see the forest for the trees."

The effects of two world wars in fifty years have again changed the face of California. They have done more: they have created a new California, the like of which has never been seen before.

A few figures will make the facts clear. In 1900 California ranked twenty-first in population among the states of the Union. By 1940 it had moved up to fifth. When the national census for 1950 is taken, it will doubtless have passed Pennsylvania and will rank second only to New York. The day will come, before the year 2000, when New York will be passed and California will lead the nation. Most of this gain has been along the Royal Highway, and most of the Royal Highway gain has been in southern California in the Los Angeles metropolitan area. One third of all the people who live on the Pacific Coast, according to a survey made by *Fortune* magazine, now live in southern California, or roughly, that area between Mission San Diego de Alcalá and Mission San Luís Obispo de Tolosa, an area in which there were only a few Franciscan padres and a sprinkling of Indians less than two hundred years ago.

The University of California, with its student body of 48,000, today ranks third in size for American educational institutions and is gaining on the first two, New York University and the College of the City of New York. Scholastically the university's standards have been consistently high since its first graduating class in 1873.

The annual income from agriculture in California has passed the billion mark, but industry, a nonentity in 1900, has passed agriculture. The Bank of America has become the largest financial institution of its kind, not only in California, or in the nation, but in the world. During World War II the oil industry produced more than three quarter of a million barrels a day. Mining and lumbering increased proportionately. Shipbuilding amazed the nation, and 10,000-ton freighters were built not in a matter of weeks, or even days, but in hours. As for aviation, the production of aircraft in southern California could not be matched by Germany, Italy and Japan combined, and the Axis powers lost that all-important control of the air.

Naturally, all this meant a new California and a new type of civilization along the Royal Highway. While the pastoral aspect of rural California will continue to exist, and agriculture will always be one of the leading divisions of labor (note the boom in lettuce in the Salinas Valley, now often referred to as the state's lettuce bowl), the twentieth century has seen the passing of the last vestiges of the frontier, and California must be described as an industrial state. It has been estimated that the peak of employment of workers by industry, off since the war boom in 1945, will again be reached by 1950 and will then be surpassed. But as always with contemporary events, we are in the forest and must look beyond the single tree. The motion-picture industry, for example, unknown before 1910 and unaccountable as always, has not had a very happy last two years. But press, radio and television have. Who can say where the "movies" will be by 1975? Nonexistent, perhaps, swallowed up by television—or could it be vice versa?

But regardless of the chaos of adjustments within adjustments, wheels will continue to roll along the Royal Highway. It is today, and will inevitably become more so, one of the most important arteries of traffic in the nation. We can, in fact, go all the way back to Ordóñez de Montalvo, and if we are born to live on this earth for a span, consider ourselves lucky if we may spend some of that time in what the Spanish author of 1510 called "an island named California, very close to the Terrestrial Paradise," beside its most important highway which the Franciscans named El Camino Real.

APPENDIX, BIBLIOGRAPHY,
ACKNOWLEDGMENTS
AND INDEX

APPENDIX A

GOVERNORS OF CALIFORNIA

I. THE SPANISH GOVERNORS

Gaspar de Portolá, governor of Las Californias, Alta and Baja, 1768-1770.

Felipe de Barri, governor of Las Californias, residing at Loreto, 1770-1775.

Felipe de Neve, governor of Las Californias, residing at Loreto from March 4, 1775; at Monterey from February 3, 1777, to September 10, 1782.

Pedro Fages, September 1782, to April 1791.

José Antonio Roméu, April 16, 1791, to April 9, 1792.

José Joaquín de Arrillaga, governor *ad interim,* April 1792, to October 1794.

Diego de Borica, governor, October 1794, to January 1800.

José Joaquín de Arrillaga, governor *ad interim,* 1800 to 1804. Constitutional governor from 1804 to 1814.

José Argüello, acting governor from 1814 to 1815.

Pablo Vicente Sola, governor from August 15, 1815, to November 22, 1822.

II. THE MEXICAN GOVERNORS

Pablo Vincente Sola, holdover from the Spanish regime to November 1822.

Luís Argüello, acting governor, 1822-1825.

José María de Echeandía, 1825-1831.

Manuel Victoria, 1831-1832.

Pío Pico (twenty days), 1832.

José María Echeandía (in the south only), 1832-1833.

Agustín Vicente Zamorano (in the north only), 1832-1833.

José Figueroa, 1833-1835.

José Castro (acting governor), 1835-1836.
Nicolás Gutiérrez (acting governor four months), 1836.
Mariano Chico (three months), 1836.
Nicolás Gutiérrez (acting governor three months), 1836.
Juan Bautista Alvarado (first revolutionary, then constitutional governor), 1836-1842.
Manuel Micheltorena, 1842-1845.
Pío Pico, 1845-1846.
José María Flores, 1846-1847.

III. AMERICAN GOVERNORS UNDER MILITARY RULE

Commodore John D. Sloat, July 7, 1846.
Commodore Robert F. Stockton, July 29, 1846.
Captain John C. Frémont, January 19, 1847.
General Stephen W. Kearny, March 1, 1847.
Colonel Richard B. Mason, May 31, 1847.
General Persifor F. Smith, February 28, 1849.
General Bennett Riley, April 12, 1849.

IV. GOVERNORS OF THE STATE OF CALIFORNIA

Name	Politics	Date of Inauguration
Peter H. Burnett	Ind. Dem.	Dec. 20, 1849
John McDougal	Ind. Dem.	Jan. 9, 1851
John Bigler	Dem.	Jan. 8, 1852
John Neely Johnson	Amer.	Jan. 9, 1856
John B. Weller	Dem.	Jan. 8, 1858
Milton S. Latham	Lecomp. D.	Jan. 9, 1860
John G. Downey	Lecomp. D.	Jan. 14, 1860
Leland Stanford	Rep.	Jan. 10, 1862
Frederick F. Low	Union	Dec. 10, 1863
Henry H. Haight	Dem.	Dec. 5, 1867
Newton Booth	Rep.	Dec. 8, 1871
Romauldo Pacheco	Rep.	Feb. 27, 1875
William Irwin	Dem.	Dec. 9, 1875
George C. Perkins	Rep.	Jan. 8, 1880

Name	Politics	Date of Inauguration
George Stoneman	Dem.	Jan. 10, 1883
Washington Bartlett	Dem.	Jan. 8, 1887
Robert W. Waterman	Rep.	Sept. 13, 1887
Henry H. Markham	Rep.	Jan. 8, 1891
James H. Budd	Dem.	Jan. 11, 1895
Henry T. Gage	Rep.	Jan. 4, 1899
George C. Pardee	Rep.	Jan. 7, 1903
James N. Gillett	Rep.	Jan. 9, 1907
Hiram W. Johnson	Prog. Rep.	Jan. 3, 1911
William D. Stephens	Rep.	Mar. 15, 1917
Friend W. Richardson	Rep.	Jan. 8, 1923
Clement C. Young	Rep.	Jan. 4, 1927
James Rolfe, Jr.	Rep.	Jan. 6, 1931
Frank F. Merriam	Rep.	Jan. 2, 1934
Culbert L. Olson	Dem.	Jan. 2, 1939
Earl Warren	Rep.	Jan. 4, 1943

APPENDIX B

I. THE TWENTY-ONE MISSIONS

(With dates of their foundings and their founders)

1. San Diego de Alcalá, July 16, 1769. Junípero Serra.
2. San Carlos Borroméo, June 3, 1770. Junípero Serra.
3. San Antonio de Padua, July 14, 1771. Junípero Serra.
4. San Gabriel Arcángel, September 8, 1771. Junípero Serra.
5. San Luís Obispo de Tolosa, September 1, 1772. Junípero Serra.
6. San Francisco de Asís, October 9 (or 8), 1776. Francisco Palou.
7. San Juan Capistrano, November 1, 1776. Fermín Francisco de Lasuén.
8. Santa Clara, January 12, 1777. Tomás de la Peña.
9. San Buenaventura, March 31, 1782. Junípero Serra.
10. Santa Barbara, December 4, 1786. Fermín Francisco de Lasuén.
11. Purísima Concepción, December 8, 1787. Fermín Francisco de Lasuén.

12. Santa Cruz, September 25 (or August 28), 1791. Fermín Francisco de Lasuén.
13. Nuestra Señora de la Soledad, October 9, 1791. Fermín Francisco de Lasuén.
14. San José de Guadalupe, June 11, 1797. Fermín Francisco de Lasuén.
15. San Juan Bautista, June 24, 1797. Fermín Francisco de Lasuén.
16. San Miguel Arcángel, July 25, 1797. Fermín Francisco de Lasuén.
17. San Fernando Rey de España, September 8, 1797. Fermín Francisco de Lasuén.
18. San Luís Rey de Francia, June 13, 1798. Fermín Francisco de Lasuén.
19. Santa Inés, September 17, 1804. Estevan Tapis.
20. San Rafael Arcángel, December 14, 1817. Vicente Francisco Sarría.
21. San Francisco Solano (Sonoma), July 4, 1823. José Altimira.

II. PRESIDENTS OF THE MISSIONS

Fray Junípero Serra 1769-1784
Fray Francisco Palou 1784-1785
Fray Fermín Francisco Lasuén 1785-1803
Fray Estevan Tapis 1803-1812
Fray José Señan 1812-1815
Fray Mariano Payeras 1815-1819
Fray José Señan 1819-1823
Fray Vicente Francisco Sarría 1823-1825
Fray Narciso Durán 1825-1827
Fray José Bernardo Sánchez 1827-1831
Fray Narciso Durán 1831-1838
Fray José Joaquín Jimeno 1838-1844
Fray Narciso Durán 1844-1846

BIBLIOGRAPHY

Ament, William Sheffield and R. D. Hunt: *Oxcart to Airplane.* Powell Publishing Co., Los Angeles, 1929.

American Guide Series: Northern California. *Monterey Peninsula.* Stanford University Press, 1941.

Atherton, Gertrude: *California: An Intimate History.* Boni & Liveright, New York, 1927.

———: *Rezánov.* F. S. Stokes & Co., New York, 1906.

Bancroft, Hubert Howe: *The History of California.* The History Co., San Francisco, 1882.

Bell, Major Horace: *On the Old West Coast.* William Morrow Co., New York, 1930.

Bell, Major Horace: *Reminiscences of a Ranger.* Wallace Hebberd, Santa Barbara, 1927.

Belle, Frances P.: *Joaquin Murrieta.* Regan Publishing Corp., Chicago, 1925. (Translated from the Spanish of I. Paz.)

Berger, John A.: *The Franciscan Missions of California.* Doubleday & Co., New York, 1948.

Bolton, Herbert Eugene: *Anza's California Expeditions.* University of California Press, Berkeley, 1930.

———: *Kino's Historical Memoir of Pimeria Alta.* University of California Press, Berkeley, 1948.

———: *Outpost of Empire.* Alfred A. Knopf, New York, 1931.

———: *Spanish Exploration in the Southwest, 1542-1706.* Charles Scribner's Sons, New York, 1907.

Burns, Walter Noble: *The Robin Hood of El Dorado.* Coward-McCann, Inc., New York, 1932.

Cain, Henry L.: *A Short History of Mexico.* El Modelo, Mexico, D.F. 1935.

Caughey, John Walton: *Gold Is the Cornerstone.* University of California Press, Berkeley and Los Angeles, 1948.

Cendrars, Blaise: *Sutter's Gold.* Harper & Bros., New York, 1926.

Chapman, Charles E.: *A History of California: The Spanish Period.* The Macmillan Co., New York, 1921.

335

Palou, Francisco: *Life of Junípero Serra.* George Wharton James, Pasadena, 1913.

Pattie, James Ohio: *The Personal Narrative of James O. Pattie of Kentucky.* John H. Wood, Cincinnati, 1831.

Paul, Rodman W.: *California Gold.* Harvard University Press, Cambridge, 1947.

Paxson, Frederic L.: *History of the American Frontier.* Houghton, Mifflin Co., Boston, 1924.

Priestley, Herbert Ingraham: *Franciscan Explorations in California.* Arthur H. Clark Co., Glendale, Calif., 1945.

Repplier, Agnes: *Junípero Serra.* Doubleday Doran & Co., New York, 1933.

Rice, William B.: *The Los Angeles Star.* University of California Press, Berkeley and Los Angeles, 1947.

Robinson, W. W.: *Land in California.* University of California Press, Berkeley and Los Angeles, 1947.

Rogers, David Banks: *Prehistoric Man of the Santa Barbara Coast.* Santa Barbara Museum of Natural History, 1929.

Royce, Josiah: *California: A Study of American Character.* Alfred A. Knopf, New York, 1948.

Salvator, Ludwig Louis: *Los Angeles in the Sunny Seventies.* McCallister & Zeitlin, Los Angeles, 1929.

Sánchez, Nellie van de Grift: *A Short History of California.* See Hunt, R. D.

———: *Spanish Arcadia.* Powell Publishing Co., Los Angeles, 1929.

Solis, Don Antonio de: *Conquista de Mexico.* V. Baudry, Libreria Europea, Paris, 1858.

Southern California Writers Project: *Los Angeles, A Guide to the City.* Hastings House, New York, 1941.

———: *Santa Barbara, A Guide to the Channel City.* Hastings House, New York, 1941.

Stewart, George R.: *Names on The Land.* Random House, New York, 1945.

Underhill, Reuben L.: *From Cowhides to Golden Fleece.* Stanford University Press, Palo Alto, 1939.

Vancouver, George: *A Voyage of Discovery to the North Pacific and Around the World.* Robinson and Edwards, London, 1798.

Van Dyke, T. S.: *Millionaires of a Day.* Fords, Howard & Hulbert, New York, 1890.

Van Nostrand, Jeanne: *California Pictorial*. University of California Press, Berkeley, 1948.

Von Dornum, Elsa: *A Short History of Mexico*. El Modelo, Mexico, D.F. 1935.

Wagner, Henry R.: *Juan Rodriguez Cabrillo*. California Historical Society, San Francisco, 1941.

Watson, Douglas S.: *The Founding of the Californian Missions*. Nueva California Press, San Francisco, 1934.

Wheat, Carl I.: *The Pioneer Press of California*. Biobooks, Oakland, 1948.

ACKNOWLEDGMENTS

A LIST of acknowledgments is always an unsatisfactory thing, not because of those persons or institutions who are included, but because of those who may unintentionally and regretably be left out. With this risk in mind, I wish to make a statement of thanks for the good assistance of the following individuals:

John McRae, Jr., Ruth Teiser, Phil Townsend Hanna, Michael Harrison, Myrtle M. McKittrick, Dick Thomason, Edward Weston, Ray Hewitt, August Frugé, Edith Coulter, W. W. Robinson, Leslie E. Bliss, Frances B. Eblen.

Also I wish to express my thanks for the co-operation of the following libraries, publishing houses and institutions:

The Huntington Library, The University of California Library, The California State Library, The Bancroft Library, The Bobbs-Merrill Company, Inc., A. S. Barnes and Company, Binfords & Mort, William Morrow Company, The University of California Press, The California Historical Society, The Society of California Pioneers, The Santa Barbara Chamber of Commerce, The Security-First National Bank of Los Angeles, The California Mission Trails Association.

E. C.

INDEX

341

River of the Sweet Name of Jesus of the Earthquakes, the, 56
Robbins, Thomas, 145
Robidoux, Antoine, 162
Rodeo de las Aguas, 103
Rogers, Harrison G., 150
Rogue River, 24
Rojo, Manuel, 287
"Rose Bowl," 313
Rough and Ready, 254
Rover, the, 145
Rowan, Capt. James, 114
Russia, 40, 44
Russian River, 40, 119

Sachem, the, 45
Sacramento, 204, 260, 270
Sacramento River, 204, 208
Sacramento Valley, 222
St. Francis Hotel (Los Angeles), 257
St. Francis Hotel (San Francisco), 49, 319
St. Louis the Bishop of Tolosa, *see* Mission San Luís Obispo de Tolosa
Salinan Indians, 17
Salinas, Las, 103
Salinas River, 56, 59, 60
Salinas Valley, 58, 121, 271, 293, 327
Salt Lake City, 289
Salvatierra, Juan María, 40, 41, 186
Samarkand Hotel (Santa Barbara), 318
San Antonio, Tex., 289
San Antonio, the, 51, 52, 54, 56, 64, 65, 66, 67, 68, 71, 73, 76
San Agustín, the, 35
San Ardo, 59
San Blas, 74, 75, 76
San Buenaventura, 129; 250
San Carlos, the, 51, 52
San Diego, 15, 21, 52, 54, 63, 64, 65, 68, 76, 86, 88, 100, 101, 130, 169, 173, 188, 223, 228, 233, 250, 255, 256, 260, 261, 289, 292, 297, 307
San Diego Bay, 15, 21, 37, 38
San Diego County, 18, 79
San Fernando Rey de España, 170

San Fernando Valley, 57, 169
San Francisco, 15, 49, 76, 86, 100, 101, 221, 255, 261, 292, 299, 324
San Francisco Bay, 15, 23, 26, 35, 37, 49, 50, 61, 67, 70, 74, 286, 320
San Francisco Bulletin, 288
San Gabriel Mission, 57
San Joaquin River, 160
San Joaquin Valley, 207, 272, 291
San Jose, 86, 98, 100, 189, 250, 260, 293
San José, the, 54, 64
San Juan Bautista, 272
San Juan Capistrano, 133
San Luis Obispo, 23, 34, 58, 250, 271, 292
San Marcos Pass, 231
San Mateo, 107
San Miguel Bay, 37
San Miguel Isl., 20, 22, 23, 24, 25
San Pedro, 222
San Pedro Bay, 37
San Pascual, 231
San Rafael, 219
San Salvador, the, 20, 24
San Simeon Highway, 59. *See also* State Route 1
Santa Ana, 310
Santa Ana, the, 34, 35, 36
Santa Ana River, 56
Santa Barbara, 20, 23, 25, 37, 58, 81, 86, 101, 250, 261, 292, 293, 299
Santa Barbara Channel, 22, 57
Santa Barbara Channel Islands, 23
Santa Clara River, 57
Santa Cruz, 293, 294
Santa Cruz County Park, 60
Santa Cruz Isl., 128
Santa Lucia Mts., 23, 58, 59
Santa Maria Inn (Santa Ynez), 319
Santa Maria River, 56
Santa Monica, 21, 169, 280
Santa Monica Mts., 22, 57
Santa Rosa, the, 123, 124, 125, 126, 128
Santa Susana Mts., 57
Santa Ynez, 271
Santa Ynez River, 56

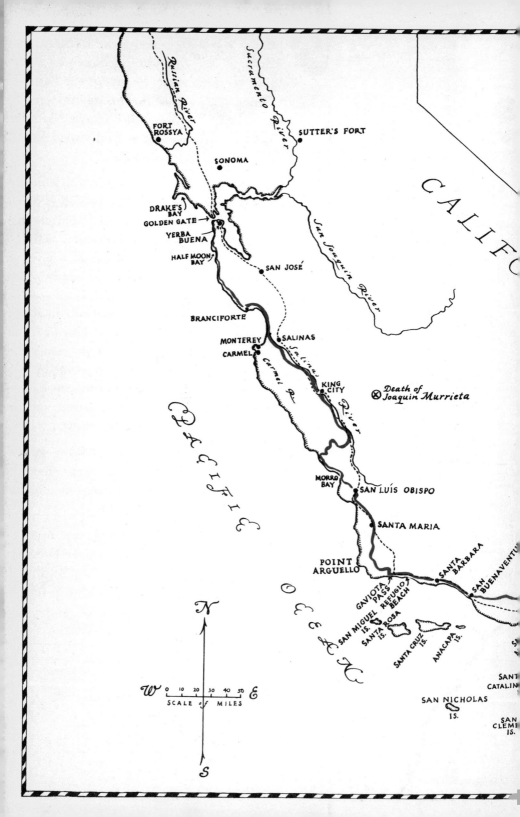

FORT
ROSSYA

Russian River

Sacramento River

SUTTER'S FORT

SONOMA

CALIFO

DRAKE'S
BAY
GOLDEN GATE→
YERBA
BUENA

HALF MOON
BAY

San Joaquin River

SAN JOSÉ

BRANCIFORTE

MONTEREY
CARMEL

SALINAS

Salinas River

Carmel R.

KING
CITY

⊗ Death of
Joaquin Murrieta

PACIFIC

MORRO
BAY

SAN LUIS OBISPO

SANTA MARIA

POINT
ARGUELLO

SANTA
BARBARA

GAVIOTA
PASS

SAN
BUENAVENTUR

OCEAN

SAN MIGUEL
IS.

REFUGIO
BEACH

SANTA ROSA
IS.

SANTA CRUZ
IS.

ANACAPA
IS.

SAN
CATALIN

N

W   E
0 10 20 30 40 50
SCALE of MILES

SANTA
CATALIN

SAN NICHOLAS
IS.

SAN
CLEME
IS.

S